RELIGIOUS EDUCATION

By

Dr. Adam Paul Patteti
Professor
Department of Education
Maulana Azad National Urdu University
College of Teacher Education
Darbhanga - 846 001
Bihar (INDIA)

&

Ismail Thamarasseri
Assistant Professor
Department of Education
Central University of Kashmir
Srinagar - 190 004
J&K (INDIA)

DPH

DISCOVERY PUBLISHING HOUSE PVT. LTD.
NEW DELHI-110 002

Published by:
Namit Wasan
DISCOVERY PUBLISHING HOUSE PVT. LTD.
4383/4B, Ansari Road, Darya Ganj
New Delhi-110 002 (India)
Phone : +91-11-23279245; 23253475; 43596065
E-mail : discoverybooksindia@gmail.com
discoverypublishinghouse@gmail.com
namitwasan9@gmail.com
web : www.discoverypublishinggroup.com

***Edition:* 2020**

ISBN: 978-93-5056-766-1

Religious Education

Printed at:
Infinity Imaging Systems
Delhi

Preface

One of the most ancient civilizations of the world, India can take legitimate pride in having been a civilizational unity without a break for more than 5000 years. We all are the part of this great civilization and culture. Our contribution in the field of art, sculpture, architecture, mathematics, science, medicine etc., is well known. Some of the oldest, deepest and most sublime philosophical thought and literature was born in India. We have several historical monuments or great archeological value spread over the entire country. These include: forests, palaces, temples etc. As to this territory had the honour of being the birth place of several great religions like: Hinduism, Buddhism, Jainism and Sikhism. Our past has shown us the path of peace, love, non-violence and truth. As citizens of this country, it is the responsibility of all of us to work for the preservation of this rich heritage and its cultural values and live in love and harmony. These are the foundations of our citizenship. All of us are supposed to maintain the dignity of the constitution, by not indulging in any activities in violation of the letter of spirit of the constitution. Our is a vast country with many languages, sub-cultures, religions and ethnic diversities, but the essential unity of the country is epitomized in the one constitution, one flag, one people and one citizenship. We are governed and guided by this constitution irrespective of caste, religion, race, sex etc. We must put the nation above our narrow personal interests and then only we will be able to protect our hard-earned freedom and sovereignty.

The Education Commission (1964-66) said on Religious Education and Education About Religion; "We suggest that a syllabus giving all chosen information about each of the major religions should be included as a part of the course in citizenship or as a part of general education to be introduced in schools and colleges up to the first degree. It should be highlighting the fundamental similarities in the great religions of the world and the emphasis they place the cultivation of certain broadly comparable moral and spiritual values". Dr. B.R. Ambedkar explains, "Secular state doesn't mean that it shall not take in to consideration the religious sentiments of the people. That entire secular state means is that this parliament shall not be competent to impose any particular religion upon the rest of the people. This is the only limitation that the constitution recognizes.

This book will introduce the students and readers to Religious Education in Secular India. In India like: secular, plural and multi-religious country it's an important topic need to be discussed. The authors hope this book is useful for those who interested in education in general and students of B.Ed., M.Ed., B.A. Education, and M.A. Education at different universities in particular. In this book, the authors has drawn materials and data from various sources such as: Government websites other URL's, standard works, journals, publications, reports, etc., the names of which have been duly incorporated in the Bibliography given to the end of work. The authors express their gratitude to the writers, editors, publishers and other bodies of all these works. The authors shall ever remain obliged to their teachers, parents, friends, colleagues, family members and students for their kind directions guidance and assistance. To them all, authors offer their grateful thanks to M/s. Discovery Publishing House Pvt. Ltd., New Delhi who came forward willingly undertakes the publishing of this book.

Dr. Adam Paul Patteti
Ismail Thamarasseri

Contents

CHAPTER

1 Hinduism and its Impact on Indian Society

INTRODUCTION

Indian society has been tasted the fruits of various religions since its beginning. In general we may had the more Hindu population but the society never confined to that particular religion only. The study of the various religions of India clearly says that it is not only Hindus but every religion in India had their own benefits from the government of India.

Concern to the Hindu religion it have been deep rooted into the Indian society. The concepts like: Dharma, Ahimsa etc., have been provided global wise importance to the Indian religions. Bhakti movement was another form of the Hinduism, which intended to revive the dogmatic elements of Hinduism.

Jainism created nonviolent basis for the Indian society. As we know, India always moved through non-violent policies to solve various problems. Its reached it independence also through its non violent measures only. Hence we cannot deny the influence of any religion on Indian society.

Buddhism which started in the 600 B.C., have been moved with its solution to various social problems and social evils. Sikkhism moved with various principles related to the protection of their own traditions. Islam have been started as an order to propagate the preachings of Mohammad. It have been influenced the Indian society very quickly.

Christianity is the only religion for the first time influenced Indians in intellectual manner by improving the education facilities. It also concern towards the upliftment of the downtrodden communities. In altogether it can be said that without the conglomeration of these religious Indian society is no more. Because Indian society is a composite society.

Hinduism

Hinduism is the predominant religion of the Indian subcontinent. Hinduism is often referred to as Sanâtana Dharma, a Sanskrit phrase meaning 'the eternal law', by its practitioners. Hindu beliefs vary widely, with concepts of God and/or gods ranging from Panentheism, pantheism, monotheism, polytheism, and atheism with Vishnu and Shiva being the most popular deities. Other notable characteristics include a belief in reincarnation and karma, as well as personal duty, or dharma.

Among its roots is the historical Vedic religion of Iron Age of India, and as such Hinduism is often stated to be the 'oldest religious tradition' or 'oldest living major tradition.' It is formed of diverse traditions and types and has no single founder. Hinduism is the world's third largest religion after Christianity and Islam, with approximately a billion adherents, of whom about 905 million live in India. Other countries with large Hindu populations can be found across southern Asia.

Hinduism's vast body of scriptures are divided into Sruti ('revealed') and Smriti ('remembered'). These scriptures discuss theology, philosophy and mythology, and provide information on the practice of dharma (religious living). Among these texts, the *Vedas* and the *Upanishads* are the foremost in authority, importance and antiquity. Other major scriptures include: the *Tantras*, the *Agama*, the *Purânas* and the epics *Mahâbhârata* and *Râmâyana*. The *Bhagavad Gîtâ*, a treatise from the *Mahâbhârata*, spoken by Krishna, is sometimes called a summary of the spiritual teachings of the *Vedas*.

Etymology

Hindû is the Persian name for the Indus River, first encountered in the Old Persian word *Hindu* corresponding to Vedic Sanskrit *Sindhu*, the Indus River. The Rig Veda mentions the land of the Indo-Aryans as *Sapta Sindhu* (the land of the seven rivers in northwestern South Asia, one of them being the Indus). This corresponds to *Hapta* in the *Avesta* (*Vendidad or Videvdad* 1.18) – the sacred scripture of Zoroastrianism. The term was used for those who lived in the Indian sub-continent on or beyond the 'Sindhu'. In Islam the Arabic texts – *al-Hind* (the Hind) also refers to 'the land of the people of modern day India'.

The Persian term (Middle Persian *Hindûk*, New Persian *Hindû*) entered India with the Delhi Sultanate and appears in South Indian and Kashmiri texts from at least 1323 CE, and increasingly so during British rule. Since the end of the 18th century the word has been used as an umbrella term for most of the religious, spiritual, and philosophical traditions of the sub-continent, excluding the distinct religions of Sikhism, Buddhism, and Jainism.

The term *Hindu* was introduced to the English. It generally denotes the religious, philosophical, and cultural traditions native to India.

Typology

Hinduism as we know it can be subdivided into a number of major currents. Of the historical division into six darshanas, only two schools, Vedanta and Yoga survive. The main divisions of Hinduism today are Vaishnavism, Shaivism, Smartism and Shaktism. The vast majority of present day Hindus can be categorized under one of these four groups, *(i)* although there are many other, *(ii)* partly overlapping, *(iii)* allegiances and *(iv)* denominations.

McDaniel (2007) distinguishes six more generic 'types' of Hinduism, in an attempt to accommodate a variety of views on a rather complex object:

1. Folk Hinduism, as based on local traditions and cults of local deities at acommunal level and spanning thorough to pre-historic times or at least prior to written Vedas.
2. Vedic Hinduism as still being practiced by traditionalist Brahmins, for example shrautins.
3. Vedantic Hinduism, for example Advaita (Smartism), as based on philosophical approach of the Upanishads.
4. Yogic Hinduism, especially based on the Yoga Sutras of Patanjali.

5. 'Dharmic' Hinduism or 'daily morality', based on the notion of Karma, and societal norms such as: Hindu marriage customs etc.
6. Bhakti or devotionalism, especially as in Vaishnavism.

Definitions

The characteristic of comprehensive tolerance to differences in belief and Hinduism's dogmatic openness makes it difficult to define it as a religion according to the traditional Western conceptions. While Hinduism is a clear practical concept to the majority of adherents, many expressed a problem arriving at a definition of the term, mainly because of the wide range of traditions and ideas incorporated or covered by it. While sometimes referred to as a religion, it is more often defined as a religious tradition, it is therefore described as both the oldest of the world's religions and most diverse in religious traditions. Most Hindu traditions revere a body of religious or sacred literature, the Vedas, although there are exceptions to it; some religious traditions regard certain particular rituals as essential for salvation, but a variety of views on it co-exist; some Hindu philosophies postulate a theistic ontology of creation, sustenance, and destruction of the universe, yet some Hindus are atheists. Hinduism is sometimes characterized with the belief in reincarnation (*samsara*) determined by the law of karma, and that salvation is freedom from this cycle of repeated birth and death, however other religions of the region, such as: Buddhism and Jainism, also believe in this, outside of the scope of Hinduism. Hinduism is therefore viewed as the most complex of all the living, historical world religions. Despite its complexity Hinduism is not only one of the numerically largest, but also the oldest living major tradition on earth, with roots reaching back into the prehistory.

A definition of Hinduism, given by the first Vice President of India and prominent theologian, Sarvepalli Radhakrishnan states that it is not 'just a faith', but in itself related to the union of reason and intuition, he explicitly suggests, that it can not be defined, but is only to be experienced. Similarly some academics are suggesting that Hinduism can be seen as a category with 'fuzzy edges', rather than a well defined and rigid entity. Some forms of religious expression are central to Hinduism, while others are not as central but still within the category. Based on that, Ferro-Luzzi has developed a 'Prototype Theory approach' to the definition of Hinduism.

Hinduism has been perceived as one of the world religions we know today only since the 19th century, when the term 'Hinduism' started being used by leaders of Hindu reform movements or revivalists, and, often considered to be biased, Western orientalists or the 'first Indologists'. However it is clearly accepted that sources of Hinduism and the 'streams' which feed in to it are very ancient, extending back to the Indus Valley civilization and earliest expressions of historical Vedic religion. It is not an accepted view that Hinduism is the construction of Western orientalists to make sense of the plurality of religious phenomena originating and based on the Vedic traditions, however some have suggested it is.

Problems with the single definition or of what is actually meant by the term 'Hinduism' are often attributed to the fact that Hinduism does not have a single or common historical founder. Hinduism, or as some say 'Hinduisms', does not have a single system of salvation and has different goals according to each sect or denomination. The forms of Vedic religion are seen, not as an alternative to Hinduism but as its earliest form, and there is little justification for the divisions found in much western scholarly writing between Vedism, Brahmanism, and Hinduism. Some suggest that Hinduism does not have a 'unified system of belief encoded in declaration of faith or a creed'. It is therefore a very different kind of religion in these respects to the monolithic tradition of Islam, while some suggest there are stronger affinities with the structure of Judaism.

From the western point of view, the understanding of Hinduism was mediated by Western notions of what religion is and how it relates to more ancient forms of belief. It is further complicated by the frequent use of the term 'faith' as a synonym for 'religion'. Some academics and many practitioners refer to Hinduism with a native definition, as 'Sanâtana Dharma', a Sanskrit phrase meaning 'the eternal law' or 'eternal way'.

Vedic Religion

The Vedic period religions laid the foundation of the religious practices that are continued till date in modern India. These religions arose from the sacred scriptures that were composed during the Vedic period. These scriptures founded the very base of Hinduism in India. The scriptures that talk of the various religious practices are basically the four Vedas namely: Rig Veda, Yajur Veda, Sama Veda and Atharva Veda. The Upanishads are also considered to be a part of the Vedas and contain valuable information regarding the rituals and religions of Vedic Age.

The principles of religions in Vedic Era were basically laid down by the priests, who were the highest class of people in the society. They were the ones who performed the rituals, chanted hymns and read out holy texts in temples and functions. The texts recorded in the Vedas were supposed to have divine power and were to be chanted perfectly with the right tone, pronunciation and emphasis. This was believed to make the hymns effective to the hilt and gain the maximum power out of it.

Religion in Early Vedic Period

Religion in early Vedic period revolved around crude forms of worshipping which basically includes: nature worship. This means that people in the early Vedic period worshipped different forms of nature as god like: sun, earth, moon, wind, rain, and other natural phenomena. Since there were no scientific explanations for natural phenomena like: rain, thunder, wind, etc., people feared them and thus worshipped them. Chanting of prayers and hymns were a common practice to invoke the Gods and it was normal to sacrifice animals in the name of religion.

Religion in Later Vedic Period

The later Vedic age saw the increase in powers of the priests and they formed the highest class in the society. Religious practices were refined and worship of Gods in the form of idols gained importance. Animal sacrifice also increased during this period. With rituals and hymns taking centre stage, the evolution of Hindu religion took place. Nature worship gave rise to new beliefs and new Gods. The duty of imparting the religious know how to people was the duty of the priests.

EARLY HINDUISM

The pantheistic scheme of salvation just described, generally known as the Vedanta teaching, found great favor with the Brahmins and has been maintained as orthodox Brahmin doctrine down to the present day. But it made little progress outside the Brahmin caste. The mass of the people have little interest in an impersonal Brahmâ who was incapable of hearing their prayers, nor had they any relish for a final end which meant the loss forever of conscious existence. And so, while the priestly ascetic was chiefly concerned with meditation on his identity with Brahmâ, and with the practice of mortification to secure freedom from all desires, the popular mind was still bent on prayer, sacrifices, and other good works in honor of the Vedic deities. But at the same time, their faith in the efficacy of these traditional gods could not be but weakened by the Brahmin teaching that freedom from rebirth was not to be obtained by acts of worship to personal deities who were powerless to secure even for themselves eternal conscious bliss. The result was popular development of special cults of two of the old gods, now raised to the position of supreme deity, and credited with the power to secure a lasting life of happiness in heaven.

It was in the priestly conception of the supreme personal Brahmá that the popular mind found its model for its new deities. Brahmá was not a traditional god, and seems never to have been a favorite object of cult with the people. Even today, there are but two temples to Brahmá in all India. His sub-ordination to the great impersonal all-god did not help to recommend him to the popular mind. Instead we find two of the traditional gods honored with special cults, which seem to have taken rise independently in two different parts of the country and, after acquiring a local celebrity, to have spread in rivalry over the whole land. One of these gods was the ancient storm-god Rudra, destructive in tempest and lightning, renewing life in the showers of rain, sweeping in lonely solitude over mountain and barren waste. As the destroyer, the reproducer, and the type of the lonely ascetic, this deity rapidly rose in popular esteem under the name of Siva, the blessed. The other was Vishnu, originally one of the forms of the son-god, a mild beneficent deity, whose genial rays brought gladness and growth to living creatures. His solar origin was lost sight of as he was raised to the position of supreme deity, but one of his symbols, the discus, points to his earlier character.

These two rival cults seem to have arisen in the fourth or fifth century B.C. As in the case of the personal god Brahmá, neither the worship of Siva nor of Vishnu did away with the honoring of the traditional gods and goddesses, spirits, heroes, sacred rivers and mountains and trees, serpents, earth, heaven, sun, moon, and stars. The pantheism in which the Hindu mind is inevitably cast saw in all these things emanations of the supreme deity, Siva or Vishnu. In worshiping any or all, he was but honoring his supreme god. Each deity was credited with a special heaven, where his devotees would find after death an unending life of conscious happiness. The rapid rise in popular esteem of these cults, tending more and more to thrust Brahminism proper in to the background, was viewed by the priestly caste with no little concern. To quench these cults was out of the question; and so, in order to hold them in at least nominal allegiance to Brahminism, the supreme god Brahmá was associated with Vishnu and Siva as a triad of equal and more or less interchangeable deities in which Brahmá held the office of creator, or rather evolver, Vishnu of preserver, and Siva of dissolver. This is the so-called Tri-murti (tri-form), or trinity, altogether different from the Christian concept of three eternally distinct persons in one Godhead, and hence offering no legitimate ground for suggesting a Hindu origin for the Christian doctrine.

More remarkable was the intimate association of other new deities – the creations of the religious fancies of the common people – with the gods Siva and Vishnu. With Siva two popular gods came to be associated as sons. One was Ganesha, lord of troops and mischievous imps, who has remained ever since a favorite object of worship and is invoked at the beginning of every undertaking to ensure success. The other was Scanda, who seems in great measure to have replaced Indra as the god of battle. Beyond the doubtful derivation of the name Scanda from Alexander, there is nothing to indicate that either of these reputed sons of Siva had ever lived the lives of men. Not so the gods that enlarged the sphere of Vishnu's influence. In keeping with Vishnu's position as god of the people, two of the legendary heroes of the remote past, Rama and Krishna, whom popular enthusiasm had raised to the rank of gods, came to be associated with him not as sons, but as his very incarnations. The incarnation of a god descending from heaven to assume a human of animal form as a sort of savior, and to achieve some signal benefit for mankind, is known as an avatar. The idea antedates Buddhism and, while applied to Siva and other gods, became above all a characteristic of Vishnu.

Popular fancy loved to dwell on his avatar as a fish to save Manu from the devastating flood, as a tortoise to recover from the depths of the sea precious possessions for gods and men, as a boar to raise the submerged earth above the surface of the waters, but most of all as the god-men Rama and Krishna, each of whom delivered the people from the yoke of a tyrant. So popular became the cults of Rama and Krishna that Vishnu himself was largely lost sight of. In time the Vishnuites became divided into two rival schisms: the Ramaites, who worshipped Rama as supreme deity, and the Krishnaites, who gave this honor rather to Krishna, a division that has persisted down to the present day. The evidence of the early existence of these innovations on Brahmin belief is to be found in the two great epics known as the 'Ramayana' and the 'Mahabharata.' Both are revered by Brahmins, Sivaites and Vishnuites alike, particularly the latter poem, which is held to be directly revealed. In the 'Ramayana,' which belongs to the period 400-300 B.C., the legendary tales of the trials and the triumphs of the hero Rama and his faithful wife Sita were worked into a highly artificial romanbtic poem, largely in the interests of Vishnu worship. The 'Mahabharata,' the work of many hands, was begun about the fifth century B.C. under Brahmin influence, and in the folowing centuries received additions and modifications, in the interests now of Vishnuism now of Sivaism, till it assumed its final shape in the sixth century of the Christian Era. It is a huge conglomeration of stirring adventure, popular legend, myth, and religious speculation. The myth centres chiefly on the many-sided struggle for supremacy between the evil tyrants of the land and the hero Arjuna, aided by his four brothers. The role that Krishna plays is not an integral part of the story and seems to have been interpolated after the substance of the epic had been written. He is the charioteer of Arjuna and at the same time acts as his religious advisor. Of his numerous religious instructions, the most important is his metrical treatise known as the 'Bhagavad-gita,' the Song of the Blessed One, a writing that has exercised a profound influence on religious thought in India. It dates from the second or third century of the Christian era, being a poetic version of a late Upanishad, with its pantheistic doctrine so modified as to pass for a personal revelation of Krishna. While embodying the noblest features of Brahmin ethics, and insisting on the faithful performance of caste-duties, it proclaims Krishna to be the superior personal all-god who, by the bestowal of special grace helps on his votaries to the attainment of eternal bliss. As an important means to this end, it inculcates the virtue of Bhakti that is a loving devotion to the deity, analogous to the Christian virtue of charity. Unhappily for the later development of Vishnuism, the Krishna of the 'Bhagavad-gita' was not the popular conception. Like most legendary heroes of folk-lore, his character was in keeping with the crude morals of the primitive age that first sounded his praises. The narrative portions of the epic show him to have been sly and unscrupulous, guilty in word and deed of acts which the higher Brahmin conscience would reprove. But it is in the fuller legendary story of his life as given in the so-called 'Hari-vansa,' a later supplement to the epic, and also in some of the Puranas of the ninth and tenth centuries of our era, that the character of the popular Krishna appears in its true light. Here we learn that Krishna was one of eight sons of noble birth, whom a Herod-like tyrant was bent on destroying. The infant god was saved from the wicked designs of the king by being secretly substituted for a herdsman's babe. Krishna grew up among the simple country-people, performing prodigies of valor, and engaging in many amorous adventures with the Gopis, the wives and daughters of the herdsmen. Eight of these were his favorites, but one he loved best of all, Radha. Krishna finally succeeded in killing the king, and brought peace to the kingdom.

Between this deified Hindu Hercules and Our Divine Lord, there is no ground for comparison, one only for contrast. That the idea of incarnate deity should be found in pre-Christian Hindu thought is not so remarkable when we consider that it answers to thc yearning of the human heart for union with God. But what is at first sight astonishing is to find in the religious writings subsequent to the 'Mahabharata' legendary tales of Krishna that are almost identical with the stories of Christ in the canonical and apocryphal Gospels. From the birth of Krishna in a stable, and his adoration by shepherds and magi, the leader is led on through a series of events the exact counterparts of those related of Our Divine Lord. Writers hostile to Christianity seized on this chain or resemblances, too close to be mere coincidence, in order to convict the Gospel writers of plagiarism from Hindu originals. But the very opposite resulted. All Indianists of authority are agreed that these Krishna legends are not earlier than the seventh century of the Christian Era, and must have been borrowed from Christian sources.

LATER OR SECTARIAN HINDUISM

The steady weakening of Brahmin influence, in consequence of the successive waves of foreign conquest, made it possible for the religious preferences of the huge, heterogeneous population of India to assert themselves more strongly. Both Sivaism and Vishnuism departed more and more strongly from traditional Brahminism, and assumed a decidedly sectarian character towards the older religion and also towards each other. With this weakening of Brahmin influence they absorbed the grosser elements of low-grade popular worship, and became abused by the accretion of immoral rites and groveling superstitions. While, on the one hand, the practice of asceticism was pushed to its utmost extremes of fanaticism, on the other the doctrine of bhakti was perverted into a system of gross sexual indulgence, for which the amours of Krishna and the Gopis served as the model and sanction. The Brahmin-caste distinctions were broken down, and an equality of all men and women was asserted, at least during the ceremonies of public worship. The Brahmin rites were in great measure replaced by others particular to each cult and held to be all-sufficient for salvation. Everywhere splendid temples arose to Siva, Vishnu, and his two human avatars; idols and phallic symbols innumerable filled the land; and each rival cult lauded its own special deity as supreme, sub-ordinating all others to it, and looking down with more or less contempt on forms of worship other than its own. One factor which contributed strongly to the degradation of these sectarian forms of religion was the veneration of the Sakti, or female side, of these deities. Popular theology would not rest until each deity was supplemented with a wife, in whom the active nature of the god was personified. With Brahmá was associated an ancient river-goddess, Sarasvati, honored as the patroness of letters. Vishnu's Sakti was Sri, or Lakshmi, patroness of good fortune. With Siva the destroyer there was associated the terrible, blood-thirsty, magical goddess Durga, or Kali, formerly delighting in human victims, now appeased with sacrifices of goats and buffaloes. Rama had his consort, Sita, and Krishna his favorite Gopi, Radha. The worship of these

Saktis, particularly Siva's consort Durga-Kali, degenerated into shocking orgies of drunkenness and sexual immorality, which even today are the crying scandal of Hinduism.

Such were the sectarian developments of post-epic times. They found expression in the inferior, quasi-historic Puranas, of the seventh and following centuries, and in the Tantras, which are more modern still, and teach the symbolic magic of Sakti-worship. Neither of these classes of writings is regarded by orthodox Brahmin as canonical.

Of the two hundred million adherents of Hinduism today, only a few hundred thousand can be called orthodox Brahmin worshipers. Sivaism and Vishnuism have overshadowed the older religion like a rank growth of poisonous weeds. In their main outlines, these two great sects have retained the characteristics of the Purana period, but differences of view on minor points have lead to a multiplication of schismatic divisions, especially among Vishnu-worshipers. Both sects, which today are fairly tolerant of each other, have a number of devotional and liturgical practices that are alike in kind, though marked by differences in sectarian belief. Both Sivaite and Vishnuite lay great stress on the frequent recital of the numerous names of their respective supreme gods, and to facilitate this piety, each carries with him, often about his neck, a rosary, varying in material and the number of beads according as it is dedicated to Siva or Vishnu. Each sect has initiation rites, which are conferred upon the young at the age of reason and in which the officiating guru puts a rosary around the neck of the applicant and whispers into his ear the mantra, or sacred motto, the recital of which serves as a profession of faith and is of daily obligation. Another rite common to both is that in which the presiding officer brands on the body of the worshiper with hot metal stamps the sacred symbols of his sect, the trident and the linga of Siva, or the discus and conch-shell (or lotus) of Vishnu.

But in their highest act of ceremonial worship the two sects differ radically. The Sivaite takes his white stone pebble, the conventional phallic emblem which he always carries with him, and while muttering his mantra, sprinkles it with water and applies to it cooling Bilva leaves. Owing to its simplicity and cheapness, this rite is much in vogue with the ignorant lower classes. The Vishnu rite is less degrading but more childish. It consists of an elaborate and costly worship of the temple image of Vishnu, or more often of Rama, or Krishna. The image is daily awakened, undressed, bathed, decked with rich robes and adorned with necklaces, bracelets, crowns of gold and precious stones, fed with choice kinds of food, honored with flowers, lights, an incense, and then entertained with vocal and instrumental music, and with dancing by the temple girls of doubtful virtue, consecrated to this service. As Krishna is generally worshipped in the form of a child-image, his diversion consists largely in the swinging of his image, the spinning of tops, and other games dear to the heart of the child.

Siva, too, has his temples, vying in magnificence with those of Vishnu, but in all these, the holy place is the linga-shrine, and the temple worship consists in the application of water and Bilva leaves to the stone symbol. The interior walls of these, and of Vishnu temples as well, are covered with shocking representations of sexual passion and yet, strange to say, these forms of religion, while giving a sanction to the indulgence of the lowest passions, at the same time inspire other devotees to the practice of the severest asceticism. They wander about in lonely silence, naked and filthy, their hair matted from long neglect, their bodies reduced to mere skin and bones by dint of incredible fasts. They will stand motionless for hours under the blazing son, with their emaciated arms uplifted toward heaven. Some go about with face ever turned upwards. Some are known to have kept their fists tightly clenched until their growing nails protruded through the backs of their hands.

Concept of God

Hinduism is a diverse system of thought with beliefs spanning monotheism, polytheism, panentheism, pantheism, monism, and atheism. It is sometimes referred to as henotheistic (*i.e.,* involving devotion to a single god while accepting the existence of others), but any such term is an overgeneralization.

Most Hindus believe that the spirit or soul – the true 'self' of every person, called the *âtman* – is eternal. According to the monistic/ pantheistic theologies of Hinduism (such as: Advaita Vedanta school), this *Atman* is ultimately indistinct from Brahman, the supreme spirit. Hence, these schools are called non-dualist. The goal of life, according to the Advaita school, is to realize that one's *âtman* is identical to Brahman, the supreme soul. The Upanishads state that whoever becomes fully aware of the *âtman* as the innermost core of one's own self realizes an identity with Brahman and thereby reaches *moksha* (liberation or freedom).

Dualistic schools (see Dvaita and Bhakti) understand Brahman as a Supreme Being who possesses personality, and they worship him or her thus, as Vishnu, Brahma, Shiva, or Shakti, depending on the sect. The *âtman* is dependent on God, while *moksha* depends on love towards God and on God's grace. When God is viewed as the supreme personal being (rather than as the infinite principle), God is called *Ishvara* ('The Lord'), *Bhagavan* ('The Auspicious One') or *Parameshwara* ('The Supreme Lord'). However interpretations of *Ishvara* vary, ranging from non-belief in *Ishvara* by followers of Mimamsakas, to identifying *Brahman* and *Ishvara* as one, as in Advaita. There are also schools like the Samkhya which have atheistic leanings.

Post-Vedic Religions

Vedic religion was gradually formalized and concluded into Vedanta, which is the primary institution of Hinduism. Vedanta considers itself the 'essence' of the Vedas. The Vedic pantheon was interpreted by a unitary view of the universe with Brahman seen as immanent and transcendent, since the Middle Upanishads also in personal forms of the deity as Ishvara, Bhagavan, or Paramatma. There are also conservative schools which continue portions of the historical Vedic religion largely unchanged until today (see Srauta, Nambudiri).

During the formative centuries of Vedanta, traditions that opposed Vedanta and which supported the same, emerged. These were the nastika and astika respectively.

- Hinduism is an umbrella term for *astika* traditions in India.
    - Puranas, Sanskrit epics;
    - The classical schools of Hindu philosophy, of which only Vedanta is extant;
    - Shaivism;
    - Vaishnavism;
    - Bhakti;
    - Shrauta traditions, maintaining much of the original form of the Vedic religion;

Vedic Brahmanism of Iron Age India co-existed and closely interacted with the non-Vedic (*nastika*) Shramana traditions. These were not direct outgrowths of Vedism, but separate movements influenced by Brahmanical traditions.

- Jainism, from the 6th century BC.
- Buddhism, from ca. 500 BC; declined in India over the 8th to 12th centuries in favour of Puranic Hinduism.

Rituals of Worship

Vedic Culture

The Vedic period has been broadly classified into two categories: *(i)* the Early and *(ii)* Later Vedic Periods. This has been done according to the way the transition in the style of culture and society took place. The Vedic period society developed rapidly as time passed by. In Vedic age, culture and society developed from the crude form to the refined form as more and more people came to settle and started to contribute their own ideas to reform the society. With the development in society and culture during Vedic era, historians had to divide the era according to the developments.

Society and Culture in Early Vedic Period

Society in the early Vedic period was basically semi nomadic in nature as people were still learning to settle permanently. They did settle on small patches of land, but moved as soon as the resources over there were depleting. They started to domesticate wild animals and train them as farm animals. As the population in these semi-nomadic groups increased, they settled permanently as moving with a large group was next to impossible. They then started to do farming on a large scale and resorted to full time farming. Their culture was that of a typical tribe. They had a tribal chief who was the governing head of the tribe. He was helped by a group of wise and experienced men in performing his duties.

Society and Culture in Later Vedic Period

The society in the later Vedic period increased in size as people began to live in large settlements that had all facilities for the people. The size of the agricultural fields grew in size. During this time, kingship evolved into the hereditary form in which the son of a ruling chief gets the throne after the chief. The priestly class developed and occupied the highest position in the society. Another significant development during the later Vedic age was that of the caste division of the society. The society was divided into four castes namely Brahmanas, Kshatriyas, Vaishyas and Shudras. The Brahmanas were the priestly class who occupied the highest position in the society. The Kshatriyas were the warriors; the Vaishyas were the service class like: businessmen and peasants. The Shudras were the lowest class of people who did jobs like: removing garbage, cleaning up, etc.

The vast majority of Hindus engage in religious rituals on a daily basis, Most Hindus observe religious rituals at home but observation of rituals greatly vary among regions, villages, and individuals. Devout Hindus perform daily chores such as: worshiping at the dawn after bathing (usually at a family shrine, and typically includes: lighting a lamp and offering foodstuffs before the images of deities), recitation from religious scripts, singing devotional hymns, meditation, chanting mantras, reciting scriptures etc. A notable feature in religious ritual is the division between purity and pollution. Religious acts presuppose some degree of impurity or defilement for the practitioner, which must be overcome or neutralised before or during ritual procedures. Purification, usually with water, is thus a typical feature of most religious action. Other characteristics include a belief in the efficacy of sacrifice and concept of merit, gained through the performance of charity or good works, that will accumulate over time and reduce sufferings in the next world. Vedic rites of fire-oblation (*yajna*) are now only occasional practices, although they are highly revered in theory. In Hindu wedding and burial ceremonies, however, the *yajña* and chanting of Vedic mantras are still the norm. The rituals, upacharas, change with time. For instance, in the past few hundred years some rituals, such as: sacred dance and music offerings in the standard Sodasa Upacharas set prescribed by the Agama Shastra, were replaced by the offerings of rice and sweets.

Occasions like birth, marriage, and death involve what are often elaborate sets of religious customs. In Hinduism, life-cycle rituals include *Annaprashan* (a baby's first intake of solid food), *Upanayanam* ('sacred thread ceremony' undergone by upper-caste children at their initiation into formal education) and *Shraadh* (ritual of treating people to feasts in the name of the deceased). For most people in India, the betrothal of the young couple and the exact date and time of the wedding are matters decided by the parents in consultation with astrologers. On death, cremation is considered obligatory for all except *sanyasis*, *hijra* and children under five. Cremation is typically performed by wrapping the corpse in cloth and burning it on a pyre.

The Vedic Literature

Scriptures

Hinduism is based on "the accumulated treasury of spiritual laws discovered by different persons in different times". The scriptures were transmitted orally in verse form to aid memorization, for many centuries before they were written down. Over many centuries, sages refined the teachings and expanded the canon. In post-Vedic and current Hindu belief, most Hindu scriptures are not typically interpreted literally. More importance is attached to the ethics and metaphorical meanings derived from them. Most sacred texts are in Sanskrit. The texts are classified into two classes: *Shruti* and *Smriti.*

Shruti

Shruti (lit: that which is heard) primarily refers to the *Vedas*, which form the earliest record of the Hindu scriptures. While many Hindus revere the Vedas as eternal truths revealed to ancient sages (*Zcis*), some devotees do not associate the creation of the Vedas with a god or person. They are thought of as the laws of the spiritual world, which would still exist even if they were not revealed to the sages. Hindus believe that because the spiritual truths of the Vedas are eternal, they continue to be expressed in new ways.

There are four *Vedas* (called *(i) Zig-, (ii) Sâma- (iii) Yajus-* and *(iv) Atharva-*). The *Rigveda* is the first and most important Veda. Each Veda is divided into four parts: the primary one, the *Veda proper*, being the *Samhitâ*, which contains sacred *mantras*. The other three parts form a three-tier ensemble of commentaries, usually in prose and are believed to be slightly later in age than the *Samhitâ*. These are: the *Brâhmanas*, *Âranyakas*, and the *Upanishads*. The first two parts were subsequently called the *Karmakânda* (ritualistic portion), while the last two form the *Jñânakanda* (knowledge portion). While the *Vedas* focus on rituals, the *Upanishads* focus on spiritual insight and philosophical teachings, and discuss Brahman and reincarnation.

Smritis

Hindu texts other than the *Shrutis* are collectively called the *Smritis* (memory). The most notable of the smritis are the epics, which consist of the *Mahâbhârata* and the *Râmâyana*. The *Bhagavad Gîtâ* is an integral part of the *Mahabharata* and one of the most popular sacred texts of Hinduism. It contains philosophical teachings from *Krishna*, an incarnation of *Vishnu*, told to the prince Arjuna on the eve of a great war. The *Bhagavad Gîtâ*, spoken by Krishna, is described as the essence of the *Vedas*. However Gita, sometimes called *Gitopanishad*, is more often placed in the Shruti, category, being Upanishadic in content. The Smritis also include: the *Purânas*, which illustrate Hindu ideas through vivid narratives. There are texts with a sectarian nature such as: *Devî Mahâtmya*, the *Tantras*, the *Yoga Sutras*, *Tirumantiram*, *Shiva Sutras* and the *Hindu Âgamas*. A more controversial text, the *Manusmriti*, is a prescriptive lawbook which epitomizes the societal codes of the caste system.

History and Literature

Scholars sometimes distinguish Vedism, the religion of ancient India based on the Vedas, from Hinduism, although it is difficult to pinpoint a time that demarcates them. The Vedas were hymns of the Aryans, who invaded in the 2d millennium BC.

Vedism stressed hope for a future existence in heaven and lacked the concepts of karma and rebirth; Hinduism characteristically includes karma and rebirth, and the greatest hope is for eventual release from their sway.

The Vedic deities were somewhat different from those which dominate in Hinduism, although scholars have traced the origins of Vishnu and Shiva back to Vedic counterparts. Later Vedism is sometimes called Brahmanism because of the authority accorded the Brahmins, or priests, who performed the ritual Vedic sacrifice. However, the challenge of non-Vedic religions, notably Buddhism and Jainism, led to the replacement of the rigid Brahmanical rules by more relaxed and varied forms of worship.

Although the Vedas continue to be spoken of as the final authority in Hinduism, other texts of equal importance exist. Thus, a literature was developed for each of the four aims of life: various Dharmasastras, such as: the Code of Manu, which detail the duties of class and station; Kamasastras, such as: the Kamasutras of Vatsyayana, handbooks of pleasure, erotic and otherwise; the Arthasastra, attributed to Kautilya (fl. 300 BC), which, like Machiavelli's The Prince, offers advice to a ruler as to how to keep the throne; and the philosophical literature of the various systems, which deals with liberation and how to achieve it.

In addition, certain collections of tales came to be widely known in popular life, especially the two great epics, the Mahabarata and the Ramayana. The Mahabharata tells of five princes who were cheated out of their kingdom and who, after a period of banishment in the forest, returned to fight a victorious and righteous war to regain it. An especially beloved portion of this epic is the section called the

Bhagavad Gita, in which Arjuna, one of the brothers, is counseled by his charioteer Krishna, an incarnation of Lord Vishnu. The Ramayana tells the story of the ideal Hindu man, Rama, whose wife Sita is abducted by a demon, and of Rama's journey to Sri Lanka to recapture her. Both epics are filled with didactic tales, edifying poems, and fables. It is probably through their constant retelling in the village that Hinduism is most efficiently disseminated from generation to generation. Another source of Hindu lore is the Puranas, collections of legends and myths.

The period from roughly 500 BC to 1000 AD is sometimes spoken of as that of classical Hinduism. It was during this period that the major literature was composed, the great philosophical systems developed, and the basic Vaishnava and Shaiva sects organized. After 1000, beginning in south India somewhat earlier, a spirit of devotional fervor coupled with social reform swept through India, and the period from that time until near the present is known as the bhakti period. During this time the forms of religious worship changed and diversified further. Singing of devotional songs and poems in the vernacular rather than in Sanskrit, the language in which practically all classical Hindu literature was written, is one example. Direct approach to the god was emphasized, and the mediating role of the priest somewhat curtailed. Love, a sentiment common to all but particularly to the most ordinary villager, is now celebrated as the way to the highest end; some bhakti philosophies hold that liberation is not the supreme goal and that loving service to God is a higher one.

Recent developments in Hinduism are indicative of a movement away from certain aspects of classical practice, such as: Suttee, a widow's suicide at her husband's funeral; caste distinctions; and even karma and rebirth.

The Four Vedas are the Sacred Books of the Hindu

Hinduism emphasizes the necessity of escaping from material life and of extinguishing desire. Hinduism is very ritualistic and includes extreme self denial and self punishment. Cows are considered sacred as are rivers. Most Hindus believe in the transmigration of souls (reincarnation), where when a person dies, his soul enters the body of a newborn child or even the body of an animal. Over and over. Therefore, devout Hindus will not kill even a fly. They are vegetarians, lest by eating meat they become cannibals.

The caste system in India is directly related to their religious beliefs. About 2500 years before Christ, a white people called the Aryans came to India (probably from Persia.) The Aryans formed a caste system in order to maintain the purity of their blood and to maintain white supremacy. Originally, they recognized only four castes:

1. *Brahmans,* (highest) priests and scholars.
2. *Kshatriyas,* (next) nobles and warriors.
3. *Vaisyas,* (next) farmers and merchants.
4. *Sudras,* (lowest) serfs and slaves.

Later, these four castes multiplied until today where there are thousands of castes in India. Only Hindus practice the caste system; it is abandoned if a Hindu becomes a Mohammedan or a Christian.

The castes became hereditary which meant that all sons are necessarily members of the same caste as their father and that he has to follow his father's occupation. The 7000 modern castes even include a caste of thieves!

If someone is expelled from his caste or has no caste by birth, he is known as an Untouchable, a pariah, and such a person is in a hopeless and pitiable condition. There are currently more than 60,000,000 untouchables in India.

Hinduism teaches that anyone born into a lower caste or an Untouchable is being punished for the sins committed in his past life. If such a person is calmly resigned to his fate and lives rightly, he will be elevated in caste in his next life. This premise tends to make the members of the lower castes and the untouchables submissive to the terrible economic and social conditions under which they live.

Brahma is the chief god, the omnipresent one who is father of the Brahman Trinity. He has four heads, three of which (representing their Trinity) can be seen from any point of view.

Brahma (the creator)
Vishnu (the preserver)
Siva (the destroyer of evil)

Vaishnavism

Vaishnavism is a tradition of Hinduism, distinguished from other schools by its worship of Vishnu or his associated avatars, principally as Rama and Krishna, as the original and supreme God. This worship in different perspectives or historical traditions addresses monotheistic

God under the names of Narayana, Krishna, Vâsudeva or more often 'Vishnu', and their associated avatars. It is principally monotheistic in its philosophy, but not exclusive. Its beliefs and practices, especially the concepts of Bhakti and Bhakti Yoga, are based largely on the Upanishads, and associated with the Vedas and Puranic texts such as: the Bhagavad Gita, and the Padma, Vishnu and Bhagavata Puranas.

The followers of Vaishnavism are referred to as *Vaishnava(s)* or *Vaishnavites*. According to recent statistics, a majority of Hindus are Vaishnavas, with the vast majority living in India. Awareness, recognition, and growth of the belief has significantly increased outside of India in recent years. The Gaudiya Vaishnava branch of the tradition has significantly increased the awareness of Vaishnavism internationally, since the mid-1900s, largely through the activities and geographical expansion of the Hare Krishna movement, primarily through ISKCON and more recently, through several other Vaishnava organizations conducting preaching activities in the West.

Etymology

The term *Vaishnavism* entered the English language in the 19th century. It was formed by attaching the suffix *-ism* to Sanskrit *Vaishnava* (IAST: vaicGava), which is the *vriddhi* form of *Vishnu* meaning 'relating, belonging, or sacred to Vishnu' or 'a worshipper or follower of Vishnu'.

Principal Historic Branches

Bhagavatism, early Ramaism and Krishnaism, merged in historical Vishnuism, a tradition of Historical Vedic religion, distinguished from other traditions by its primary worship of Vishnu. Vaishnavism is historically the first structured Vaishnava religion as "Vishnuism, in a word, is the only cultivated native sectarian native religion of India." Although it is usual to speak of Vishnu as the source of the avataras, this is only one of the names by which the God of Vaishnavism is known. The other names include Narayana, Vasudeva and Krishna; each the name of a divine figure with attributed supremacy, which each associated tradition of Vaishnavism, believes to be distinct. For example, in the Krishnaism branch of Vaishnavism, such as: the Gaudiya Vaishnava, Nimbaraka and Vallabhacharya traditions, devotees worship Krishna as the supreme form of God, Svayam Bhagavan, in contrast to the belief of the devotees of the Vishnu tradition.

Principal Beliefs

Supreme God

The principal belief of Vishnu-centered sects is the identification of Vishnu or Narayana as the one Supreme God. This belief contrasts with the Krishna-centered traditions, such as: Vallabha Sampradaya and Gaudiya Vaishnavas, in which Krishna is considered to be the Supreme God and the source of all avataras. The belief in the supremecy of Vishnu is based upon the many avatars (incarnations) of Vishnu listed in the Puranic texts, which differs from other Hindu deities such as: Ganesh, Surya or Durga. The latter are instead classified as demi-gods or devas. Vaishnavites consider Shiva, one of the Hindu Trimurti (Trinity) as subservient to Vishnu, and a Vaishnava himself. Swaminarayan, founder of the Swaminarayan faith, differs with this view and holds that Vishnu and Shiva are different aspects of the same God. Notably, the Swaminarayan view is a minority view among Vaishnavites.

A few Vaishnava schools also identify the God of the Abrahamic religions with Vishnu, which is however problematic, since Yahweh was originally only one of the middle-eastern deities and not a monotheistic God. Another distinguishing feature of the Vaishnava teachings, is that God (Vishnu and/or Krishna) 'is a real person and His variegated creation is also real'.

Worship

Vaishnava theology includes: the central beliefs of Hinduism such as: reincarnation, samsara, karma, and the various Yoga systems, but with a particular emphasis on devotion (bhakti) to Vishnu through the process of Bhakti yoga, often including singing Vishnu's name's (bhajan), meditating upon his form (dharana) and performing deity worship (puja). The practices of deity worship are primarily based on texts such as: Pañcaratra and various Samhitas.

Within their worship Vaishnava devotees consider that Vishnu is within them, as the Antaryami or the God within and as the foundation of their being; which is a part of the definition of the name Narayana. Unlike other schools of Hinduism whose goal is liberation (moksha), or union with the Supreme Brahman, the ultimate goal of Vaishnava practice is an eternal life of bliss (ananda) in service to Vishnu, or one of his many avatars, in the spiritual realm of 'Vaikuntha', which lies beyond the temporary world of illusion (maya). The three features of the Supreme as described in the Bhagavata Purana – Brahman, Paramatma and Bhagavan – are viewed as the *Universal Vishnu*, *Vishnu within the Heart*, and *Vishnu the personality* respectively.

Initiation

Vaishnavas commonly follow a process of initiation (diksha), given by a guru, under whom they are trained to understand Vaishnava practices. At the time of initiation, the disciple is traditionally given a specific mantra, which the disciple will repeat, either out loud or within the mind, as an act of worship to Vishnu or one of his avatars. The practice of repetitive prayer is known as japa. The system of receiving initiation and training from a spiritual master is based on injunctions throughout the scriptures held as sacred within the Vaishnava traditions:

"*Just try to learn the truth by approaching a spiritual master. Inquire from him submissively and render service unto him. The self-realized souls can impart knowledge unto you because they have seen the truth.*" (Bhagavad Gita)

"*One who is initiated into the Vaishnava mantra and who is devoted to worshiping Lord Vishnu is a Vaishnava. One who is devoid of these practices is not a Vaishnava.*" (Padma Purana)

The scriptures specific to the Gaudiya Vaishnava group also state that one who performs an act of worship as simple as chanting the name of Vishnu or Krishna can be considered a Vaishnava by practice:

"*Who chants the holy name of Krishna just once may be considered a Vaishnava. Such a person is worshipable and is the topmost human being.*" (Chaitanya Charitamrita)

Attitude toward Scriptures

Vaishnava traditions refer to the writings of previous acharyas in their respective lineage or *sampradya* (see below) as authoritative interpretations of scripture. While many schools like: Smartism and Advaitism encourage interpretation of scriptures philosophically and metaphorically and not too literally, Vaishnavism stresses the literal meaning (*mukhya vritti*) as primary and indirect meaning (*gauna vritti*) as secondary: *sâkshâd upadesas tu shrutih* – "The instructions of the shruti-shâstra should be accepted literally, without *fanciful or allegorical interpretations*." This is an example that even within hindu religion there exists fundamentalism – the literal interpretations of religious mythology, similar to christian fundamentalists of various cults.

Vaishnava Sampradayas

Within Vaishnavism there are four main disciplic lineages (sampradayas), each exemplified by a specific Vedic personality. The four sampradayas follow subtly different philosophical systems regarding the relationship between the soul (jiva) and God (Vishnu or Krishna), although the majority of other core beliefs are identical.

Lakshmi Sampradaya

- *Philosophy*: Vishishtadvaita ('qualified nondualism'), espoused by Ramanujacharya See Sri Vaishnavism.

Brahma Sampradaya

- *Philosophies*: Dvaita ('dualism'), espoused by Madhvacharya, and Achintya Bheda Abheda (literally 'inconceivable difference and non-difference'), espoused by Chaitanya Mahaprabhu (see Gaudiya Vaishnavism).

Rudra Sampradaya

- *Philosophy*: Shuddhadvaita ('pure nondualism'), espoused by Vishnuswami and Vallabhacharya.

Kumara Sampradaya

- *Philosophy*: Dvaitadvaita ('duality in unity'), espoused by Nimbarka.

Other Branches and Sects

- The Ramanandi movement, begun by Ramananda.
- Mahapuruxiya Dharma, espoused by Sankardeva.
- Vaisnava-Sahajiya, a tantric school

History

Main Article: Historical Vishnuism

The monotheistic worship of Vishnu was already well developed in the period of the Itihasas. Hopkins says 'Vishnuism, in a word, is the only cultivated native sectarian native religion of India.' Vaishnavism is expounded in a part of the Mahabharata known as the Bhagavad Gita, which contains the words of Krishna, one the avatars of Vishnu.

Many of the ancient kings, beginning with Chandragupta II (Vikramaditya) were known as Parama Bhagavatas, or Bhagavata Vaishnavas.

Vaishnavism flourished in South India during the seventh to tenth centuries CE, and is still commonplace, especially in Tamil Nadu, as a result of the twelve Alvars, saints who spread the sect to the common people with their devotional hymns. The temples which the Alvars visited or founded are now known as Divya Desams. Their poems in praise of Vishnu and Krishna in Tamil language are collectively known as *Naalayira* (Divya Prabandha).

In later years Vaishnava practices increased in popularity due to the influence of sages like: Ramanujacharya, Madhvacharya, Manavala Mamunigal, Vedanta Desika, Surdas, Tulsidas, Tyagaraja, and many others.

In his *The Religions of India*, Edward Washburn Hopkins presents an accepted distinction as to the assumption that Vishnuism is associated with Vedic Brahmanism, and was part of Brahmanism. Krishnaism was adopted much later, and it is for this reason, amongst others, that despite its modern iniquities Shiva has appealed more to the Brahmans than Krishna. It's only later that Vishnuism merged with Krishnaism.

Large Vaishnava communities now exist throughout India, and particularly in Western Indian states, such as: Rajasthan and Gujarat. Important sites of pilgrimage for Vaishnavs include: Guruvayur Temple, Sri Rangam, Vrindavan, Mathura, Ayodhya, Tirupati, Puri, Mayapur and Dwarka.

Since the 1900s Vaishnavism has spread from within India and is now practiced in many places around the globe, including: America, Europe, Africa, Russia and South America. This is largely due to the growth of the ISKCON movement, founded by A.C. Bhaktivedanta Swami Prabhupada in 1966.

Puranic Epics

Two great Indianepics, Ramayana and Mahabharata, are an important part of Vaishnava philosophy, theology, and culture.

The Ramayana describes the story of Rama, an avatar of Vishnu, and is taken as a history of the 'ideal king', based on the principles of dharma, morality and ethics. Rama's wife Sita, his brother Lakshman and his devotee/follower Hanuman all play key roles within the Vaishnava tradition as examples of Vaishnava etiquette and behaviour. Ravana, the evil king and villain of the epic, plays the opposite role of how not to behave.

The Mahabharata is centered around Krishna, another avatar of Vishnu, and details the story of a dynastic war between two families of cousins, with Krishna and the Pandavas, five brothers, playing pivotal roles in the drama. The philosophical highlight of the work is the chapter covering a conversation between Arjuna and Krishna prior to the final battle, individually known as the Bhagavad Gita. The Bhagavad Gita, though influential in most philosophies of Hinduism, is of particular importance to Vaishnavas because it is believed to be an accurate record of the very words spoken by Krishna himself. Depending on the Sampradaya or Vaishnava group one follows, Krishna is regarded either as a full avatar of Vishnu, non-different from him, or as the source of all avatars including Vishnu himself, a notion held only within the Gaudiya and Nimbarka branches of Vaishnavism.

Both works are often reenacted in part as dramas by followers of Vaishnavism, especially on festival days concerning each of the specific avatars. The Bhagavad Gita is widely studied as a theological textbook and is rendered in numerous English translations and world languages.

Shaivism

Shaivism, names the oldest of the four sects of Hinduism. Followers of Shaivism, called 'Shaivas,' and also 'Saivas' or 'Saivites,' revere Shiva as the Supreme Being. Shaivas believe that Shiva is All and in all, the creator, preserver, destroyer, revealer and concealer of all that is. Shaivism is widespread throughout India, Nepal, and Sri Lanka, mostly. Notable areas of the practice of Shaivism also include parts of Southeast Asia like: Malaysia, Singapore, and Indonesia.

History

It is very difficult to determine the early history of Shaivism. The *Svetâsvatara Upanishad* (400 - 200 BCE) is the earliest textual exposition of a systematic philosophy of Shaivism. As explained by Gavin Flood, the text proposes: a theology which elevates Rudra to the status of supreme being, the Lord (Sanskrit: Îsa) who is transcendent yet also has cosmological functions, as does Siva in later traditions.

During the Gupta Dynasty (c. 320 - 500 CE) Puranic religion developed and Shaivism spread rapidly, eventually throughout the subcontinent, spread by the singers and composers of the Puranic narratives.

General Features

Sacred ash came to be used as a sign of Shaivism. Devotees of Shiva wear it as a sectarian mark on their foreheads and other parts of their bodies with reverence. The Sanskrit words *bhasma* and *vibhuti* can both be translated as 'sacred ash'.

Major Schools

Shaivism has many different schools showing both regional variations and differences in philosophy. Shaivism has a vast literature that includes texts representing multiple philosophical schools, including non-dualist (*abheda*), dualist (*bheda*), and non-dual-with-dualism (*bhedâbheda*) perspectives.

Alexis Sanderson's review of Shaivite groups makes a broad distinction into two groups, with further subdivisions within each group:

- Vedic, Puranic.
- *Non-Puranic.*

These devotees are distinguished by undergoing initiation (*dîksa*) into a specific cult affiliation for the dual purposes of obtaining liberation in this life (*mukti*) and/or obtaining other aims (*bhukti*). Sanderson subdivides this group further into two sub-groups:

Those which follow the outer or higher path (*atimârga*), seeking only liberation. Among the atimârga groups two are particularly important, the Pâsupatas and a sub-branch, the Lâkula, from whom another important sect, the Kâlâmukhas, developed.

Those which follow the path of mantras (*mantramârga*), seeking both liberation and worldly objectives.

The following are concise summaries of some of the major schools of Shaivism, along with maps showing the primary areas of origin or present-day influence and concentration of each school in areas of the Indian sub-continent.

Home Worship

People also worship Shiva at home. They have natural lingam-shaped stones to which they perform ablution flower-worship and Nivedhanam, a type of food-offering.

It is also common to have small shrines or altars dedicated to Lord Shiva, with images of his sons Ganesha or Skanda, other household deities, or his consort.

BRAHMINISM

By Brahminism is meant the complex religion and social system which grew out of the polytheistic nature-worship of the ancient Aryan conquerors of northern India, and came, with the spread of their dominion, to be extended over the whole country, maintaining itself, not without profound modifications, down to the present day. In its intricate modern phases it is generally known as Hinduism.

BRAHMIN TEXTS

Our knowledge of Braḥminism in its earlier stages is derived from its primitive sacred books, originally oral compositions, belonging to the period between 1500-400 B.C.

First of all, there are four Vedas (Veda means wisdom) dating from 1500 to 800 B.C., and consisting of a collection of ancient hymns (riks), the so-called Rig-Veda, in praise of the many gods; Of the Sama-veda, compiled from parts of the Rig-Veda as a song-service for the soma-sacrifice; of the Yajur-Veda, a liturgy composed partly of ancient hymns and partly of other prayers and benedictions to be used in the various forms of sacrifice; and of the Atharva-Veda, a collection of popular exorcisms and magical incantations largely inherited from primitive Aryan days.

Next in order are the Brahmanas (about 1000-600 B.C.). They are a series of verbose and miscellaneous explanations of the texts, rites, and customs found in each of the four Vedas, composed expressly for the use of the Brahmins, or priests. They are followed (800-500 B.C.) by the so-called Upanishads, concerned chiefly with pantheistic speculations on the nature of deity and the end of man; and lastly, by the Sutras (600-400 B.C.), which are compendious guides to the proper observance of the rites and customs. The most important are the Grhya-Sutras, or house-guides, treating of domestic rites, and the Dharma-sutras, or law-guides, which were manuals of religious and social customs. Being meant for layman as well as priest, they reflect the popular, practical side of Brahminism, whereas the Brahmanas and Upanishads show us the religion on its priestly, speculative side. Closely related to the law-guides is the justly famed metrical treatise, Manava-Dharma-Sastra, known in English as the Laws of Manu. It belongs probably to the fifth century B.C. These, together with the two sacred epics of a later age, the 'Ramayana,' and the 'Mahabharata,' embrace what is most important in sacred Brahmin literature.

EARLY BRAHMINISM OR VEDISM

The religion of the Vedic period proper was comparatively simple. It consisted in the worship of many deities, great and small, the personified forces of nature. Prominent among these were Varuna, the all-embracing heaven, maker and lord of all things and upholder of the moral law; the sun-god, variously known as Surya, the enemy of darkness and bringer of blessings; as Pushan the nourisher; Mitra, the omniscient friends of the good, and the avenger of deceit; as Savitar the enlightener, arousing men to daily activity, and as Vishnu, said to have measured the earth in three great strides and to have given the rich pastures to mortals; the god of the air, Indra, like: Mars, also, the mighty god of war, who set free from the cloud-serpent Ahi (or Vritra), the quickening rain; Rudra, later known as Siva, the blessed one, the god of the destructive thunderstorm, an object of dread to evil-doers, but a friend to the good; Agni, the fire-god, the friend and benefactor of man, dwelling on their hearths, and bearing to the gods their prayers and sacrificial offerings; Soma, the god of that mysterious plant whose inebriating juice was so dear to the gods and to man, warding off disease, imparting strength and securing immortality.

There were no temples in this early period. On a small mound of earth or of stones the offering was made to the gods, often by the head of the family, but in the more important and complicated sacrifices by the priest, or Brahmin, in union with the householder. The object of every sacrifice was to supply strengthening food to the gods and to secure blessings in return. Human victims, though rare, were not wholly unknown, but animal victims were at this period in daily use. First in importance were the horse, then the ox or cow, the sheep, and the goat. Offerings of clarified butter, rice, wheat, and other kinds of grain were also very common. But dearer to the gods than any of these gifts, and rivaling the horse-sacrifice in solemnity, was the offering of the inebriating juice of the Soma-plant, the so-called Soma-sacrifice. Hymns of praise and petitions, chiefly for the good things of life, children, health, wealth, and success in undertakings, accompanied these sacrificial offerings. But the higher needs of the soul were not forgotten. In hymns of Varuna, Mitra, and the other gods there are striking texts expressing a sense of guilt and asking for forgiveness. At a time when the earlier Hebrew scriptures were silent as to the rewards and punishments awaiting man in the future life, we find the ancient rik-bards giving repeated expression to their belief in a heaven of endless bliss for the just, and in an abyss of darkness for the wicked.

Devotion to the Pitris (Fathers), or dead relatives, was also a prominent element in their religion. Although the Pitris mounted to the heavenly abode of bliss, their happiness was not altogether independent of the acts of devotion shown them by the living. It could be greatly increased by offerings of Soma, rice, and water; for like the gods they were thought to have bodies of air-like texture, and to enjoy the subtile essence of food. Hence, the surviving children felt it a sacred duty to make feast-offerings, called Sraddhas, at stated times to their departed Pitris. In return for these acts of filial piety, the grateful Pitris protected them from harm and promoted their welfare. Lower forms of nature-worship also obtained. The cow was held in reverence. Worship was given to trees and serpents. Formulae abounded for healing the diseased, driving off demons, and averting evil omens. Witchcraft was dreaded, and recourse to ordeals was common for the detection of guilt.

POPULAR BRAHMINISM

In the period that saw the production of the Brahmanas and the Upanishads, the Vedic religion underwent a twofold change. On the practical side there was an exuberant growth of religious rites and of social restrictions and duties, while on the theoretical side, Vedic belief in the efficacy of personal deities was subordinated to a pantheistic scheme of salvation. Thus the earlier religion developed on the one hand into popular, exoteric Brahminism, and on the other hand into priestly, esoteric Brahminism. The former is reflected in the Brahmanas and the Sutras; the latter in the Upanishads.

The transformation to popular Brahminism was largely due to the influence of the Brahmins, or priests. Owing to their excessive fondness for symbolic words and forms, the details of ritual became more and more intricate, some assuming so elaborate a character as to require the services of sixteen priests. The sacrifice partook of the nature of a sacramental rite, the due performance of which was sure to produce the desired end, and thus became an all-important centre around which the visible and invisible world revolved. Hence it merited liberal fees to the officiating priests. Still it was not a mere perfunctory rite, for if performed by an unworthy priest it was accounted as both useless and sacrilegious. In keeping with this complicated liturgy was the multitude of prayers and rites which entered into the daily life of both priest and layman. The daily recitation of parts of the Vedas, now venerated as divine revelation, was of first importance, especially for the Brahmins. It was a sacred duty for every individual to recite, morning and evening, the Savitri, a short prayer in honor of the vivifying sun. A scrupulous regard for ceremonial purity, surpassing even that of the Jewish Pharisee, gave rise to an endless succession of purifactory rites, such as: baths, sprinkling with water, smearing with ashes or cow-dung, sippings of water, suppressions of breath – all sacramental in character and efficacious for the remission of sin. There is reason to believe that the consciousness of guilt for sin committed was keen and vivid, and that in the performance of these rites, so liable to abuse, a penitential disposition of soul was largely cultivated.

In popular Brahminism of this period the idea of retribution for sin was made to embrace the most rigorous and far-reaching consequences, from which, save by timely penance, there was no escape. As every good action was certain of future recompense, so every evil one was destined to bear its fruit of misery in time to come. This was the doctrine of karma (action) with which the new idea of rebirth was closely connected. While the lasting bliss of heaven was still held out to the just, different fates after death were reserved for the wicked, varying, according to the nature and amount of guilt, from long periods of torture in a graded series of hells, to a more or less extensive series of rebirths in the forms of plants, animals, and men. From the grade to which the culprit was condemned, he had to pass by slow transition through the rest of the ascending scale till his rebirth as a man of honorable estate was attained. This doctrine gave rise to restrictive rules of conduct that bordered on the absurd. Insects, however repulsive and noxious, might not be killed; water might not be drunk till it was first strained, lest minute forms of life be destroyed; carpentry, basket-making, working in leather, and other similar occupations were held in disrepute, because they could not be carried on without a certain loss of animal and plant life. Some zealots went so far as to question the blamelessness of tilling the ground on account of the unavoidable injury done to worms and insects. But on the other hand, the Brahmin ethical teaching in the legitimate sphere of right conduct is remarkably high. Truthfulness, obedience to parents and superiors, temperance, chastity, and almsgiving were strongly inculcated. Though allowing, like other religions of antiquity, polygamy and divorce, it strongly forbade adultery and all forms of unchastity. It also reprobated suicide, abortion, perjury, slander, drunkenness, gambling, oppressive usury, and wanton cruelty to animals. Its Christianlike aim to soften the hard side of human nature is seen in its many lessons of mildness, charity towards the sick, feeble, and aged, and in its insistence on the duty of forgiving injuries and returning good for evil. Nor did this high standard of right conduct apply simply to external acts. The threefold division of good and bad acts into thought, words, and deeds finds frequent expression in Brahmánic teaching.

Intimately bound up in the religious teaching of Brahminism was the division of society into rigidly defined castes. In the earlier, Vedic period there had been class distinctions according to which the warrior class (Kshatriyas, or Rajanas) stood first in dignity and importance, next the priestly class (Brahmins), then the farmer class (Vaisyas), and last of all, the servile class of conquered natives (Sudras). With the development of Brahminism, these four divisions of society became stereotyped into exclusive castes, the highest place of dignity being usurped by the Brahmins. As teachers of the sacred Vedas, and as priests of the all-important sacrifices, they professed to be the very representatives of the gods and the peerage of the human race. No honor was too great for them, and to lay hands on them was a sacrilege. One of their chief sources of power and influence lay in their exclusive privilege to teach the youth of the three upper castes, for education then consisted largely in the acquisition of Vedic lore, which only priests could teach. Thus the three upper castes alone had the right to know the Vedas and to take part in the sacrifices, and Brahminism, far from being a religion open to all, was exclusively a privilege of birth, from which the despised caste of Sudras was excluded.

The rite of initiation into Brahminism was conferred on male children only, when they began their studies under a Brahmin teacher, which took place generally in the eighth year of the Brahmin and in the eleventh and twelfth years for the Kshatriya and the Vaisya respectively. It consisted in the investiture of the sacred cord, a string of white cotton yarn tired together at the ends, and worn like a deacon's stole, suspended on the left shoulder. The investiture was a sort of sacrament in virtue of which the youth was freed from guilt contracted from his parents and became Dvi-ja, twice-born, with the right to learn the sacred Vedic texts and to take part in the sacrifices. The period of studentship was not long for members of the warrior and farmer castes, but for the young Brahmin, who had to learn all the Vedas by heart, it consumed nine years or more. During this period, the student was subjected to severe moral discipline. He had to rise before the sun, and was not allow reclining until after sunset. He was denied rich and dainty foods, and what he ate at his two daily meals he had to beg. He was expected to observe the strictest chastity. He was bound to avoid music, dancing, gambling, falsehood, and disrespect to superiors and to the aged, covetousness, anger, and injury to animals.

Marriage was held to be a religious duty for every twice-born. It was generally entered upon early in life, not long after the completion of the time of studentship. Like the initiation rite, it was a solemn sacramental ceremony. It was an imperative law that the bride and groom should be of the same caste in the principal marriage; for, as polygamy was tolerated, a man might take one or more secondary wives from the lower castes. For certain grave reasons, the household might repudiate his wife and marry another, but a wife on her part had no corresponding right of divorce. If her husband died, she was expected to remain for the rest of her life in chaste widowhood, if she would be honored on earth, and happy with him in heaven. The later Hindu practice known as the Suttee, in which the bereaved wife threw herself on the funeral pyre of her husband, seems at this period to have been unknown. All knowledge of the Vedic texts was withheld from woman, but she had the right to participate with her husband in the sacrifices performed for him by some officiating priest. One important sacrifice remained in his own hands – the morning and evening offering of hot milk, butter, and grain to the fire on the hearth, which was sacred to Agni, and was kept always burning.

A strong tendency to asceticism asserted itself in the Brahminism of this period. It found expression in the fasts preceding the great sacrifices, in the severe penances prescribed for various kinds of sin, in the austere life exacted of the student, in the conjugal abstinence to be observed for the first three days following marriage and on certain specified days of the month, but, above all, in the rigorous life of retirement and privation to which not a few devoted their declining years. An ever increasing number of householders, chiefly Brahmins, when their sons had grown to man's estate, abandoned their homes and spent the rest of their lives as ascetics, living apart from the villages in rude huts, or under the shelter of trees, eating only the simplest kinds of food, which they obtained by begging, and subjecting themselves to extraordinary fasts and mortifications. They were known as Sannyasis, or Yogis, and their severity of life was not so much a penitential life for past offenses as a means of acquiring abundant religious merits and superhuman powers. Coupled with these mortifications was the practice of Yogi (union). They would sit motionless with legs crossed, and, fixing their gaze intently on an object before them, would concentrate their thought on some abstract subject until they lapsed into a trance. In this state they fancied they were united with the deity, and the fruit of these contemplations was the pantheistic view of religion which found expression in the Upanishads, and left a permanent impress on the Brahmin mind.

PANTHEISTIC BRAHMINISM

The marked monotheistic tendency in the later Vedic hymns had made itself more and more keenly felt in the higher Brahmin circles till it gave rise to a new deity, a creation of Brahmin priests. This was Prabjapati, lord of creatures, omnipotent and supreme, later known as Brahmá, the personal creator of all things. But in thus looking up to a supreme lord and creator, they were far removed from Christian monotheism. The gods of the ancient pantheon were not repudiated, but were worshipped still as the various manifestations of Brahmá. It was an axiom then, as it has been ever since with the Hindu mind, that creation out of nothing is impossible. Another Brahmin principle is that every form of conscious individuality, whether human or Divine, implies a union of spirit and matter. And so, outside the small school of thinkers who held matter to be eternal, those who stood for the supreme personal god explained the world of visible things and invisible gods as the emanations of Brahmá. They arrived at a personal pantheism. But speculation did not end here. To the prevailing school of dreamy Brahmin ascetics, whose teachings are found in the Upanishads, the ultimate source of all things was not the personal Brahmá, but the formless, characterless, unconscious spirit known at Atman (self), or, more commonly Brahmâ. (Brahmâ is neuter, whereas Brahmá, personal god, is masculine.) The heavens and the earth, men and gods, even the personal deity, Brahmá, were but transitory emanations of Brahmâ, destined in time to lose their individuality and be absorbed into the great, all-pervading, impersonal spirit. The manifold external world thus had no real existence. It was Maya, illusion. Brahmâ alone existed. It alone was eternal, imperishable.

This impersonal pantheism of the Brahmin ascetics led to a new conception of the end of man and of the way of salvation. The old way was to escape rebirths and their attendant misery by storing up merits of good deeds so as to obtain an eternal life of conscious bliss in heaven. This was a mistake. For so long as man was ignorant of his identity with Brahmá and did not see that his true end consisted in being absorbed into the impersonal all-god from which he sprang; so long as he set his heart on a merely personal existence, no amount of good works would secure his freedom from rebirth. By virtue of his good deeds he would, indeed, mount to heaven, perhaps win a place among the gods but after a while his store of merits would give out like oil in a lamp, and he would have to return once more to life to taste in a new birth the bitterness of earthly existence. The only way to escape this misery was through the saving recognition of one's identity with Brahmâ. As so as one could say from conviction, 'I am Brahmâ,' the bonds were broken that held him fast to the illusion of personal immortality and consequently to rebirth. Thus, cultivating, by a mortified life, freedom form all desires, man spent his years in peaceful contemplation till death put an end to the seeming duality and he was absorbed in Brahmâ like a raindrop in the ocean.

THE PURANIC NATURE OF HINDUISM

Vedic, Puranic and Non-Puranic

These devotees are distinguished by undergoing initiation (*dîksa*) into a specific cult affiliation for the dual purposes of obtaining liberation in this life (*mukti*) and/or obtaining other aims (*bhukti*). Sanderson subdivides this group further into two subgroups:

Those which follow the outer or higher path (*atimârga*), seeking only liberation. Among the atimârga groups two are particularly important, the Pâsupatas and a sub-branch, the Lâkula, from whom another important sect, the Kâlâmukhas, developed.

Those which follow the path of mantras (*mantramârga*), seeking both liberation and worldly objectives.

The following are concise summaries of some of the major schools of Shaivism, along with maps showing the primary areas of origin or present-day influence and concentration of each school in areas of the Indian sub-continent.

Puranic Epics

Two great Indianepics, Ramayana and Mahabharata, are an important part of Vaishnava philosophy, theology, and culture.

The Ramayana describes the story of Rama, an avatar of Vishnu, and is taken as a history of the 'ideal king', based on the principles of dharma, morality and ethics. Rama's wife Sita, his brother Lakshman and his devotee/follower Hanuman all play key roles within the Vaishnava tradition as examples of Vaishnava etiquette and behaviour. Ravana, the evil king and villain of the epic, plays the opposite role of how not to behave.

The Mahabharata is centered on Krishna, another avatar of Vishnu, and details the story of a dynastic war between two families of cousins, with Krishna and the Pandavas, five brothers, playing pivotal roles in the drama. The philosophical highlight of the work is the chapter covering a conversation between Arjuna and Krishna prior to the final battle, individually known as the Bhagavad Gita. The Bhagavad Gita, though influential in most philosophies of Hinduism, is of particular importance to Vaishnavas because it is believed to be an accurate record of the very words spoken by Krishna himself. Depending on the Sampradaya or Vaishnava group one follows, Krishna is regarded either as a full avatar of Vishnu, non-different from him, or as the source of all avatars including Vishnu himself, a notion held only within the Gaudiya and Nimbarka branches of Vaishnavism.

Both works are often reenacted in part as dramas by followers of Vaishnavism, especially on festival days concerning each of the specific avatars. The Bhagavad Gita is widely studied as a theological textbook and is rendered in numerous English translations and world languages.

CHAPTER

2 Bhakti Movement

INTRODUCTION

The *Bhakti movement* was a Hindu religious movement in which the main spiritual practice was loving devotion to God, or *bhakti*. The devotion was directed towards a particular form of God, such as: Shiva, Vishnu, Murukan or Shakti. The bhakti movement started in southern India and slowly spread north during the later half of the Indian medieval period (800-1700 CE).

A *bhakta* is a devotee of a particular form of God, such as: Vishnu, Krishna or Rama. In common use it means 'one who follows the path of bhakti', often referred to as bhakti yoga.

A *bhagat* is a holy person who leads humanity towards God. A Bhagat is an Eastern equivalent to a Christian Saint. A Bhagat may also be a guru, in which case he would have a huge following or sangat.

CHIEF SAINTS OF BHANKTHI MOVEMENT

Indian Bhakti Preachers

There are some personalities that are known as the saints of Bhakti movement and they are widely respectable.

Ramanuja

The first great exponent of Bhakti was Ramanuja. He lived in the eleventh century. He asked his followers to worship Vishnu. He did not believe in Sankara's Advaita doctrine according to which the universal soul and the individual souls are one. According to Ramanuja the individual souls exhale from him but are not essentially one with the Supreme Reality. He, therefore, preached that the individual souls should seek His grace by love and devotion to him. His teachings appealed to large numbers of man in South India.

Ramananda

Ramananda flourished in North India in the fourteenth century. He entirely discarded the theory of caste system by birth. He preached the worship of Rama and Sita. Persons of all castes became his disciples. Among his chief disciples there was a barber, a chamar and a weaver. He preached in Hindi, which was the language of the common man in northern India. His followers are worshippers of Rama whom they regard an incarnation of Vishnu.

Kabir

The life of Kabir is totally unknown to the humankind. A true proponent of the Bhakti Movement Kabir was a holy soul who further preached about the unity of Hindu and Muslim.

Guru Nanak

Nanaka was born in 1469 in the village to Talwandi. Presently the place is known as Nankana in the Sheikhupura district of West Punjab. His parents belonged to Khatri caste. His father Kalu was the Patwari of the village. Nanaka was educated in the village school. From his boyhood he showed a religious bent of mind and paid no attention to his studies.

Vallabhacharya

Vallabhacharya was a Tailang Brahmana. He preached the worship of Vishnu in the form of Krishna. He was born in 1479 in the Telugu country. He visited Mathura, Vrindaban and many other sacred places and finally settled at Benaras.

Chaitanya

Chaitanya was the greatest saint who preached the worship of Krishna and Radha. Chaitanya was born at Navadwipa in 1486. His father Jagannatha Misra was a religious and scholarly man and his mother Sachi was also a pious and religious minded lady. Chaitanya as a boy was an exceptionally brilliant student.

Bhakti movements are Hindu religious movements in which the main spiritual practice is the *fostering of loving devotion to God*, called bhakti. They are monotheistic movements generally devoted to worship of Shiva or Vishnu or Shakti.

Origins

The Bhakti Movement was essentially founded in South India and later spread to the North during the late medieval period. The notion of 'Bhakti' (loosely translated as devotional love to God) is of antiquity. A nascent consciousness of what 'Bhakti' constitutes is already to be found in the earliest Vedas, especially in relation to deities such as: Varuna. A clearer expression of Bhakti began to be formed during the so-called Epic Period and the Puranic periods of Hindu history. Texts such as: the Bhagavad Gita and the BhagavataPurana clearly explore Bhakti Yoga or the Path of Devotion as a means to salvation. The Bhakti Movement itself is a historical-spiritual phenomenon that crystallized in South India during Late Antiquity. It was spearheaded by devotional mystics (later revered as Hindu saints) who extolled devotion and love to God as the chief means of spiritual perfection. The Bhakti movement in South India was spearheaded by the sixty-three Nayanars (Shaivite devotees) and the twelve Alvars (Vaishnavaite devotees). Among the earliest Shaivite mystics was Karaikkal Amaiyar, who probably lived around the late 5th century AD or perhaps the early 6th century. She was said to be a contemporary of the Vaishnavaitesaints Bhuttalwar and Peialwar. Kannapa Nayanar was also an early Shaiva Bhakti saint. But most famous among the Shaiva Bhaktisaints were the 'Nalvar' (The Four Eminent Ones), namely: *(i)* Sundarar, *(ii)* Appar, *(iii)* Sambandar and *(iv)* Manikkavasagar. Their devotional hymns are ecstatic, lyrical and moving. The Vaishnavaite Bhakti movement was contemporaneous with the Shaiva Bhakti movement. The hymns of the twelve alvars are held together as the 'Nalayira Divya Prabandham' and recited (as are the Shaiva texts) in temple rituals. Whilst all the saints are held in great reverence, Aandaal (or Godadevi) in particular holds a special place among the Vaishnavasaints. Not only is she the only female Vaishnava saint but also her hymns are among the best expressions of bridal mysticism in the Hindu religion. The twelve Alvars and the sixty-three Nayanars nurtured the incipient bhakti movement in South India under the Pallavas and Pandyas in the fifth to seventh centuries AD. They constitute South India's 75 Apostles of Bhakti and were greatly influential in determining the expression of faith in South India. The path of devotion as expounded by these mystics would later be incorporated into Ramanuja and Madhva philosophical systems. During the 12th and 13th centuries A.D., the Virashaiva movement and, during the rule of the Vijayanagar Empire in South India, the Haridasa movement spread from present-day Karnataka. The Virashaiva movement spread the philosophy of Basavanna, a Hindu reformer. The seeds of Carnatic music were sown, and the philosophy of Madhvacharya was propagated by the Kannada Haridasas. The Haridasa movement presented, like the Virashaiva movement, another strong current of Bhakti, pervading the lives of millions. The Haridasas presented two groups – Vyasakuta and Dasakuta. The former were required to be proficient in the Vedas, Upanishads and other Darshanas, while the Dasakuta merely conveyed the message of Madhvacharya through the Kannada language to the people. The philosophy of Madhvacharya was preserved and perpetuated by his eminent disciples like: Vyasatirtha or Vyasaraja Naraharitirtha, Vadirajatirtha, Sripadaraya, Jayathirtha and others. In the fifteenth century, the Haridasa movement took shape under Sripadaraya of Mulbagal; but his disciple Vyasatirtha provided it a strong organizational base. He was intimately associated with the Vijayanagar Empire, where he became a great moral and spiritual force. His eminent disciples were Purandaradasa and Kanakadasa. Yakshagana, as a theater form emerged as an offshoot of this movement in Karnataka. The late Bhakti movement led to the proliferation of regional poetic literature in the various vernacular languages of India. The Bhakti movement in what is now Karnataka resulted in a burst of poetic Kannada literature in praise of Lord Vishnu. Some of its leaders include Purandara Dasa and Kanaka Dasa, whose contributions were essential to Carnatic music. The later Carnatic Trinity is also no doubt a product of this long Bhakti Movement. The Bhakti movement began to spread to the North during the late medieval ages when North India was under Muslim domination. There was no grouping of the mystics into Shaiva and Vaishnava devotees as it was in the South. The movement was spontaneous and the various mystics had their own version of devotional expression. Unlike in the South where devotion was centered on Shiva and Vishnu (in all his forms), the Northern devotional movement was more or less centered on Rama and Krishna, both of whom were incarnations of Vishnu. Though this did not mean that the cult of Shiva or of the Devi went into decline. In fact for all of its history the Bhakti movement co-existed peacefully with the other movements in Hinduism. It was initially considered unorthodox as it rebelled against caste distinctions and made disregarded Brahmanic rituals which according to Bhaktisaints not necessary for salvation. In the course of time however, owing to its immense popularity among the masses (and even royal patronage) it became 'orthodox' and continues to be one of the most important modes of religious expression in modern India. In the period between the 14-17th centuries, a great bhakti movement swept through Northern India initiated by a loosely associated group of teachers or 'Sants'. Caitanya, Vallabha, Meera Bai, Kabir, Tulsi Das, Tukaram and other mystics spearheaded the Bhakti movement in the North. Their teachings were that people could cast aside the heavy burdens of ritual and caste and the subtle complexities of philosophy and simply express their overwhelming love for God. This period was also characterized by a spate of devotional literature in vernacular prose and poetry in the ethnic languages of the various Indian states or provinces.

As aforementioned whilst many of the Bhakti mystics focused their attention on Krishna or Rama, it did not necessarily mean that the cult of Shiva was marginalized. The growth of the Vira-Shaiva and the older Shaiva Siddhanta schools in this period, which incorporated Bhakti into their teachings are testimony to the growth of the Shaiva faith in this period. In the thirteenth century Basava founded the Vira-Shaiva school or Virashaivism. He rejected the caste system, denied the supremacy of the Brahmins, condemned ritual sacrifice and insisted on bhakti and the worship of the one God, Shiva. His followers were called Vira-Shaivas, meaning 'stalwart Shiva-worshipers'. The Saiva-Siddhanta school is a form of Shaivism (Shiva worship) found in the south and is of hoary antiquity. It incorporates the teachings of the erstwhile Shaivanayanars and espouses the belief that Shiva is Brahman and his infinite love is revealed in the divine acts of the creation, preservation and destruction of the universe, and in the liberation of the soul.

Seminal Bhakti works in Bengali include the many songs of Ramprasad Sen. His pieces (known as Shyama Sangeet, or Songs of the Dark Mother) are still actively sung today in West Bengal. Coming from the 17th century, they cover an astonishing range of emotional responses to Ma Kali, detailing complex philosophical statements based on Vedanta teachings and more visceral pronouncements of his love of Devi. Using inventive allegory, Ramprasad had 'dialogues' with the Mother Goddess through his poetry, at times chiding her, adoring her, celebrating her as the Divine Mother, reckless consort of Shiva and capricious Shakti, the universal female creative energy, of the cosmos.

The Nature of the Bhakti Movement

Generally speaking the religious movement of this period that lies between 300-1550 A.D. was non-ritualistic and mainly based on Bhakti. It emphasized a religion or faith, which was essentially Hindu but reflected the vigorous monotheism of Islam. All Bhakti cults are essentially monotheistic. It is immaterial whether he is called Siva, Krishna or Devi. They all symbolize the One and the Eternal. It is the religion, philosophy and social thinking that were created during this revival, which enabled Hinduism to reassert itself in the following period. In the religious life of India the glory of the period is most resplendent. Ramanand, Kabir, Mira, and Vallabhacharya in the north, Chaitanya in Bengal, Madhva, Vedanta Desika and numerous others in the south give to the religious life of the period a vitality that Hinduism never seems to have enjoyed before.

Characteristics of Bhakti Movement

One chief characteristic of the Bhakti movement can be mentioned as belief in one God. A devotee could worship God by love and devotion. The second characteristic of the Bhakti movement was that there was no need to worship idols or to perform elaborate rituals for seeking his grace. The third feature on which the Bhakti saints laid stress was the equality of all castes. There was no distinction of high or low as far as the devotion to God was concerned. The fourth feature was the emphasis, which these saints laid on Hindu-Muslim unity. According to these saints all men irrespective of their religion are equal in the eyes of God.

The saints preached in the language of the common people. They did not use Sanskrit, which was the language of the cultured few.

These saints laid stress on purity of heart and practice of virtues like: truth, honesty, kindness, and charity. According to these saints only virtuous man could realize God. These saints considered God as omnipresent and omnipotent. Even a householder could realize God by love and devotion. Some saints regarded God as formless or Nirguna while others consider him as having different forms or Saguna.

The basic principles of the Bhakti movement namely: love and devotion to one personal god and the unity of God were mainly Hindu. But as a result of contact with Islam more emphasis was laid on these principles than performance of outward rituals such as: Yajiias, fasts, going to sacred places, bathing in the Ganges or worship of images.

The Movement had two main objects in view. *One* was to reform Hindu religion to enable it withstand the onslaught of Islamic propaganda. *Two* was to bring about a compromise between Hinduism and Islam.

EFFECTS OF BHAKTHI MOVEMENT

Factors that helped the Development of the Bhakti Movement

There were a number of factors, which contributed to the rise, and growth of the Bhakti movement during the medieval period. The first important factor was the destruction of Hindu temples by the invaders. They destroyed idols of Hindu gods and goddesses. The Hindus lost faith in the dependability of their religious rites and, therefore, chose the path of love and devotion.

The second factor can be presumed as the persecution of Hindus by the Muslim rulers, who tried to convert them to Islam and imposed jaziya if they were not prepared to become followers of Islam.

The third factor was the ill treatment of the lower classes in Hindu society by the persons of upper castes. The people of the lower castes had to suffer injustice and cruelties. So the teachings of the Bhakti saints who preached equality of castes as far as the devotion to God was concerned appealed to the people of lower castes.

The fourth factor was the elaborate rituals that the common man disliked. The Bhakti saints preached the path of devotion and discarded all rituals hence it appealed to the common man. The fifth factor was the enthusiasm and the inspiration of the Bhakti saints. They tried to remove the evils of Hindu society and gave it a new vigor and vitality.

The sixth factor was the inner vitality of Hindu religion that resulted in an intellectual and moral revival of Hinduism. This Hinduism affected every aspect of thought and generated new moral forces, which helped to revitalize Hindu life, and gave it the dynamism. In the sphere of religion and normal thinking in law, in literature and even in political ideals, a new life came into being in India by the middle of the 16th century which KM. Panikkar termed the first Indian Renaissance.

BRAHMA SAMAJ

Brahmo Samaj (Bengali *Bramho Shômaj*) is the societal component of Brahmoism. "It is without doubt the most influential socio-religious movement in the evolution of Modern (*Greater*) India." It was conceived as reformation of the prevailing Bengal of the time and began the Bengal Renaissance of the 19th century pioneering all religious, social and educational advance of the Hindu community in the 19th century. From the *Brahmo Samaj* springs Brahmoism, the most recent of legally recognised religions in India and Bangladesh, reflecting its non-syncretic "foundation of Rammohun Roy's reformed spiritual Hinduism (contained in the 1830 Banian deed) and scientifically invigorated by inclusion of root Hebraic – Islamic creed and practice."

Meaning of Names

The *Brahmo Samaj* is a community of people assembled for orderly public meeting, discussion or worship of the Eternal, Immutable Supreme Being, Author and Preserver of the Universe, "but not under or by any other name designation or title peculiarly used for and applied, to any particular being or beings by any man or set of men whatsoever". The *Brahmo Samaj* represents a body of men who are struggling, in India, to establish the worship of the Supreme Being in spirit as opposed to the prevailing idolatry of the land."

Brahmo (*bramho*) literally means 'one who worships Brahman', and *Samaj* (*Shômaj*) mean 'community of men'.

History and Timeline

On 20 August 1828 the first assembly of the *Brahmo Sabha* (progenitor of the Brahmo Samaj) was held at the North Calcutta house of *Feringhee* Kamal Bose. This day is celebrated by Brahmos as *Bhadrotsab* (*Bhadrotshôb* 'Bhadro celebration'). This *Sabha* was convened at Calcutta by religious reformer Raja Rammohun Roy for his family and friends settled there. The *Sabha* regularly gathered on Saturday between seven o'clock to nine o'clock. These were essentially informal meetings of Bengali Brahmins (the 'twice born'), accompanied by Upanishadic recitations in Sanskrit followed by Bengali translations of the Sanskrit recitation and singing of Brahmo hymns composed by Rammohun. These meetings were open to all Brahmins and there was no formal organization or theology as such.

On 8 January 1830 influential progressive members of the closely related Kulin Brahmin clan (scurrilously described as Pirali Brahminie. Ostracised for service in the Mughal *Nizaamat* of Bengal) of Tagore (*Thakur*) and Roy (*Vandopâdhyây*a) *zumeendar* family mutually executed the Trust deed of Brahmo Sabha for the first Adi Brahmo Samaj (place of worship) on Chitpore Road (now Rabindra Sarani), Kolkata, India with Ram Chandra Vidyabagish as first resident superintendent. On 23 January 1830 or 11th *Magh*, the *Adi Brahmo* premises were publicly inaugurated (with about 500 Brahmins and 1 Englishman present). This day is celebrated by Brahmos as *Maghotsab* মাঘো[]সব *Maghotshôb* 'Magh celebration').

In November 1830 Rammohun Roy left for England.

Decline of Brahmo Sabha

With Rammohun's departure for England in 1830, the affairs of Sabha were effectively managed by Trustees Dwarkanath Tagore and Pandit Ram Chandra Vidyabagish, with Dwarkanath instructing his *diwan* to manage affairs. Weekly service were held consonant with the Trust directive, consisting of three successive parts: recitation of the Vedas by Telegu Brahmins in the closed apartment exclusively before the Brahmin members of the congregation, reading and exposition of the Upanishads for the general audience, and singing of religious hymns. The reading of the Vedas was done exclusively before the Brahmin participants as the orthodox Telegu Brahmin community and its members could not be persuaded to recite the Vedas before Brahmins and non-Brahmins alike.

By the time of Rammohun's death in 1833 near Bristol (UK), attendance at the *Sabha* dwindled and the Telugu Brahmins surreptitiously revived idolatry. The *zumeendars*, being preoccupied in business, had little time for affairs of *Sabha*, and flame of *Sabha* was almost extinguished.

Foundation of Samaj

On 7th Pous 1765 Shaka (1843) Debendranath Tagore and twenty other Tattwabodhini stalwarts were formally invited by Pt. Vidyabagish into the Trust of Brahmo Sabha. The Pous Mela at Santiniketan starts on this day which is considered as foundation of the 'Adi' (First) *Brahmo Samaj* which was named the Calcutta *Brahmo Samaj*. The other Brahmins who took the First Covenant are:

- Shridhar Bhattacharya.
- Shyamacharan Bhattacharya.
- Brajendranath Tagore.
- Girindranath Tagore, brother of Debendranath Tagoreand father of Ganendranath Tagore.
- Anandachandra Bhattacharya.
- Taraknath Bhattacharya.
- Haradev Chattopadhyaya.
- Shyamacharan Mukhopadhyaya.
- Ramnarayan Chattopadhyaya.
- Sashibhushan Mukhopadhyaya.

First Schism

The admittance of Keshub Chandra Sen (a non-Brahmin) into the Calcutta Brahmo Samaj in 1857 while Debendranath was away in Simla caused considerable stress in the movement, with many old Tattvabodhini Brahmin members leaving the Samaj and institutions due to his high-handed ways. These events took place intermittently from 1859, coming to a head publicly between the period of 1 August 1865 till November 1866 with many tiny splinter groups styling themselves as *Brahmo*. The most notable of these groups styled itself 'Brahmo Samaj of India'. This period is referred to in the histories of these secessionists as the 'First Schism'.

Spread of Influence

Although the *Brahmo Samaj* movement was born in Kolkata, the idea soon spread to the rest of India. That happened to be the period when the railways were expanding and communication was becoming easier. Outside Bengal presidency some of the prominent centres of Brahmo activity were: Punjab, Sind, and Bombay and Madras presidencies. Even to this day, there are several active branches outside West Bengal. Bangladesh BrahmoSamaj at Dhaka keeps the lamp burning.

Social and Religious Reform

In all fields of social reform, including abolition of the caste system and of the dowry system, emancipation of women, and improving the educational system, the *Brahmo Samaj* reflected the ideologies of the Bengal Renaissance. Brahmoism, as a means of discussing the dowry system, was a central theme of Sarat Chandra Chattopadhyay's noted 1914 Bengali language novella, *Parineeta*.

All Brahmo marriages were thereafter solemnised under this law which required the affirmation 'I am not Hindu, nor a Mussalman, nor a Christian'. The Special Marriages Act 1872 was repealed by the new Special Marriages Act in 1954 which became the secular Marriage law for India. The old Special Marriages Act of 1872 was allowed to live on as the Hindu Marriage Act 1955 for Hindus – Brahmo Religionists are excluded from this Act; which is applicable, however, to Hindus who follow the BrahmoSamaj. On May 5, 2004 the Supreme Court of India, by order of the Chief Justice, dismissed the Government of West Bengal's 30 year litigation to get Brahmos classified as Hindus. The matter had previously been heard by an 11 Judge Constitution Bench of the Court (the second largest bench in the Court's history). As of 2007 the statutory minimum age for Brahmos to marry is 25(M)/21(F) *vs.* 21(M)/18(or 15F) for Hindus.

It also supported social reform movements of people not directly attached to the *Samaj*, such as: Pandit Iswar Chandra Vidyasagar's movement which promoted widow re-marriage.

Doctrine

The following doctrines, as noted in Renaissance of Hinduism, are common to all varieties and offshoots of the *Brahmo Samaj*:

- Brahmo Samajists have no faith in any scripture as an authority.
- Brahmo Samajists have no faith in Avatars.
- Brahmo Samajists denounce polytheism and idol-worship.
- Brahmo Samajists are against caste restrictions.
- Brahmo Samajists make faith in the doctrines of Karma and Rebirth optional.

RAMAKRISHNA MISSION

Mission together have 166 branch centres all over India and in different parts of the world.

The Motto

The Mission is a registered Society laying emphasis on rendering welfare services undertaken with a spiritual outlook. The service activities are rendered looking upon all as veritable manifestation of the Divine. The Motto of the organization is *Atmano Mokshartham Jagad-hitaya Cha*. Translated from Sanskrit आत्मनोमोक्षार्थम्जगद्धितायच it means *For one's own salvation, and for the good of the world.*

Math and Mission

Strictly speaking, the Ramakrishna Math is a monastic order, and the Ramakrishna Mission is the part of the organization that carries on activities such as: disaster relief, operation of schools and charitable hospitals, and other work. However, because the humanitarian activities of the movement are more well-known than the monastic order, and because the monks of the order perform a great deal of the humanitarian work, 'Ramakrishna Mission' is popularly used to refer to both institutions.

Monastic Order

After the passing away of their Master Sri Ramakrishna in 1886 the young disciples organized themselves into a new monastic order. The original monastery at Baranagar known as: Baranagar Math was sub-sequently moved to two other places before finally being shifted in January 1899 to a newly acquired plot of land at Belur in Howrah district by Swami Vivekananda. This monastery, known as Belur Math, serves as the Mother House for all the monks of Ramakrishna Order who live in the various branch centres of Ramakrishna Math and/or Ramakrishna Mission in different parts of India and the world. All members of the Order undergo training and ordination (Sannyasa) at Belur Math. A candidate for monastic life is treated as a pre-probationer during the first year of his stay at any centre, and as a probationer during the next four years. At the end of this period he is ordained into celibacy (Brahmacharya) and is given certain vows (Pratijna), the most important of which are chastity, renunciation and service. After a further period of four years, if found fit, he is ordained into (Sannyasa) and given the ochre (gerua) clothes to wear.

Activities

The Ramakrishna Mission has its own hospitals, charitable dispensaries, maternity clinics, tuberculosis clinics, and mobile dispensaries. It also maintains training centres for nurses. Orphanages and homes for the elderly are included in the Mission's field of activities, along with rural and tribal welfare work.

In educational activities, the Ramakrishna Mission has established some the renowned educational institutions in India, having its own colleges, vocational training centres, high schools and primary schools, teacher's training institutes, as well as schools for the visually handicapped. The Ramakrishna Mission has also involved in disaster relief operations during famine, epidemic, fire, flood, earthquake, cyclone and communal disturbances.

In a speech made in 1993, Federico Mayor, Director-General of UNESCO, stated: I am indeed struck by the similarity of the constitution of the Ramakrishna Mission which Vivekananda established as early as 1897 with that of UNESCO drawn up in 1945. Both place the human being at the centre of their efforts aimed at development. Both place tolerance at the top of the agenda for building peace and democracy. Both recognize the variety of human cultures and societies as an essential aspect of the common heritage.

Controversies

To a large extent, the Ramakrishna Mission has avoided controversies through its policy of non-involvement in politics.

In 1980, however, in an act that caused 'considerable debate' within the Order, the Mission petitioned the courts to have their organization and movement declared a non-Hindu minority religion. It is possible that this was because they believed there was a danger that the local marxist government would take control of its schools unless it could invoke the extra protection the Indian constitution accords to minority religions. The Supreme Court of India ruled against the Mission in 1995. The leadership today embraces the Mission's status as a Hindu organization.

ARYA SAMAJ

Aum, considered by the Arya Samaj to be the highest and most proper name of God. Arya Samaj (Sanskrit*âryasamâja* आर्यसमाज 'Noble Society') is a Hindu reform movement founded in India by Swami Dayananda in 1875. He was a sannyasi (renouncer) who believed in the infallible authority of the Vedas. Dayananda advocated the doctrine of karma and reincarnation, and emphasized the ideals of brahmacharya (chastity) and sanyasa (renunciation).

The Founding of the Arya Samaj

Vedic Schools

Between 1869 and 1873, Swami Dayanand, a native of the Princely State of Gujarat, made his first earnest attempt at affecting a substantial and lasting reform in his native India. This attempt took the form of the establishment of several so-called 'Vedic Schools' which, in contradistinction to other public schools at the time, put a marked emphasis on attempting to impart Vedic values, culture and religion to its students. The first was established at Farrukhabad in 1869 and reported 50 students as being enrolled in its first year. This initial success led to the founding of four additional schools in rapid succession at *(i)* Mirzapur (1870), *(ii)* Kasganj (1870), *(iii)* Chhalesar (1870) and *(iv)* Varanasi (1873).

The Vedic Schools represented the first practical application of Swami Dayanand's vision of religious and social reform. They enjoyed a mixed reception. On the one hand, students were not allowed to perform traditional *murtipuja* at the school, and were instead expected to perform sandhya (a form of meditative prayer using mantras from the Vedas) and participate in agnihotra twice daily. Also, disciplinary action was swift and not infrequently severe. On the other hand, all meals, lodging, clothing and books were given to the students free of charge, and the study of Sanskrit was opened to non-Brahmins. The most noteworthy feature of the Schools was that only those texts which accepted the authority of the Vedas were to be taught. This, in the opinion of Swami Dayanand, was critical for the spiritual and social regeneration of Vedic culture in India.

Due primarily to organizational problems, the Vedic Schools soon ran into many difficulties. Swami Dayanand had considerable trouble finding qualified teachers who agreed with his views on religious reform, and there existed a paucity of textbooks which he considered suitable for instruction in Vedic culture. Funding was sporadic, attendance fluctuated considerably, and tangible results in the way of noteworthy student achievement were not forthcoming. Consequentially, some of the schools were forced to close shortly after opening. As early as 1874, it had become clear to Swami Dayanand that, without a wide and solid base of support among the public, setting up schools with the goal of imparting a Vedic education would prove to be an impossible task. He therefore decided to invest the greater part of his resources in the clear formulation and widespread propagation of his ideology of reform. Deprived of the full attention of Swami Dayanand, the Vedic School system all but collapsed shortly thereafter, and the last of the remaining schools (Farrukhabad) was finally closed down in 1876 due to Muslim takeover.

Adi Brahmo Samaj

While traveling (1872-73), Swami Dayanand came into close and extended contact with several of the leading Indian intellectuals of the age, including Navin Chandra Roy, Raj Narayan Bose, Debendranath Tagore and Hemendranath Tagore all of whom were actively involved in the Brahmo Samaj. This reform organization, founded in 1828, held many views similar to those of Swami Dayanand in matters both religious (*e.g.*, a belief in monotheism and the eternality of the soul) and social (*e.g.*, the need to abolish the hereditary caste system and uplift the masses through education). Debendranath Tagore had written a book entitled *Brahmo Dharma*, which serves as a comprehensive manual of religion and ethics to the members of that society, and Swami Dayanand had studied it thoroughly while in Calcutta.

Although Swami Dayanand was persuaded on more than one occasion to join the Brahmo Samaj, there existed several points of contention which the Swami simply could not overlook, the most important being the position of the Vedas. Swami Dayanand held the Vedas to be divine revelation, and refused to accept any suggestions to the contrary. Despite this difference of opinion, however, it seems that the members of the BrahmoSamaj and Swami Dayanand parted on good terms, the former having publicly praised the latter's visit to Calcutta in several journals and the latter having taken inspiration from the former's activity in the social sphere.

The Light of Truth

Swami Dayanand made several changes in his approach to the work of reforming Hindu society after having visited Calcutta. The most significant of these changes was that he began lecturing in Hindi. Prior to his tour of Bengal, the Swami had always held his discourses and debates in Sanskrit. While this gained him a certain degree of respect among both the learned and the common people alike, it prevented him from spreading his message to the broader masses. The change to Hindi allowed him to attract increasingly larger crowds, and as a result his ideas of reform began to circulate among the lower classes of society as well.

After hearing some of Swami Dayanand's speeches delivered in Hindi at Varanasi, Raj Jaikishen Das, a native government official there, suggested that the Swami publish his ideas in a book so that they might be distributed among the public. Witnessing the slow collapse of the Vedic Schools due to a lack of a clear statement of purpose and the resultant flagging public support, Swami Dayanand recognized the potential contained in Das' suggestion and took immediate action.

From June to September 1874, Swami Dayanand dictated a comprehensive series of lectures to his scribe, Pundit Bhimsen Sharma, which dealt with his views and beliefs regarding a wide range of subjects including God, the Vedas, Dharma, the soul, science, philosophy, childrearing, education, government and the possible future of both India and the world. The resulting manuscript was edited by Sharma and others, and was eventually published under the title Satyarth Prakash or The Light of Truth in 1875 at Varanasi. This voluminous work would prove to play a central role in the establishment and later growth of the organization which would come to be known as the Arya Samaj.

Principles of Arya Samaj

On the 24th of June, 1877, the second major Arya Samaj was established at Lahore. However, the original list of 28 rules and regulations drafted by Dayanand for the Rajkot Arya Samaj and used for the Bombay Arya Samaj were deemed by the Lahore community to be too unwieldy. Therefore, it was proposed that the principles should be reduced and simplified, while the bylaws should be removed to a separate document. Everyone present, including Swami Dayanand, agreed, and the 10 Principles of the Arya Samaj as they are known around the world today came into existence.

All subsequently established branches of the Arya Samaj have been founded upon the Lahore principles. However, each new branch of the Society has a degree of freedom in determining the exact bylaws under which it shall operate. Everyone who wishes to become a member of the Society must agree to uphold these principles in their entirety. However, nothing beyond these 10 Principles has any binding force on any member of the Arya Samaj. For this reason, the early Samaj proved to be attractive to individuals belonging to various religious communities, and enjoyed a notable degree of support from segments of the Hindu, Sikh and Muslim populations of Indian society.

Drawing what are seen to be the logical conclusions from these principles, the Arya Samaj also unequivocally condemns practices such as: polytheism, idolatry, iconolatry, animal sacrifice, ancestor worship, pilgrimage, priestcraft, the belief in avatars or incarnations of God, the hereditary caste system, untouchability and child marriage on the grounds that all these lack Vedic sanction.

The Arya Samaj and the Theosophical Society

There continues to this day a considerable controversy regarding the exact nature of the relationship which existed between the Arya Samaj and the Theosophical Society from 1877 to 1882. What follows is a report of the chain of events as understood by members of the Arya Samaj today. (For the version of the Theosophical Society, see the article: Theosophical Society of the Arya Samaj.)

Relations with Sikhs

In 1875, the Arya Samaj established itself in Punjab, and some of its members began stating publicly that Sikhism should be considered a branch of Hinduism using what was seen as derogatory language in reference to Sikh Gurus and their writings. Leaders in the Sikh community, however, showed resolve in maintaining the status of their religion as independent and unique, and the statements of the AryaSamaj activists were summarily denounced as acts of aggression with the intent of destroying Sikh religious identity. It was also alleged that the Arya Samaj, which had taken an increasingly active role in certain Sikh Gurdwaras, was introducing practices that were contrary to Sikh principles and behaving in ways which would prove detrimental to the Sikh faith. In response, organizational efforts such as: Singh Sabha and Gurdwara Sudhar Movement were launched for countering Arya Samaj influence and peacefully reclaiming control of Sikh Gurdwaras.

Arya Samaj's teachings are in lines with the Sikh religion. Many Sikhs were influenced by Arya Samaj. For example, Indian freedom fighter Sardar Bhagat Singh was earlier a follower of Arya Samaj along with his grandfather, Sardar Ajit Singh. However he wrote a book, 'Why I am an Atheist' after being influenced by socialist ideals. His last photograph however indicates that he returned to Sikhism. Gurubani says: 'Ved Katev Kaho Mat Jhoote, JhootaVoh Jo Na Vichare', 'Ved Path Paapaan Mati Laye' and cites many other examples. However Sikhs do not accept the Vedas and the tenth Sikh pontificate, Guru Gobind Singh clearly mentioned, "Ram Rahim Puran Kuranamekkahe mat eknamanyo. Simrit Shastra Ved Sabhebahubhedkahe hum eknajanyo" (Meaning that Ram and Raheem, Puran and Kuran say many things, but I do not believe in them. The Smriti and Shastra and Ved all say many things, but I accept not even a single one).

CHAPTER

3 Jainism and its Educational Implications

INTRODUCTION

It is a common misconception among people that Jainism religion was started by Lord Mahavira. The truth is that Jainism existed long before Lord Mahavira was born. Lord Mahavira reformed Jainism and gave it more exposure. Thus, the history and origin of Jainism dates back to many centuries before Lord Mahavira was born. The religion of Jainism is based on philosophy and the concept of Dharma. Read on this section which is essentially an introduction to Jainism.

The Jains basically follow the teachings of 24 Tirthankaras or Enlightened spiritual leaders. Lord Mahavira was the 24th and last Tirthankara. He lived in approximately around 6th Century B.C. The Jains have influenced many cultures with their teachings and philosophies. They emphasize on non-violent form of living and treating all life forms with respect. They believe that self-control is essential for the attainment of omniscience or infinite knowledge. The realization of infinite knowledge leads to Moksha or Nirvana.

The Jains are supposed to be the most educated religious community of India. Some of India's oldest libraries are of the Jains. The Jains are essentially of two types:

1. *Digambaras*: Jains who believed that monks should not wear clothes.
2. *Shwetambaras*: Jains who believed that monks can wear only white clothes.

The 24th and last Tirthankara of the Jains, Lord Mahavira is much revered among the Jains. His teachings and philosophies continue to inspire numerous people even today. He was born in a royal family and denounced his royal family life to attain spiritual knowledge like: the Buddha. He was named Vardhamana Mahavira because when he was born his father, king Siddhartha prospered like anything. Vardhamana means increasing and the king credited his growing success and prosperity to the birth of his son. The life of Swami Mahavir is very interesting and is given here as a short story.

Origin of Janism

Lord Mahavira was born roughly around 599 B.C. He was born in the royal family of Kshatriyakund, a part of the republic of Vaishali. His father was King Siddhartha and his mother was Queen Trishala. It is said that when the queen conceived Lord Mahavira, she had fourteen auspicious dreams that were a premonition of the greatness of the child that was to be born. The prosperity of the King grew day-by-day. The king attributed his success to his new born child and named him Vardhamana, which means 'ever increasing'. Vardhamana had a lavish childhood and lived like a proper prince. He did many great things in his childhood like saving his friend from a poisonous snake, fighting a monster, etc., that proved that he was no ordinary child. This earned him the name 'Mahavira'. He was born with all worldly pleasures and luxuries but somehow he was never attracted by them. When he was in his late 20's his parents died. That is when he decided to become a monk. He left all his worldly possessions including clothing and went into seclusion to become a monk.

After 12 years of strict meditation and ascetic lifestyle, he finally gained enlightenment and spiritual knowledge and came to be known as Lord Mahavira. He gave up food and learnt to control his desires and wants. After gaining enlightenment, he preached what he had learnt to all those who needed it. He traveled far and wide barefoot spreading his divine knowledge and words of wisdom for thirty years. Numerous people were inspired by him and converted to Jainism. He left his mortal form around 527 B.C at the age of 72. The Jains celebrate this day as Diwali the day when Lord Mahavira attained liberation is the last day on the Hindu calendar that is celebrated as Diwali.

HISTORY OF SPREAD OF JAINISM

Jainism has been a major cultural, philosophical, social and political force since the dawn of civilization in Asia, and its ancient influence has been noted in other religions, including Buddhism and Hinduism.

This pervasive influence of Jain culture and philosophy in ancient Bihar may have given rise to Buddhism. The Buddhists have always maintained that during the time of Buddha and Mahavira (who, according to the Pali canon, were contemporaries), Jainism was already an ancient, deeply entrenched faith and culture there. (For connections between Buddhism and Jainism see Buddhism and Jainism). Over several thousand years, Jain influence on Hindu philosophy and religion has been considerable, while Hindu influence on Jain rituals may be observed in certain Jain sects. Certain Vedic Hindu holy books contain beautiful narrations about various figures who were adopted by Jains as Tirthankars (*e.g.,* Lord Rishabdev).

For instance, the concept of *puja* is Jain. The Vedic Religion prescribed *yajnas* and *havanas* for pleasing god. *Puja* is a specifically Jain concept, arising from the Kannada words, 'pu' (flower) and 'ja' (offering).

With 10 to 12 million followers, Jainism is among the smallest of the major world religions, but in India its influence is much greater than these numbers would suggest. Jains live throughout India. Maharashtra, Rajasthan and Gujarat have the largest Jain populations among Indian states. Karnataka, Bundelkhand and Madhya Pradesh have relatively large Jain populations. There is a large following in Punjab, especially in Ludhiana and Patiala, and there used to be many Jains in Lahore (Punjab's historic capital) and other cities before the Partition of 1947, after which many fled to India. There are many Jain communities in different parts of India and around the world. They may speak local languages or follow different rituals but essentially follow the same principles.

Outside India, the United States, United Kingdom, Canada and East Africa (Kenya, Tanzania and Uganda) have large Jain communities. Jainism is presently a strong faith in the United States and several Jain temples have been built there. American Jainism accommodates all the sects. Smaller Jain communities exist in Nepal,

South Africa, Japan, Singapore, Malaysia, Australia, Fiji, and Suriname. In Belgium the very successful Indian diamond community, almost all of whom are Jain, are also establishing a temple to strengthen Jain values in and across Western Europe.

Denominations

It is generally believed that the Jain *sangha* divided into two major sects, *(i)* Digambar and *(ii)* Svetambar, about 200 years after Mahâvîra's nirvana. Some historians believe there was no clear division until the 5th century. In the book *Outlines of Jainism*, it states. "It seems certain that even at the time of Mahâvîra the two sects were in existence, though he was able to maintain at least a semblance of unity between them. The final 'parting of ways' came much later". The best available information indicates that the chief Jain monk, Acharya Bhadrabahu, according to the Svetambara version of the split between the two sects, foresaw a 12-year famine and led about 12,000 Digambar followers to southern India.

Twelve years later they returned to find the Svetambara sect, and in 453 the Valabhi council edited and compiled the traditional Svetambara scriptures.

The differences between the two sects are minor and relatively obscure. Digambar Jain monks do not wear clothes because they believe clothes, like other possessions, increase dependency and desire for material things, and desire for anything ultimately leads to sorrow. Svetambar Jain monks, on the other hand, wear white, seamless clothes for practical reasons, and believe there is nothing in Jain scripture that condemns wearing clothes. Sadhvis (nuns) of both sects wear white. In Sanskrit, *ambar* refers to a covering generally, or a garment in particular. *Dig*, an older form of *disha*, refers to the cardinal directions. *Digambar* therefore means 'covered by the four directions', or 'sky-clad'. *Svet* means white and Svetambars wear white garments.

Digambars believe that women cannot attain moksha in the same birth, while Svetambars believe that women may attain liberation and that Mallinath, a Tirthankar, was a woman. The difference is because Digambar asceticism requires nudity. As nudity is impractical for women, it follows that without it they cannot attain moksha. This is based on the belief that women cannot reach perfect purity (yathakhyata), 'Their lack of clothes can, therefore, be a hindrance to their leading a holy life'. The earliest record of this belief is contained in the Prakrit Suttapahuda of the Digambara mendicant Kundakunda (c. second century A.D.)

Digambars believe that Mahavir was not married, whereas Svetambars believe Mahavir was married and had a daughter. The two sects also differ on the origin of Mata Trishala, Mahavira's mother.

Sthanakavasis and Digambars believe that only the first five lines are formally part of the Namokara Mantra (the main Jain prayer), whereas Svetambaras believe all nine form the mantra. Other differences are minor and not based on major points of doctrine.

THIRTHANKARAS

The statue of Gomateshwara of Digambar tradition in Shravanabelagola, Karnataka is the tallest monolith of its kind in the world.

Like other Indian religions, knowledge of the truth (*dharma*) is considered to have declined and revived cyclically throughout history. Those who rediscover dharma are called *Tirthankara*. The literal meaning of *Tirthankar* is 'ford-builder', or god. Jains, like: Buddhists, compare the process of becoming a pure human to crossing a swift river, an endeavour requiring patience and care. A ford-builder has already crossed the river and can therefore guide others. One is called a 'victor' (Skt: *Jina*) because one has achieved liberation by one's own efforts. Like Buddhism, the purpose of Jain dharma is to undo the negative effects of karma through mental and physical purification. This process leads to liberation accompanied by a great natural inner peace.

Having purified one's soul of karmic impurities, a *tirthankar* is considered omniscient, and a role model. Identified as god, these individuals are called *bhagavan*, lord (*e.g.,* Bhagavan Rishabha, Bhagavan Parshva, etc.). Tirthankar are not regarded as gods in the pantheistic or polytheistic sense, but rather as examplars who have awakened the divine spiritual qualities which lie dormant in each of us. There have been 24 Tirthankaras in what the Jains call the 'present age'. The last two Tirthankaras: Parsva and Mahavira (the 23rd and 24th) are historical figures whose existence is recorded.

Mahavira established the fourfold community (*chaturvidhisangha*) of monks, nuns, and male and female laypersons. The 24 Tirthankaras, in chronological order, are Adinath (Rishabhnath), Ajitnath, Sambhavanath, Abhinandannath, Sumatinath, Padmaprabha, Suparshvanath, Chandraprabha, Pushpadanta (Suvidhinath), Sheetalnath, Shreyansanath, Vasupujya, Vimalnath, Anantnath, Dharmanath, Shantinath, Kunthunath, Aranath, Mallinath, Munisuvrata, Nami Natha, Neminath, Parsva (Parshvanath) and Mahavir (Vardhamana).

Jain Monks and Nuns

In India there are thousands of Jain Monks, in categories like: Acharya, Upadhyaya and Muni. Trainee ascetics are known as Ailaka and Ksullaka in the Digambartradition. There are two categories of ascetics, *(i) Sadhu* (monk) and *(ii) Sadhvi* (nun). They practice the five *Mahavratas*, three *Guptis* and five *Samitis*:

Five Mahavratas

1. *Ahimsa*: Non-violence in thought, word and deed.
2. *Satya*: Truth which is (hita) beneficial, (mita) succinct and (priya) pleasing.
3. *Acaurya*: Not accepting anything that has not been given to them by the owner.
4. *Brahmacarya*: Absolute purity of mind and body.
5. *Aparigraha*: Non-attachment to non-self objects.

Three Guptis

1. *Managupti*: Control of the mind.
2. *Vacanagupti*: Control of speech.
3. *Kayagupti*: Control of body.

Five Samitis

1. *Irya Samiti*: Carefulness while walking.
2. *Bhasha Samiti*: Carefulness while communicating.
3. *Eshana Samiti*: Carefulness while eating.
4. *Adana Nikshepana Samiti*: Carefulness while handling their fly-whisks, water gourds, etc.
5. *Pratishthapana Samiti*: Carefulness while disposing of bodily waste matter.

Male Digambara monks do not wear any clothes and are nude. They practice non-attachment to the body and hence, wear no clothes. Shvetambara monks and nuns wear white clothes. Shvetambaras believe that monks and nuns may wear simple un-stitched white clothes as long as they are not attached to them. Jain monks and nuns travel on foot. They do not use mechanical transport.

Digambar followers take up to eleven *Pratimaye* (oath). Monks take all eleven oaths. They eat only once a day. The Male Digambarmonk (*Maharajji*) eat standing at one place in their palms without using any utensil.

The hand with a wheel on the palm symbolizes the Jain Vow of Ahimsa, meaning non-violence. The word in the middle is 'Ahimsa.' The wheel represents the dharmacakra, to halt the cycle of reincarnation through relentless pursuit of truth.

Jain monks and nuns practice strict asceticism and strive to make their current birth their last, thus ending their cycle of transmigration. The laity, who pursues less rigorous practices, strives to attain rational perception and to do as much good as possible and get closer to the goal of attaining freedom from the cycle of transmigration. Following strict ethics, the laity usually chooses professions that revere and protect life and totally avoid violent livelihoods.

Jains practice *Samayika*, which is a Sanskrit word meaning *equanimity* and derived from *samaya* (the soul). The goal of *samayika* is to attain equanimity. *Samayika* is begun by achieving a balance in time. If this current moment is defined as a moving line between the past and the future, *samayika* happens by being fully aware, alert and conscious in that moving time line when one experiences *atma*, one's true nature, and common to all life forms. *Samayika* is especially significant during *Paryushana*, a special period during the monsoon, and is practiced during the *Samvatsari Pratikramana* ritual.

Jains believe that *Devas* (demi-gods or celestial beings) cannot help *jiva* to obtain liberation, which must be achieved by individuals through their own efforts. In fact, Devas themselves cannot achieve liberation until they reincarnate as humans and undertake the difficult act of removing karma. Their efforts to attain the exalted state of *Siddha*, the permanent liberation of *jiva* from all involvement in worldly existence, must be their own.

The strict Jain Ethical code for monks/nuns is:

- *Ahimsa* (Non-violence).
- *Satya* (truth).
- *Achaurya* or *Asteya* (non-stealing).
- *Brahmacharya* (Celibacy).
- *Aparigraha* (Non-attachment to temporal possessions).

Common men and women also have the five vows of non-violence, truth, non-stealing, celibacy and non-possession. It is not possible to observe these vows completely in day-to-day life and therefore followed to a limited extent. As these vows are limited in their scope, they are called 'Anuvratas'. Apart from these, additionally there are seven vows designed to assist the householders in their spiritual journey.

Non-violence includes vegetarianism. Jains are expected to be non-violent in thought, word, and deed, both toward humans and toward all other living beings, including their own selves. Jain monks and nuns walk barefoot and sweep the ground in front of them to avoid killing insects or other tiny beings. Even though all life is considered sacred by the Jains, human life is deemed the highest form of life. For this reason, it is considered vital never to harm or upset any person.

For laypersons, *brahmacharya* means either confining sex to marriage or complete celibacy. For monks and nuns, it means complete celibacy.

While performing holy deeds, Svetambara Jains wear cloths, *muhapatti*, over their mouths and noses to avoid saliva falling on texts or revered images. It is incorrect to say that this is to avoid accidentally inhaling insects. Many healthy concepts are entwined. For example, Jains drink only boiled water. In ancient times, a person might get ill by drinking unboiled water, which could prevent equanimity, and illness may engender intolerance.

True spirituality, according to enlightened Jains, starts when one attains *Samyakdarshana*, or true perception. Such souls are on the path to moksha, striving to remain in the nature of the soul. This is characterized by knowing and observing only all worldly affairs, without *raag* (attachment) and *dwesh* (repulsion), a state of pure knowledge and bliss. Attachment to worldly life collects new karmas, and traps one in birth, death, and suffering. Worldly life has a dual nature (for example, love and hate, suffering and pleasure, etc.), for the perception of one state cannot exist without the contrasting perception of the other.

Jain Dharma shares some beliefs with Hinduism. Both believe in karma and reincarnation. However, the Jain version of the Ramayana and Mahabharata is different from Hindu beliefs, for example. Generally, Hindus believe that Rama was a reincarnation of God, whereas Jains believe he attained moksha (liberation) because they are free from any belief in a creator god.

Along with the Five Vows, Jains avoid harboring ill will and practice forgiveness. They believe that *atma* (soul) can lead one to becoming *parmatma* (liberated soul) and this must come from one's inner self. Jains refrain from all violence (Ahimsa) and recommend that sinful activities be avoided.

Mahatma Gandhi was deeply influenced (particularly through the guidance of ShrimadRajchandra) by Jain tenets such as peaceful, protective living and honesty, and made them an integral part of his own philosophy.

Jainism has a distinct idea underlying Tirthankar worship. The physical form is not worshiped, but their Gunas (virtues, qualities) are praised. Tirthankaras remain role-models, and sects such as the Sthanakavasi stringently reject statue worship.

Most Jains fast at special times, like during festivals (known as *Parva. Paryushana and Ashthanhika* are the main *Parva*s which occurs 3 times in a year), and on holy days (eighth and fourteenth days of the moon cycle). Paryushana is the most prominent festival, lasting eight days for Svetambara Jains and ten days for Digambars, during the monsoon. The monsoon is considered the best time of fasting due to lenient weather. However, a Jain may fast at any time, especially if s/he feels some error has been committed. Variations in fasts encourage Jains to do whatever they can to maintain self-control.

A unique ritual in this religion involves a holy fasting until death; it is called *sallekhana*. Through this one achieves a death with dignity and dispassion as well as no more negative karma. When a person is aware of approaching death, and feels that s/he has completed all duties, s/he willingly ceases to eat or drink gradually. This form of dying is also called *Santhara/Samaadhi*. It can be as long as 12 years with gradual reduction in food intake. Considered extremely spiritual and creditable, with all awareness of the transitory nature of human experience, it has recently led to a controversy. In Rajasthan, a lawyer petitioned the High Court of Rajasthan to declare *santhara* illegal. Jains see *santhara* as spiritual detachment, a declaration that a person has finished with this world and now chooses to leave. This choice however requires a great deal of spiritual accomplishment and maturity as a pre-requisite.

JAINA ETHICS AND RELIGION

Principles and Beliefs

Jainism differs from other religions in its concept of God. Accordingly, there is no overarching Supreme Being, divine creator, owner, preserver or destroyer. Every living soul is potentially divine and the Siddhas, those who have completely eliminated their karmic bonds to end their cycle of birth and death, have attained God-consciousness.

A *Jain* is a follower of *Jinas* ('conquerors'), identifies specially gifted human beings who rediscover the *dharma,* become fully liberated and teach the spiritual path to benefit all living beings. Practicing Jains follow the teachings of 24 special Jinas who are known as *Tirthankaras* ('ford-makers', or "those who have discovered and shown the way to salvation"). Tradition states that the 24th, and most recent, *Tirthankar* is Shri Mahavir, lived from 599 to 527 BCE. The 23rd Tirthankar, ShriParsva, is a historical person, who lived from 872 to 772 BC.

Jainism encourages spiritual development through reliance on and cultivation of one's own personal wisdom and self-control व्रत, *vrata*). The goal of Jainism is to realize the soul's true nature. 'Samyakdarshangyancharitrani moksha margah', the (triple gems of Jainism), meaning 'true/right perception, knowledge and conduct' provides the path for attaining liberation (moksha) from samsara (the universal cycle of birth and death). Moksha is attained by liberation from all karma. Those who have attained moksha are called *siddha*, 'liberated souls', and those who are attached to the world through their karma are called *samsarin* 'mundane souls'. Every soul has to follow the path, as described by the Jinas (Tirthankaras), to attain moksha.

Jaina tradition identifies Rishabha (also known as Adhinath) as the First Tirthankar of this declining (avasarpini) kalachakra (time cycle). The first Tirthankar, Rishabhdev/Adhinath, appeared prior to the Indus Valley Civilization. The swastika symbol and naked statues resembling Jain monks, which archaeologists have found among the remains of the Indus Valley Civilization, tend to support this claim.

Jains hold that the Universe and Dharma are eternal, without beginning or end. However, the universe undergoes processes of cyclical change. The universe consists of living beings ('Jîva') and non-living beings ('Ajîva'). The samsarin (worldly) soul incarnates in various life forms. Human, animal, plant, deity, and hell-being are the four forms of the samsari souls. All worldly relations of one's Jiva with other Jiva and Ajiva are based on Karma.

The main Jain prayer (*Namokar Mantra*) therefore salutes the five special categories of souls that have attained God-consciousness or are on their way to achieving it, to emulate and follow these paths to salvation. Another major characteristic of Jain belief is the emphasis on the consequences of not only physical but also mental behaviours.

Jain practices are derived from the above fundamentals. For example, the principle of non-violence seeks to minimize karmas which may limit the capabilities of the soul. Jainism views every soul as worthy of respect because it has the potential to become Siddha (Paramatma – 'pure soul'). Because all living beings possess a soul, great care and awareness is essential in one's actions in the incarnate world. Jainism emphasizes the equality of all life, advocating harmlessness towards all, whether these be creatures great or small. This policy extends even to microscopic organisms. Jainism acknowledges that every person has different capabilities and capacities and therefore assigns different duties for ascetics and householders. The 'great vows' (mahavrata) are prescribed for monks and 'limited vows' (anuvrata) are prescribed for householders.

The Five Basic Ethical Principles

There are five basic ethical principles (vows) prescribed. The degree to which these principles must be practiced is different for renunciant and householder. Thus:

1. *Non-violence (Ahimsa)* – To cause no harm to living beings.
2. *Truth (Satya)* – To always speak the truth in a harmless manner.

3. *Non-stealing (Asteya)* – To not take anything that is not willingly given.
4. *Celibacy (Brahmacarya)* – To not indulge in sensual pleasures.
5. *Non-possession (Aparigraha)* – To detach from people, places, and material things.

Ahimsa

'Non-violence', is sometimes interpreted as not killing, but the concept goes far beyond that. To achieve the goal of non-violence mind and body must harmonize thoughts, speech and actions to "the heart which knows nothing but love". There can be no thought to injure others and no speech inciting injury by others.

Satya

'Truthfulness', is also to be practiced by all people. Given that non-violence has priority, all other principles yield to it, whenever there is a conflict. For example, if speaking truth will lead to violence, it is perfectly ethical to be silent. Thiruvalluvar in his Tamil classic devotes an entire chapter clarifying the definition of 'truthfulness'.

Asteya

'Non-stealing', is the strict adherence to one's own possessions, without desire to take another's. One should remain satisfied by whatever is earned through honest labour. Any attempt to squeeze others and/or exploit the weak is considered theft. Some of the guidelines for this principle are:

- Always give people fair value for labour or product.
- Never take things which are not offered.
- Never take things that are placed, dropped or forgotten by others.
- Never purchase cheaper things if the price is the result of improper method (*e.g.,* pyramid scheme, illegal business, stolen goods, etc.)

Brahmacarya

'Monastic celibacy', is the complete abstinence from sex, which is only incumbent upon monastic. Householders, practice monogamy as a way to uphold brahmacarya in spirit..

Aparigraha

'Non-possession', is the renounciation of property and wealth, before initiation into monkhood, without entertaining thoughts of the things renounced. This is done so one understands how to detach oneself from things and possessions including home and family so one may reach *moksa*. For householders, non possession owns without attachment, because the notion of possession is illusory. The reality of life is that change is constant, thus objects owned by someone today will be property of someone else in future days. The householder is encouraged to discharge his or her duties to related people and objects as a trustee, without excessive attachment.

Jain Religion; Worship and Rituals

Every day most Jains bow and say their universal prayer, the 'Namokara Mantra', aka the Navkar Mantra, Parmesthi Mantra, Panch Namaskar Mantra, Anadhi Nidhan Mantra. Jains have built temples, or *Basadi* or *Derasar*, where images of tirthankaras are revered. Rituals may be elaborate because symbolic objects are offered and Tirthankaras praised in song. But some sects refuse to enter temples or revere images. All Jains accept that images of Tirthankaras are merely symbolic reminders of their paths to attain moksha. Jains are clear that the Jinas reside in moksha and are completely detached from the world.

Jain rituals include:

- *Pancakalyanaka Pratishtha.*
- *Pratikramana.*
- *Samayika.*
- Guru Vandana, *Chaitya Vandana*, and other sutras to honor ascetics.

Over time, some sections of Jains also pray deities, which are yakshas and yakshinis.

JAIN PHILOSOPHY

Jain philosophy (Sanskrit: Jain darsana; "जैनदर्शन deals extensively with the problems of metaphysics, reality, cosmology, ontology, epistemology and divinity. Jainism is essentially a transtheistic religion of ancient India. It is a continuation of the ancient ŒramaGa tradition which co-existed with the Vedic tradition since ancient times. The distinguishing features of Jain philosophy are its belief in independent existence of soul and matter, neither denial nor acceptance of a creative and omnipotent God, an eternal (and hence uncreated) universe, a strong emphasis on non-violence, on relativity and multiple facets of truth, and morality and ethics based on liberation of souls.

Jain philosophy explains the rationale of being and existence, the nature of the Universe and its constituents, the nature of bondage and the means to achieve liberation. It is described as ascetic because of its strong emphasis on self-control, austerities and renunciation and called a model of philosophical liberalism for its insistence that truth is relative and multifaceted and for its willingness to accommodate all possible view-points of rival philosophies. It has been compared to Western concepts of subjectivism and moral relativism. Jainism strongly upholds the individual nature of soul and personal responsibility for one's decisions; and that self-reliance and individual efforts alone are responsible for one's liberation. In this matter, it is similar to individualism and Objectivism.

In Jainism, truth or reality is perceived differently depending on different points of view, and that no single point of view is the complete truth. Jain doctrine states that an object has infinite modes of existence and qualities and, as such, cannot be completely perceived in all its aspects and manifestations, due to inherent human limitations. Only Kevalins – the omniscient beings – can totally comprehend objects and that others can knowing only a part. Consequently, no one view can represent the absolute truth. In the process, the Jains have their doctrines of relativity used for logic and reasoning –

- *Anekântavâda* – Literally, 'Non-one-endedness', 'Non-singular Conclusivity', the idea that no one perspective holds the complete truth.
- *Syâdvâda* – The theory of conditioned predication.
- *Nayavâda* – The theory of partial standpoints.

These philosophical concepts contributed immensely to Indian philosophy, especially in skepticism and relativity.

- *Karma Theory*: Karma in Jainism conveys a totally different meaning than commonly understood in the Hindu philosophy and western civilization. It is not the so called inaccessible force that controls the fate of living beings in inexplicable ways. It does not mean 'deed', 'work', nor invisible, mystical force (*adrsta*), but a complex of very fine matter, imperceptible to the senses, which interacts with the soul, causing great changes. Karma, then, is something material (*karmapaudgalam*), which produces certain conditions, like a medical pill has many effects. According to Robert Zydendos, karma in Jainism is a system of laws, but natural rather than moral laws. In Jainism, actions that carry moral significance are considered to cause consequences in just the same way as physical actions that do not carry any moral significance. When one holds an apple in one's hand and then let go of the apple, the apple will fall: this is only natural. There is no judge, and no moral judgment involved, since this is a mechanical consequence of the physical action.

IMPACT OF JAINISM ON INDIAN CULTURE AND SOCIETY

While Jains represent less than 1 per cent of the Indian population, their contributions to culture and society in India are considerable. Jainism had a major influence in developing a system of philosophy and ethics that had a major impact on all aspects of Indian culture in all ages. Scholarly research and evidences have shown that philosophical concepts considered typically Indian – Karma, Ahimsa, Moksa, reincarnation and like – either originate in the sramana school of thought or were propagated and developed by Jaina teachers.

Jains have also wielded great influence on the culture and language of Karnatak, Southern India and Gujarat most significantly. The earliest known Gujarati text, Bharat-Bahubali Ras, was written by a Jain monk. Some important people in Gujarat's Jain history were Acharya Hemacandra Suri and his pupil, the Calukya ruler Kumarapala.

Jains are among the wealthiest Indians. They run numerous schools, colleges and hospitals and are important patrons of the Somapuras, the traditional temple architects in Gujarat. Jains have greatly influenced Gujarati cuisine. Gujarat is predominantly vegetarian (see Jain vegetarianism), and its food is mild as onions and garlic are omitted. Though the Jains form only 0.42 per cent of the population of India, their contribution to the exchequer by way of income tax is an astounding 24 per cent of the total tax collected.

Jains encourage their monks to do research and obtain higher education. Jain monks and nuns, particularly in Rajasthan, have published numerous research monographs. This is unique among Indian religious groups and parallels Christian clergy. The 2001 census states that Jains are India's most literate community and that India's oldest libraries at Patan and Jaisalmer are preserved by Jain institutions.

Jain Literature

Jains have contributed to India's classical and popular literature. For example, almost all early Kannada literature and many Tamil works were written by Jains.

- Some of the oldest known books in Hindi and Gujarati were written by Jain scholars. The first autobiography in Hindi, [Ardha-Kathanaka] was written by a Jain, Banarasidasa, an ardent follower of Acarya Kundakunda who lived in Agra.
- Several Tamil classics are written by Jains or with Jain beliefs and values as the core subject.
- Practically all the known texts in the Apabhraṁsha language are Jain works.

The oldest Jain literature is in Shauraseni and Ardha-Magadhi Prakrit (Agamas, Agama-Tulya, Siddhanta texts, etc.). Many classical texts are in Sanskrit (Tatvartha Sutra, Puranas, Kosh, Sravakacara, mathematics, Nighantus etc). 'Abhidhana Rajendra Kosha' written by AcharyaRajendrasuri, is only one available Jain encyclopedia or Jain dictionary to understand the Jain Prakrit, Sanskrit, and Ardha-Magadhi and other Jain languages, words, their use and references with in oldest Jain literature. Later Jain literature was written in Apabhramsha (Kahas, rasas, and grammars), Hindi (Chhahadhala, Mokshamarga Prakashaka, and others), Tamil (Jivakacintamani and others), and Kannada (Vaddaradhane and various other texts). Jain versions of Ramayana and Mahabharata are found in Sanskrit, Prakrit, Apabhramsha and Kannada.

Jainism and other Religions

Jains are not a part of the Vedic Religion (Hinduism). Ancient India had two philosophical streams of thought: The Shramana philosophical schools, represented by Jainism, and the Brahmana/Vedic/Puranic schools represented by Vedanta, Vaishnava and other movements. Both streams are subsets of the Dharmic family of faith and have existed side by side for many thousands of years, influencing each other.

The Hindu scholar, Lokmanya Tilak credited Jainism with influencing Hinduism and thus leading to the cessation of animal sacrifice in Vedic rituals. Bal Gangadhar Tilak has described Jainism as the originator of Ahimsa and wrote in a letter printed in Bombay Samachar, Mumbai:10 Dec, 1904: "In ancient times, innumerable animals were butchered in sacrifices. Evidence in support of this is found in various poetic compositions such as the Meghaduta. Swami Vivekananda also credited Jainism as influencing force behind the Indian culture.

"What could have saved Indian society from the ponderous burden of omnifarious ritualistic ceremonialism, with its animal and other sacrifices, which all but crushed the very life of it, except the Jain revolution which took its strong stand exclusively on chaste morals and philosophical truths? Jains were the first great ascetics. "Don't injure any, do good to all that you can and that is all the morality and ethics, and that is all the work there is, and the rest is all nonsense... Throw it away." And then they went to work and elaborated this one principle, and it is a most wonderful ideal: how all that we call ethics they simply bring out from one great principle of non-injury and doing good."

- *Relationship between Jainism and Hinduism:* According to the Encyclopædia Britannica Article on Hinduism,"... With Jainism which always remained an Indian religion, Hinduism has so much in common, especially in social institutions and ritual life, that nowadays Hindus tend to consider it a Hindu sect. Many Jains also are inclined to fraternization..."
- *Independent Religion:* From the Encyclopædia Britannica Article on Jainism: "...Along with Hinduism and Buddhism, it is one of the three most ancient Indian religious traditions still in existence. ...While often employing concepts shared with Hinduism and Buddhism, the result of a common cultural and linguistic background, the Jain tradition must be regarded as an independent phenomenon. It is an integral part of South Asian religious belief and practice, but it is not a Hindu sect or Buddhist heresy, as earlier scholars believed." The author Koenraad Elst in his book, *who is a Hindu?*, summarises on the similarities between Jains and the mainstream Hindu society.
- Monier Williams, in his article of Jainism, mentions that Jainas outdo every other Indian sect in carrying the prohibition of himsa to the most prosperous extremes.

Constitutional Status of Jainism in India

In 2005 the Supreme Court of India in a judgment stated that Sikhs, Jains and Buddhists are sub-sects or 'special faiths' of Hinduism, and are governed under the ambit of Hindu laws. In the same year however, it declined to issue a writ of Mandamus towards granting Jains the status of a religious minority throughout India. The Court noted that Jains have been declared a minority in 5 states already, and left it to the rest of the States to decide on the minority status of Jain religion.

In 2006 the Supreme Court in a judgment pertaining to a state, opined that "Jain Religion is indisputably not a part of the Hindu Religion". (para 25, Committee of Management Kanya Junior High School Bal Vidya Mandir, Etah, U.P. v. Sachiv, U.P. Basic Shiksha Parishad, Allahabad, U.P. and Ors., Per Dalveer Bhandari J., Civil Appeal No. 9595 of 2003, decided On: 21.08.2006, Supreme Court of India).

JAINISM AND ITS EDUCATIONAL IMPLICATIONS

In the Jain literature the term 'Jin' denotes one who has acquired perfect control over everything of a vicious nature or worldly pleasures of life. The preachings given by such conquerors over their senses constitute Jain religion.

The founders of Jainism thought that the world was a place for various pleasures for most of the people. But when the population increased people abandoned the idea of enjoying the pleasures of life, because then they had to face various types of scarcities of life. So the ideal of enjoying pleasures was changed into performing work. Thus the world was then regarded as a place of work (Karma Bhumi). At this time fourteen Kulakars or Manus were born. These Mans (Kulkars) developed traditions, conventions and customs for establishing a good social system. Because of such a developmental work these mans were called Kulakars. (the one who works for the welfare of Kula or family was given the name Kulakar. In the Jain literature we find mention of only fourteen Kulakars. Of these fourteen, Nabhirai was the last Kulakar. Nabhiari had a son named Rikhabhadev. Rikhabhadev is considered to be the first propounder of Jainism. In fact, Jainism developed from him. In the Jain literature Lord Rikhabhadev is regarded as 'Jin' (the conqueror of all senses) or

Tirthankar. Jainism is a collection of preaching of such twenty-four Tirthankars of who Lord Rikhbhadev was the first and Lord Mahavir was the last, Lord Mahavir was born in 800 B.C. in a village named Kundagram. His father's name was Siddharth. Trishal was his mother. The Viashali area of Bihar is regarded as his birth place. Lord Mahavir would not stand the slaughtering of innocent animals in Yajan (Yagya). At the age of 30, he became disillusioned with the world and he performed hard penance for twelve years. As a result, he got light of knowledge (Gyanjyati). After this for thirty years he preached his religion known as Jainism. He obtained salvation (Nirvan) at the age of 72 years.

Principles of Jain Philosophy

According to Jain Philosophy there are three main elements in each matter – *(i)* Ulpad, *(ii)* Vyay, and *(iii)* Dhraubya. These three principal elements are respectively indicative of *(i)* Ulpati, *i.e.,* birth, origin or creation, *(ii)* Vinash, *i.e.,* destruction or annihilation, and *(iii)* Sthirat. *i.e.*, stability. The process of birth and destruction of these elements never stops. It is on this basis that Jain philosophy regards this world as changeable. But in spite of this changeability the unity of the world is maintained in the same way as a man changes from infancy to adolescence, adulthood and old age, but his unity as a man is maintained. On this basis the Jain religion believes that unchangeability is always continued along with changes.

According to Jainism this worked is eternal and endless. Jains believe that this world is not made by anyone. The world is made of Jiva, *i.e..,* spirit and Ajiva, *i.e.,* matter (which is lifeless and inanimate). The Ajiva or the matter is or five types-Pudgai, Dharma, Adharma, Akash and Kai. These five elements always remain constant. Neither they decrease nor increase. Jainism does not believe in the existence of God. Neither God creates nor destroys, simply because is (*i.e.,* God's) very concept is baseless.

Antheism (or Anishwarvad) of Jainism

As already referred to above. Jainism does not believe in the existence of God. The propounders of Jainism regard the concept of God as irrelevant. They contend that in order to prove the truthfulness of any so-called truth, 'there should be some proof', then God is not cognizable and he is out of the purview of our senses.

Jainism sees the same thing into different forms. According to this philosophy a 'truth' (Satya) may be seen with varying viewpoints. Therefore a true Jain does not stick to a particular point of view, not does he insist on his own views in the process of reasoning. He has a liberal outlook. He believes that a particular thing may be perceived in different ways. Because of this attitude a true Jain is able to maintain a Sambhav or poise or equilibrium in face of all circumstances. This attitude is known as Syadvad.

The Educational Implications of the Principle of Anekantvad

Anekantvad implies liberalism. This principle classifies that only one aspect of a thing or issue cannot be acceptable. Regarding or proposition there may be two or more sides. Therefore, in order to reach a right judgment on a certain issue, we have to take into consideration its various aspects. In the democratic era of these days it is quite natural to have various points of view regarding a certain idea. It is not possible that the stand of a teacher or that of any student in a class will be accepted by all the students, in the classes. Therefore, it is necessary to effect a co-ordination between the various views expressed by students in a class. In reaching a decision each student should have the self-satisfaction that his viewpoints have also been duty considered and the same have been accommodated in the final deliberation. This feeling on the part of the student will promote the development of his personality and will help in adopting a liberal attitude about things. On the class teaching of modern days the teacher should try to co-ordinate the various views of the students for posing a consistent whole. Evidently, the same idea must not be imposed on all students.

- *Non-violence:* Non-violence is the main basis of Jainism. In fact, it is its main philosophy of behaviour. Non-violence has been given the highest place in the life of a follower of Jainism. Violence against any inanimate or animate being is strictly prohibited in Jainism. We are very much prone to commit violence in our various simple and complex activities. Jainism enjoins that everyone should always try to avoid any kind of violence. We must not commit violence in any situation. Even to hurt anyone's feelings is a kind of violence. It is well known that because of fear of committing violence, a follower of

Jainism does not take food in the night. He keeps his lips and nostrils wrapped up with thin pieces of cloth in order to prevent entering of germs into the body through them.

Educational Implications of Non-Violence

Today the entire world is besieged with various of violence. One country wants to establish its supremacy over another through hurting its feelings. In some part of the world some battle is being fought between two countries. Extremists and terrorists are having their sway all over the world.

The Theory of Karma (The Bondage of the Being)

In Jainism the relationship between 'being' (the animate) and the inanimate (Jadm Pudgal or the body matter) has been regarded as a bondage. In Jainism the animate, the being or the 'Jiva' has been accepted as the consciousness (Chetan). The animate epitomizes unlimited knowledge (Anant Gyan), unlimited vision (Anant Darshan) unlimited prowess (Valour or Ananat Virya), and unlimited enjoyment (Bliss or Anant Anand). As a result of its deeds (Karma), ignorance (Agyanta), envelops the being (Jiva) and all these powers vanish and the 'being' (Jiva) is encircled into a bondage. If the Jiva (the being) acquires knowledge, he will recapture all these powers and obtain salvation and his form will becomes full of lustres. Here a relevant matter (Ajiva) Jainism believes that this association or bondage comes through Karmas (or deeds). Because of his bondage the one influence the other (*i.e.,* the Jiva (being), it reacts on the Pudgal *i.e.,* the body matter) and the forms of the two are changes. Because of attachments (Raga) and Malice (Dvesha) the Jiva happens to perform various deeds. A certain matter (property-Dravya) enter into the being as a result of his mental and physical activities. Consequently, the Jiva gets into a bondage.

Jainism believes that whatever the Jiva (the Being animate) gets is a result of his deeds. The colour, form of the body, age and the various senses are the results of one's deeds. This analysis of Karma is a special aspect of Jain philosophy. Jainism does not believe that God is the determiner of one's fate or destiny. In fact, Jainism does not believe in the existence of God. Whatever man gets in his life is a result of his deeds and not a kindness of God (Ishwar Kripa). The man is the maker of his 'good' or 'bad'. No unseen power influences the Jiva.

Educational Implication of the Concept of Salvation According to Jainism

Now it is not difficult to understand the educational ideas implies in the concept of salvation according to Jainism. In a way, it will not be an exaggeration to say that the ultimate purpose of education is attainment of salvation. In this sense, salvation (Moksha) and education become synonymous. If we have not attachment with worldly things our various types of drives will vanish. Then we shall be oriented towards attainment of perfection or salvation. As a result, all our activities will be directed towards seeking welfare of others. The various tools for attainment of salvation, as prescribed by Jainism may be regarded as tools for achieving ideals of education also.

CHAPTER

4

Educational Implications of Buddhism

INTRODUCTION

According to tradition Buddha was born in the year 560 BC. in Kapilavastu, on the southern border of today's Nepal, as a descendent of the distinguished clan of the Sakya. Father Suddhodana, mother Maya. He himself was called Siddhartha, married Yasodhara, and had a son Rahula. Became a wandering ascetic in the 29th year of his life.

Buddhism is a truly Indian religion for it belongs to the tradition of Indus Valley Civilization. It is essentially non-Vesic and possibly pre-Aryan world-view of India. In it the doctrine of *Karma-Samsara-jnana-mukti* was clearly defined and adopted. However, non-Aryan Yoga along with the *tapas* (austerities) of *Sannyasa* (renunciation) has been fully assimilated. Even when Buddhism has been assimilated by Hinduism, its distinctiveness cannot be denied. It has developed its own scripture. Instead of appealing to the scripture as an authority, the Buddha encouraged independent thinking without appealing to any authority. It never held the doctrine of caste and theoretically it held fast atheism (*nirishvaravada*) and salvation through ones efforts alone without taking recourse to any supernatural agency. Buddhism, unlike Hinduism, has centered round the life and teaching of its founder, Gotama, the Buddha.

Some prefer to call the teaching of the Buddha a religion, others call it a philosophy, still others think of it as both religion and philosophy. It may, however, be more correct to call it a 'way of life'. The Buddha is only a teacher who points out the way and guides the followers to their individual deliverance. A sign-board at the parting of roads, for instance, indicates directions, and it is left to the wayfarer to tread along the way watching his steps. The board certainly will not take him to his desired destination.

The Main Texts of Buddhism

The canon of the holy writings of the Buddhists is the triad of baskets, the *tripitaka*, so named according to the three baskets or collections of what they consist.

- *The Vinayapitaka*: The collection of the order for the Buddhist monks and nuns.
- *Suttapitaka:* It contains the doctrine of Buddha and a number of his dialogues.
- It is *divided* into nikayas or collection.
  - *(i) Dirghanikaya* (Long Discourses);
  - *(ii) Majjhimanikaya* (Medium Sized Discourses);
  - *(iii) Samyutta-nikaya* (Mixed Discourses);
  - *(iv) Anguttara-nikaya* (Graduated Discourses);
  - *(v) Khuddaka-nikaya* (Miscellaneous Miscourses);
- *Abhiharma-nikaya*: This contains philosophical matter and creed. For the Mahayanist *Vaipulya* Sutras and *Prajnapar-mita* Sutras are most important. *Visuddha – Magga* of *Buddha-ghosa* and Milindapanha also important works.

The chief contents of these collections consist of the teachings of Buddha and his disciples.

The Main Schools or Sects of Buddhism

There are two schools or sects in Buddhism, namely: *(i)* Mahayana and *(ii)* Hinayana.

Hinayana

Generally there are three names for Hinayana, they are: *(i)* Southern Buddhism, *(ii)* Original Buddhism, and *(iii)* Hinayana. The first name is given by European scholars. The division 'original and developed Buddhism' is based on the belief that Mahayana was only a gradual development of the original doctrine which was Hinayana, but this is not acceptable to Mahayanists.

The ideal of Hinayana is Arhatship or Arhantship. To put it in simple English, the ideal of Hinayana is individual enlightenment. The word '*yana*' is generally translated as way, path or vehicle. In his 'Survey of Buddhism', *Bhikshu Sangharaksita* suggests 'career' for '*yana*'. This seems to be the best English equivalent for '*yana*'.

Causality

Its conception of causality, *viz*; and *pratiya-samutpada*is in consonance with its conception of reality which could neither move nor change, but could only appear and disappear. Hinayanists explain *pratiya-samutpada*in a somewhat different way. They say that itya is a *taddhita* or a derivative derived from the noun *iti* which means disappearance, *itya*, therefore, means 'fit to disappear'. The affix *prati* is used in the sense of *vipsa. i.e.,* repetition implying continuous or successive action. Thus according to them *pratiyasamutpada* means *pratipratiityanamvinasinamsamutpadah i.e.,* appearance of every thing bound to disappear *i.e.,* every thing momentary. So their explanation comes to this – The evanescent momentary things appear. According to it, *pratiyasamutpada* is the causal law regulating the coming into being and disappearance of the various elements.

Nirvana

The Hinayanist believes that by the realization of *pudgalanairatmya* (not-self or unsubstantiality of the person), one could attain Nirvana. The Hinayanist says that man is unable to attain Nirvana, because Reality is hidden by the veil (*avarana*) of passions like attachment, aversion, delusion (*klesavarana).* The *klesavarana* acts as an obstacle in the way of the realization of Nirvana. The *klesavarana* has, therefore to be removed before one can attain Nirvana.

Dharma

The Hinayanists believed in certain ultimate reals, called *dharmas.* They believe that the world is composed of an unceasing flow of certain *ultimate dharmas* which are simple, momentary and impersonal. Most of them are *samskrta* (dharmas without signs). Hinayana was entirely intellectual. The main concern of the Hinayanist was to follow the eight-fold path chalked out by the Buddha. In Hinayana, it was the human aspect of the Buddha which was emphasized.

In Hinayana, the elements, although interdependent (*samskrta = pratityasamutpada),* were real. Every whole (*rasi = avayavin)* is regarded as a nominal existence (*prajnaptisat*) and only the parts or ultimate elements (*dharma*) are real (*vastu).* The individual (*pudgala*), the self (*atma*) was resolved in its component elements (*skandha – ayatana – dhatavah = anatma*); there were no real personalities (*pudgala-nairatmya*), but a congeries of flashing forces (*samskara-samuha*).

– Stcherbatsky, Theodore, '*The Conception of Buddhist Nirvana*', New Delhi: Motilal Banarsidass, 1989.

Mahayana

The *Vajjians* called themselves Mahasanghika and the rest were known as *Theravadins*. The *Mahasanghika* called themselves Mahayana and called the rest through the nickname of Hinayanyana on the whole they were progressive, liberal and in due course spread all over North India, North-west regions of Asia and China. In the due course, they developed esoteric circle and *tantra.*

Causality

Nirvana is *ajati* (unborn) and cannot be acquired. It is a state as a result of attaining *bodhi*. It cannot be described at all, not even as bliss. It is *Shunyata*.

Nirvana

Here one has to attain not *arhatva* of the individual selves, but of all beings. Hence, bodhisattva is the ideal and not nirvana but *parinirvana* has to be won. Not *buddhatva*, but *sambuddhatva* has to be acquired after many more efforts as bodhisattva.

Dharma

Mahayana in addition to *klesavarana* emphasizes the removal of *jnanavarana i.e.*, the veil over true knowledge. Hence, it takes the help of dialectic (*prasangikavnda*). Hence, even *pratitya – samutvada* has to be shown as only an initial stand, for the dialectic shows that ultimately it is also self-contradictory, leading finally to the acceptance of *shunyata.*

Both accepted the following:

- Nirvana is inexpressible, has no origin and is unchangeable.
- Nirvana has to be realized by oneself alone, without making reference to any supernatural agency.

- Personal self is lost in nirvana.
- Nirvana means tranquility.
- It means the barring out of any more *samsarika* birth.

BUDHIST PHILOSOPHY

Buddhism is one of the most remarkable development of Indian thought. It is an offshoot of later vedic thought. Buddhism is founded on the rejection of certain orthodox Hindu Philosophical concepts. It has many philosophical views with Hinduism, such as: belief in Karma, a cause and effect relationship between all that has being done and all that will be done. Events that occur are held to be direct results of previous events. The ultimate goal for both is to eliminate Karma (both good and bad), end the cycle of rebirth and suffering and attain freedom (Moksha or Nirvana). Buddhist education system (200 B.C. to 200 A.D) was founded by Lord Gautam Buddha. Gautam Buddha was primarily an ethical teacher and reformer and not a philosopher. He was concerned mainly with the problems of life. He avoided the discussion of metaphysical question because they are ethically useless and intellectually uncertain. He always discussed the most important questions of suffering, its cessation and the path leading to its cessation. Thus Buddha‘s enlightenment which he tried to share with all fellow-beings has come to be known as the four Noble Truths.

A sense of aimlessness prevailed in society during Brahmanic period due to over casteism. In such circumstances, Budhism emerged as a reaction to vedic ritualism. Budhists began to establish educational monasteries in competition to the vedic system of education. Initially, these budhistmonasteries provided education only to Budhists, but gradually they came to impart education to all classes.

Budhist education came in to existence in the 5th century B.C. Brahmanas deprived the common people of their right to education, and hence the emergence of Budhism granted the people the freedom to obtain education and to practice their religion themselves.

The budhists imparted education in Sanghas/Collective groups/ congregations. In budhism there was no opportunity for the individual to obtain education independently, away from his ‘sugham’.

Buddhism and its Educational Implications

The Life of Lord Buddha

Lord Budda has been the founder of Buddhism. He was born in 563 B.C. at Lumbini of Kapilvastu Nagar of the Kingdom of Nepal. Shuddhodan, the king of Shakya dynasty in the south of Nepal was his father. Maya Devi was his mother. At the time of birth Lord Buddha's name was Siddhartha. A week after his birth, his mother, Maya Devi died and his step-mother Majaprajapati brought him up. During the first sixteen years of his life Siddartha received an education in policy of state administration and also in military science. He was married to a girl named Yasodhara. After marriage, for three years he looked after the state affairs. During this period Siddhartha became a father to a son born from Yasodhara. The son was named Rahul. Even during his infancy Siddhartha was of peaceful nature and he evinced a tendency towards Sanyas, *i.e.*, (renouncing the world). Consequently, he became interested in Yoga an turned indifferent to worldly pleasures in the 'Shunya'. Thus all religions are depend upon others and all are changeable. All these are indescribe able also. Their indescribability (Anivarchyata) in relation to Shunya is known as 'Modhyam Marg' or middle course. According to this middle course a thing signifies completely neither 'feeling form' (Bhava Roop) nor does it indicate 'Dearth form' (Abhava Roop). The element which cannot be described the words may be appropriately regarded as 'Shunya'. Thus the philosophical purpose of 'Shunyavad' is infinitiveness. *i.e.,* Bhavatmak and not Abhavatmak (dearthness). From the practical viewpoint 'Shunyavad' refers to the cycle of birth and death and from the spiritual viewpoint Shunyavadis Nirvana or salvation.

The Impact of Buddhism

Buddhism spread in India and in many other countries of the Asian continent. Today there are very few Buddhists in India scattered here and there. But this religion particularly spread in Sri Lanka, Burma, Tibet, Russia, Mangolia, Indonesia, Vietnam, Cambodia, Thailand (Shyam), China, Japan and Korea. In Japan, China and Tibet various branches of this religion have been developed. These branches do not exist in India. Buddhism and its philosophy have immensely influenced Indian philosophical systems. Consequently, in many contexts, Buddhism has been vehementally criticized also. There are many common points between Buddhism and Brahmanism, but their basic stands are different from each other. In Indian sculpture, architecture, literature, painting and drama the impact of the character of Lord Buddha can never be forgotten. Ashok, Kanishka and Harshvardhan embraced Buddhism as immensely contributed to its growth and expansion. Due to these kings Buddhism remained as a state religion in India for long. It will not be an exaggeration to say that it is from Buddhism that the ideals of service to the people, compassionate view point to all and Moksha (salvation) have come into the Vaishnav religion (Brahmanism). Impact of Buddhism may be clearly seen on the sophists. In the Christian religion the concept of Joseph of the Greek and Roman Church appears to be compatible with Buddhism. The countries where Islam was spread were originally centres of Buddhism. Therefore the impact of Buddhism was but natural on the followers of Islam. In fact, it is a truism to remark that even today Buddhism is found as a world religion, because even now its followers are in crorers. The place of Buddhism is certain in the future world, no matter whatever other religion is propounded.

Educational Implications of Buddhism

1. *Educational Implications of the four Arya Satya (four Truths):* 'This world is full of miseries' is the first truth as viewed by Lord Buddha. He has regarded the various miseries of the world as a nature of man. If one realizes this truth from the very beginning he will do nothing which may cause may trouble to him. Then he will so conduct his life as to ensure his physical, mental, moral and spiritual development. Thus he will become a good citizen. If the parents and teachers are motivated by this first truth of Lord Buddha, children will be developed in a desirable manner and our educational system will be transformed.

In the second Arya Satya (truth) Lord Buddha says that one's ignorance is the cause of misery. Due to ignorance one gets involved into various intricacies of the world. In the third truth he says that if the drives generated due to ignorance are destroyed, then a person will rise above all attachments (Rag), rivalry, lust and anger. In fact, to obtain this victory is to achieve salvation. Through the fourth truth Lord Buddha has indicated the parth towards destruction of worldly miseries. In this indication he has spoken of eight devices (Ashiangik Marg) which may help one in getting himself free from worldly miseries.

Lord Buddha has prescribed a middle course to be followed. He had opposed to torture the body through hard penance. The middle course consists of eight devices. By following these eight devices the ultimate aim of education may be achieved. To obtain salvation (Niryan) is the ultimate end of life. Salvation is the freedom from the cycle of birth and death. In fact, this may also be accepted as the ultimate purpose of education.

2. *The Educational Implications of the Ashtangik Marg:* The first step of the Ashtangik Marg is *Samyak Drishti*, *i.e.,* the appropriate insight. This insight will help one to be away from worldly complexities. For being away, *Samyak Sankalpor* appropriate willpower is necessary. This will-power will help one to proceed towards the path of salvation. After having thus proceeded, *Samayakvachor* appropriate speech is necessary. This may be possible through control over oneself. This control will assist one towards proper behaviour with other. After achieving this control, one should exercise the restriction over his physical and mental aspirations. This type of restriction has been termed as *Samyak Marmant* which means to shun all types of violence through thought, word and deed (Mansa, Vacha and Karmana). After Samayak Marmant comes *Samyak Ajeev*, means to earn his bare living through justice. Samayak Ajeev is to be followed by *Samyak Vyayam* which purports that one should entertain only auspicious thoughts in his mind and should shun evil ones. The seventh Marg (device) as enjoined by Lord Buddha is *Samyak Smriti* which means that one should always remember the basic elements of the acquired knowledge. The eighth marg (device) is *Samyak Samadhi* which amounts to perfect concentration of attention after purifying one's inner self. Antakkaran Kshuddhi, for salvation this concentration is very necessary. Needless to add that the above Ashtangik Marg (eight devices) are full of very powerful education meanings.
3. *The Educational Implications of the Theory of Karma*: According to Lord Buddha 'sin' and piety (right cousness) are the outcomes of one's own deeds. The sinner reaps miseries both in this world and in the other beyond, and the pious (Punyatma) man harvests happiness. Due to one's own efforts

someone is rich and the idel one is poor. It is the outcome of one's own deed that one is ill and the other is healthy. One is learned and the other is ignorant. Thus the various peculiarities in the world are not God's creations but the outcomes of some deeds. Thus Lord Buddha has given the message to the mankind that one gets miseries due to his own deeds. Therefore he is quite capable of removing them. Thus the theory of Karma has been propounded very strongly. Lord Buddha firmly believes that God is not the giver of the result of any deed. In fact, the deed, itself, gives its outcome to the doer. Needless to remark that Lord Buddha's theory of Karma is pregnant with noble educational meanings. If our educational centres become imbued with the ideals of Karmavad and the parents, teachers and students begin to behave accordingly, all will be 'up and doing' and every one will be the maker of his own destiny. Then no one will curse his fate and sit idele, doing nothing. In some other contexts, we have already referred to this ideal.

4. *The Educational Implications of the Concept of Bodhisatva:* To attain *Boddhisatva* is the ultimate objective of Buddhism. This position may be accepted as the highest ideal for any person. A person enriches with this position is embedded with spiritual excellencies. The objective of Bodhisatva is to sacrifice one's life for the welfare of others. Thus long with spirituality he is equipped with the cravings for the welfare of all. He is an embodiment of compassion and benevolence. In short, it will not be too much to say that the ultimate purpose of education also should be to make each student a Bodhisatva. If this becomes possible there will be no one miserable in this world. Then one's miseries will be taken up by others as their own and they will try to remove the same. If our education succeeds in achieving this objective this very earth will become a heaven.

Since the Mahayanschool has given great importance to the ideal of Bodhisatva, the above educational implications are applicable to the Mahayan schools as well.

The four great truths of Lord Buddha's teachings are, world is full of miseries, there is a cause for misery, miseries may be wiped off and device for removing misery. Soul is not eternal. Man is himself responsible for his own miseries. Education to make the students depend upon their own efforts. The ultimate purpose of education is to sacrifice one's life for the welfare of others. Freedom from worldly fabrications provides salvations, good education should guide one to their salvations.

Buddhist System of Admission – *Pabbajja*

The *vinayapitaka*, a famous Buddhist scripture states the nature of admission. "Let him who desires to receive ordination first cut off his upper robe so as to cover one shoulder, salute the face of the *bhikshu* with his head; and sit down squatting; then let him raise his joined hands and tell them to say "I take my refuge in the Budha, I take my refuge in the Dharma, I take my refuge in Sangh".

This act of admission was called '*Pabbajja*' (going out of home). After pabbajja, the student was called as *Shramana/Samner*. The 'Samner' had to renounce all his worldly and family relationships. That 'Shraman' was given ten suggestions to follow, *i.e.*

1. Practice non-violence.
2. Speak truth.
3. Do not steal.
4. Do not collect.
5. Observe celibacy.
6. Give up luxury.
7. Renounce wealth and do not touch women.
8. Do not use fragrant things.
9. Do not eat any thing untimely.
10. Do not use soft and very comfortable bed.

Any caste could be admitted and after being he didn't belong to any caste. After admission he had change his old clothes/old ways/ manners of living. For the '*Pabajja*. The minimum age was eight years. When 'Samner' attained twenty *i.e.*, when he received 12 years education he had to under go the '*Upasampada*'. The *Upasampada* ceremony entitled a student for full-fledged membership of the monastery. '*Upasanpada*', was democratic in nature. The 'Shraman' had to present himself before all other monks. One could be admitted for '*Upasampada*' only when the majority of the monks voted in the favour of the same. After *Upasambada* the male monks were called Bhikshu and female monks Bhikshuni. After '*Upasambada*', shraman was regarded as a full-fledged member of the monastery, and his/her all worldly and family relationships ended.

Contrary to vedic education, student never came back to householder life, he cut off his worldly relationships for ever.

Nature of Buddhist Education

The Buddhist education system was residential by nature. A group of young 'Bhikshus' or monks living in a vihar under the guardianship of a common teacher, the Upadhaya or acharya who was the individual responsible for:

- Their health.
- Studies.
- Manners.
- Morals.
- Spiritual upliftment.

Student/Teacher Relationship

Students were required to serve their teachers, beg for alms, eat food thrice a day, bath themselves with pure water and live in discipline. Dr. Altekar, "a teachers relation with his new students was akin to the father-son or parental relationship".

Feminine Education

Women occupied a position inferior to men. Initially, they were prohibited from joining 'Sangha'. Later on they were granted admission. Separate monastries were established for women. Lord Buddha had regarded ladies are the source of all evils. So he had advised during his life time not to admit women in monasteries. But after some time due to the insistance of his dear pupil Ananad, Buddha had permitted women for admission with many restrictions and reservations.

Strict rules were enforced for women monks. The first two years was their probotion period. The women monks were not allowed to meet any male monk in lonliness and their residence arranged separately. They were regarded as lower in status than the male monks.

Vocational Education

The monks of a Vihar were taught spinning, weaving and sewing in order that they meet their clothing requirements. They were taught architecture that enable them to build up a maintain vihars.

Aims of Education

Buddha preached his followers the four 'Noble truths', *i.e.*

- These is sufferings in life.
- This suffering has a cause.
- This suffering could be removed by destroying its cause.
- The cause of suffering is 'Thrishna'/desire.

The most important aim of education is to show the path by which an individual can assimilate this craving or remove his desire and ultimately obtain 'Nirvan'. The desire can only be removed by following the eight noble fold path or the Arya Asthang Marga. The aim of education is to make familiar with these paths and practise in life. *i.e.,* Right views or faith, Right aspiration, Right speech, Right action, Right livelihood, Right effort, Right mindfulness and Right contemplation.

Another aim of Buddhist-education was to teach the monks the law of varna, its working and transmission of souls. The doctrine states, "A man reaps what he sows. A man acts, so shall be. Every individual is the maker of his own destiny".

Another prominent aim of education was the teaching of Ahimsa. Non-violence towards life is recognized as an integral principle of life. Other important aims of education are:

- Development of human qualities.
- Purity of behaviour.
- Obedience to religion.
- Building up of character.
- Development of power of reasoning.
- All round development of the individual.

Curriculum

Curriculum chiefly spiritual in nature, because the chief of education was to attain Salvation/Nirvan Suttanta, Vinaya and Dhamma were the main subjects. Besides these spinning, weaving, printing of cloth, tailoring, sketching, accountancy, medicine, etc were the other subjects.

Methodology

Oral method, Lecturing and Memorise themselves are well practicing methods. Special emphasis was laid on the purity of conduct, because it was thought that if one was not good in behaviour, he couldn't learn anything for his development.

At first the teacher gave a lecture on a certain topic and the students were required to listen to him with rapt attention. After wards students were expected to memorize the same. The students used to react before other fellow students what ever they had committed to memory. During this period the art of writing had developed but it couldn't touch the field of education, the writing materials were not in abundance for all.

Assembly

On the beginning (pratipada) and close (purnima) of each month learned people used to assemble together, for maintain the moral standards of the Bhikshuks. In the assembly each monk used to confess and describe his immoral behaviour frankly. The assembly used to deliberate upon such confessed immoral behaviours of various monks and impose punishments.

The Nature of Mass Education

The Vihars/monasteries support from the people in general to whom they would go for alms. So the time of begging the monks used to remove the religious doubts of people through conversations/ short and apt lectures. In this way monks tried to educate the masses.

Centres of Learning

Dr. Altekar opines that the Buddhists raised India's international stature by the high level of education in their monasteries, since students from as far as Korea, Tibet, Java and other distant centuries were attached to them.

During this period some prominent centres of education sprang up. There was no discrimination between students on any basis. Some of these centres possessed on international reputation.

Wherever Vihars/Monsteries established, educational centres too emerged. Among the most notable universities to develop during this period were the universities at, Taxila, Nalanda, Ballabhi, Vikrama Shila, Odantpuri, Nadia, Jagdalla and Mithila.

CHAPTER

5 Teachings of the Sikhism

INTRODUCTION

Sikhism is the most recent among world religions. Guru Nanak is founder of this religion. This recently has its own strengths, the most important of them being its present day relevance. It took its rise in the Punjab in the 15th century. It was born at a time when India was in a state of political upheaval, social instability and religions ritualism, externalism without much inner illumination and spiritual experience in depth true, Sikhism of Guru Nanak was largely a religions and spiritual movement, but even Guru Nanak advised his followers to resist evil even to the point of sacrifice and martyrdom Guru Nanak was essentially a religious reformist movement in the direction of saint poets of India.

Sikh is really derived from the word 'Sisya' – Hence, Sikhism is the religion of ten Gurus and their followers 'Sisyas'. Follower of the Sikhism, is called as Khalsa, and who were to be called singh, means lion – it is used for men and for the woman 'Kaur' means lioness.

Guru

The Guru occupies a very high status in Sikhism. He is indispensable. Liberation cannot be won without a Guru. But he is not an incarnation of God. He is not at end in himself but only a means. He is a humble prophet or messenger invested with the duty of showing the true-spiritual way to the people. The Guru is an intermediary between God and creation.

"The True Guru is the Boatman and the word the oars to ferry one to the other shore, where there's neither wind, nor fire, nor water, nor form, and where abideth our true Lord dispensing the True Name which takes us across. Those who were led by the Guru, reached the other shore, attuned to the True one. And they overcame their coming and going, their soul merged with the Over soul; Yea, through the guru's wisdom poise welleth up in one, and one mergeth in Truth" (Maru, Mohalla 1). "without the Guru, devotion not love for God welleth within us, nor are we ushered into the society of the saints. Without the Guru, one is blind and is involved in strife; yea through the Guru is the mind cleansed. It is by meeting with the Guru that one conquereth oneself; and one ever revelleth in the Yoga of God's Devotion. Associating with the Guru-saint, one is rid of all one's maladies. In this way one is blest with the Yoga of equipoise" (Basant, Mohalla 1). The spirit of God resides in all the human beings. But in the Guru the Divine Spirit finds its expression.

Ten Gurus

Guru Nanak was the real founder of Sikhism. He was born in 1469 in a village called Talwandi, some fifty miles south-west of Lahore. It is now in Pakistan and has been named Nankana Sahib. True, Sikhism of Guru Nanak was largely a religious and spiritual movement, but even Guru Nanak advised his followers to resist evil 'even to the point of sacrifice and martyrdom'. Later on Guru Hargobind Singh girded on two swords 'miri' (to defend and pursue political end) and 'puri (for safe guarding spiritual pursuit). But it was the last Guru Gobind Singh who infused martial spirit into his Sikh followers called 'Khalasa' and who was to be called 'Singh' (lion). The new order of Khalas had to fight in defence of their faith, home and hearth and their honour.

1. Guru Nanak (1469-1539).
2. Guru Angad (1504-1552). He introduced Gurumukhi Script.
3. Guru Amar Das (1479-1574).
4. Guru Ram Das (1534-1581).
5. Guru Arjun Dev (1563-1606).

Guru Arjun Dev built a temple 'Hari Mandir' which developed into Golden Temple in the 19th Century through the munificence of Maharaja Ranjit Singh. He also prepared what ultimately took the form of AdiGranth Sahib in 1604.

6. Guru Hargobind (1595-1644). He assumed two swords Puri and Miri and sat on a seat and called it Akal-Takht. 'Miri' stands for earthly power, and 'Puri stands for spiritual power. Thus a Guru is a soldier and a saint.
7. Guru Hari Rai (1630-1661).
8. Guru Hari Krishnan (1656-1664).
9. Guru Teg Bahadur (1621-1674).
10. Guru Gobind Singh (1666-1708).

Teachings of the Sikhism

Sikhism is wholly an Indian religion in the sense that its founders were all of Indian origin. *Secondly*, its religious scripture and teachings are wholly Hindu and hardly Muslim. With these stand points we can submit the following points as the outstanding features of Sikhism which distinguish it form any prophetic religion.

1. Sikhism filly subscribes to the four fold principles of: *(i)* Karma *(ii)* Samsara *(iii)* Jnana *(iv)* Mukti (Japuji XX, XXV). These principles are the differentiating features of any form of Hinduism, at the present time.
2. Sikhism is marked out as a Guru-centered religion much more than any other Indian tradition. True, Guru is given a place of great importance in Nyaya, Advaitism, Nathism and Kabirpanth, but the Guru is held in the highest esteem in Sikhism. Even God is called Wahe guru. The script of Guru Granth Sahib is called Gurmukhi because it is calculated to make the Sikhs God-ward last resort AdiGranth Sahib is now known as 'Guru' *i.e.,* a spiritual guide of the whole community (sangat).
3. There is the vow of five K's *i.e.,* keeping of long hair (of head and face), iron-bracelets (Kara), Kachh (under drawers), comb (Kangha) and Kripan (Sword). In one sense, they are merely external observances, but in another respect they are the vows of self-discipline, martial spirit, brotherhood and submission to the Guru. These five K's not only mark out the Sikhs form the Hindus but from all other people of the earth.

4. Unlike any other from of Hinduism, it enjoins upon the Sikhs to fight against social injustice and in defence of one's faith. Though it apperars to have some resemblance with the Muslim doctrine of Jehad, yet it appears to have arisen among the Sikhs as a result of religious persecution and social injustice in the form of Jizya. Even the first huru, Guru Nanak had advised his followers to fight against social evils. Guru Hargobind wielded the two swords of miri and puri. But it was Guru Gobind Singh who infused the amrtial spirit into the Sikhs in defence of one's faith. Hence one of the salient features of Sikhism is that there is a fusion of bhakti and Sakti and khalsa is a symbol of a saint soldier.
5. Sikhism teaches strict monotheism. The highest entity is both non-personal and attribute less and personal. In the non-attributed form it is called One-Omkara of nirahskara, and in the attributed form He is the creator, sustainer and destroyer of the world. For His devotees He is dayalu (kind) and Kripalu (compassionate).

God as both manifest and unmanifest is in accordance with Indian tradition, but is most marked I nDadu and Rai Das, the Saint poets of medieval India. To some extent even Namadeva admits the worship of Pauranic deities though his deity is essentially without attributes.

6. In consonance with strict monotheism, Sikhism does not admit avatarvada (the doctrine of incarnation) and does not believe that there can be any first and last or special prophet of God. But an earnest seeker can obtain the light divine and can be said to be a realized soul. Such a person can be a Guru, but he is not an object of worship, but only of veneration.

The refutation of avataravada is found most pronounced in Kabir by whom Guru Nanak was certainly influenced. By the way this rejection of avataravada shows that it could have no relationship with Christianity and the rejection of any special emissary of God differentiates Sikhism from Islam.

7. But Sikhism admits that there is only one God ek-Omkara (unmanifest) and also Omkara (in manifest form) with an infinite number of attributes. He can be variously named as Wage guru, Kartar (Creator), Akal (eternal), Satt-nama (the holy name). He is also known as Allah, Khuda, Karim (benevolent), rahim (merciful), and Sahib (Lord). The same Lord may be variously named and worshiped in different languages.

This is also a strongly marked feature of Kabir's teachings. On the basis of this Kabir has tried to unify the Muslim and Hindu differences.

8. Sikism is against caste, idolatry, ritualism and external observances. These features are found in most saint poets, but especially in Kabir.

9. Sikhism teaches that Maya is the creative manifestation of God, but is also the source of five traditional evils in man, namely, Kama (passion), Krodh (anger), lobha (greed), moha (infatuation) and ahamkara (egoity). These can be removed through prayer, meditation and social service.

Kabir also teaches that Maya is the power of God, called Ragunath and, that it is a great enchanting power which leads to man's spiritual fall.

10. Nama-sumirana (constant muttering) of God's name with complete surrender to him has been emphasized by Guru Nanak. This is a powerful means of winning the Grace of God.

Kabir too takes recourse to nama-sumirana, but it was Namadeva who dwelt upon this method of meditation. We must not ignore the fact that Sikhism is also known as sant-mat. Hence, it is nut natural that it should have been influenced by saint poets.

11. Sikhism prescribes bhakti for gaining release and this is also a strong feature of saint poets like: Dadu, Rai Das and Kabir.

12. Guru Nanak does not recommend sannyasa as a means of mukti. He himself was a house-holder and considers the life of a house-holder as very important in society.

13. Like Kabir (Sakhi 31. 7-9; Pada 103 of kabir Granthavali), Sikhism is beyond both Hinduism (Vedic) and Islam. Sikhism is no doubt an Indian religion and embedded in Hindu culture and world-view but is and independent religion.

14. But Sikhism does not teach that either Hinduism or Islam is wrong. It teaches both Hindus and Muslims to practice their own faiths with a view to strict moral life and social service, without caring much for rituals and external observances. In this sense it was a reformist religion.

15. Sikhism favours local language and its script is gurmukhi, which is also its distinctive feature.

Gurdwara

Gurdwara is the name given to a Sikh temple; literally it means the gateway to the Guru which implies the Adigranth. A gurdwara is a centre of congregational worship can be divided into two categories: Katha, the reading of the Holy Hymns followed by their explanations and kirtan, the singing of the humns, the latter being more common. Attached to every gurdwara is invariably a free kitchen called Langar.

Gurdwara is not a place for idol worship – not even for individual worship. It is open to all regardless of age, sex, caste or creed.

Gurdwara also plays a socio-economic role in the Sikh community. Devotees who go to a gurdwara make offerings in money or victuals. These offering are not the property of any one person but are used for the common good – for running the langar, schools, colleges and hospitals.

It is believed that the first gurdwara was erected at Emnabad where Guru Nanak met Bhai Lalo. Now-a-days you find gurwaras all over the world. A gurdwara is known form a distance by the Nishan Sahib – the Sikh standard.

Golden Temple

The Golden Temple also popularly known as Harmandir Sahib (Temple of God) or Darbar Sahib (Divine Court) situated in Amritsar is a living symbol of the spiritual and historical traditions of the Sikhs. It has been a source of inspiration to the Sikhs ever since its foundation and their chief place of pilgrimage.

The glistening temple stands in the midst of a sqare tank each side by about 150m with some 18m parakarma (path) on all four sides. A causeway about 60m long has to be covered to reach the temple which itself is 12m square and it rests upon 20m square platform. The temple has four doors, one in each direction. The marble slabs used for the embellishment of the temple proper have artistic engravings on them.

The Golden Temple has had a chequered history in line with that of the Sikh community. It has always been a major rallying point for the Sikhs. When they were facing severe persecution and were fighting for survival from their hideouts, it was captured by the Mughal rulers and razed to the ground. Around 1740 A.D. Massa Ranahar, the ruler of Amritsar desecrated it by using it as a dancing hall. He was killed by Mahtab Singh. In 1762 A.D. Ahmad Shah Abdali gunned down the temple and filled up the tank. Baba deep Singh laid down his life to save the sanctity of the Golden Temple. The construction of the Golden Temple in tis present shape was taken up in 1764 A.D. when Jassa Singh Ahluwallia laid the foundation stone. Many of the doors and domes were covered with gold plated copper sheets during the reign of Maharaja Ranjit Singh. The Golden Temple Complex got partly damaged in the army action in June 1984 to flush out terrorists as alleged by the Government.

Sikh's Ethics

Sikh's ethics can be divided into two parts they are social and personal. Under social ethics: social equality, universal brotherhood, Altruism and social service. Under personal ethics: Bhakti, contentment and courage.

1. Social equality – No caste system and sex discrimination.
2. Universal Brotherhood – Love every one in the spirit of brotherhood.
3. Altruism – The Sikhs are a casteless society. Guru Nanak did not the caste system prevalent in his days. He advised: "Know people by the light illuminating them and do not ask their caste; for in the hereafter no one is differentiated by his caste." (Asa Mohalla 1, p. 349). "God does not mind our caste of birth. So let us learn the way of truthful living; for one's deeds proclaim one's caste and respect."
4. Social Service – The concept of education in Sikhism is best summarized by 'Vidya Vichari Tan Parupkari' 9 Guru Nanak, AdiGranth, p. 356). It means: He is learned indeed who does good to others. But a person cannot do good unless he has a head full of knowledge, hands which are skilful to do service and a heart which is free vices like: egoism, greed, pride and unless it is full of spirit of service, devotion to god and humility.
5. Equipoise – means mental equilibrium – calmness of mind or temper. It is a positive value in Sikhism and occurs again and again in the AdiGranth and other writings. "He alone truly meeteth his God who meeteth Him through equipoise. And then he dieth not, nor cometh nor goeth. In the master os the servant, in the servant is the Lord" (AdiGranth, Dhanasri Mohalla 1, Ashtapadis 2). The way to equipoise is also made clear: "when a man loses Ego, he reaches the state of equipoise".

6. Bakti – Devotion (Bhakti) is common to all religions. Sikhism however, does not recognize the outward form of devotion. It lays great stress on inward devotion in the form of pure love. Guru Amardas has defined Bhakti: "Whoever experiences inward love gets release. He controls his sense through the path of truth and continence. He always remembers the Lord with the word of the Guru. This form of Bhakti is liked by God". (Majh Ashpadi, Mohalla 3). Guru Nanak also states: "Without devotion, one cannot find the True Guru; without good fortune, one cannot cherish devotion to God." (Basant, Mohalla 1).
7. Contentment – is one of the greatest ethical virtues of Sikhism. It implies a state of mind covering temperance, patience, detachment and surrender to the will of God with its necessary accompaniment of humility. Application of contentment puts restrictions on individual's passions, furies and infatuations. It demands of man to keep a check on his tendencies of worldly pursuits. It prohibits self-indulgence, greed, lust, over-eating and over sleeping. It recommends non-attachment with worldly affairs and further implies a control over egoistic and self-centered pursuits. It is stated in the AdiGranth: "The contented who dwell upon none but the Trust of the True, serve Him truly. They do not tread the path of evil. They do good and practice righteousness. They loosen worldly bonds and eat drink in moderation" (Asa, Mohalla 1, p. 467).
8. Courage – Every Sikh suppose to be a courageous to face or fight against evil practices in the world and to sacrifice himself for the cause of good.

The Impacts of Sikhism on Indian Culture and Society

1. All from of Hinduism at present accept the four pillars of: *(i)* Karma *(ii)* Samsara *(iii)* Jnana *(iv)* Mukti. Sikhism too accepts them. Therefore, Sikhism comes under the family name of 'Hinduism'.
2. Besides, at the time of the origin of Sikhism, it did not differentiate itself from caste-Hinduism. Almost on all religious occasions, Brahmin priests presided over the functions. M.A. Macauliffe in 1909 writes:

> Not withstanding the Sikh Gurus' powerful denunciation of Brahmans, secular Sikhs now rarely do anything without their assistance. Brahmans help them to be born, help them to wed, help them to die, and help their souls after death to obtain a state of bliss.

Again, Khushwant Singh observes that contrary to the instructions of the Gurus, Sighs maintain caste, go to Hindu and Sikh places of pilgrimage. Under the circumstances, how can one say that Sikhism is not Hinduism?

3. Sikhism does not accept idolatry, avatarvada (incarnation) and caste.
4. Keeping to the rejection of many external forms of devotion, pilgrimage, idolatry, caste, one Inderjit Singh, a Sikh has given the following statement of Guru Granth Sahib to show that Sikhs are not Hindus.
5. But there is little doubt that the following features differentiate a Sikh from a Hindu.
   (a) the adoption of five vows of long hair, iron bracelet, Kachh (under drawers), comb and Kirpan;
   (b) intense loyalty to the Guru 'Sir rakhe sir jathai';
   (c) belonging to Sikh Khalsa or militancy;
   (d) the adoption of Gurmukhi Script as distinguished form devanagari Script, differentiates Sikhism from Hinduism which recognizes Sanskrit in Devanagari script.

Conclusion

At present all kinds of sects are called Hindus, irrespective of their beliefs and practices. Negatively Hinduism means non-Christian, non-Muslim and non-Parsi faiths and practices. This cannot but produce confusion. We have divided Hinduism into Vedic and non-Vedic. Vedic Hinduism, excepting Arya Samaj, simply means the acceptance of the Vedas as the only religious scripture and the acceptance of caste. Non-Vedic Hinduism is largely of Jain and Buddhist tradition in which atheism, anti-avataravada, anti-casteism etc., are maintained. Kabirpanth, Gorakh Nath Panth and Sikhism are really non-Vedic Hinduism. But like all other forms of Hinduism, Sikhism has family resemblance with even the prevalent form of Sanatana Hindu Dharma.

Holy Books of Sikhism

Sri Guru Granth Sahib

The Guru Granth Sahib (Punjabi: ਗੁਰੂਗ੍ਰੰਥਸਾਹਿਬ, Gurû Granth Sâhib), or Adi Sri Guru Granth Sahib, is the Holy Scripture and the final Guru of the Sikhs. It is a voluminous text of 1430 angs (parts), compiled and composed during the period of Sikh Gurus, from 1469 to 1708. It is a collection of hymns or shabad, which describe what God is like and the right way to live.

Historical Volumes of the Siri Guru Granth Sahib

- *Kartarpur Vaali Bir*: As described above, Guru Arjun dictated the AdiGranth to Bhai Gur Das. This first volume, or Bir, was made in Amritsar and later transferred to Kartarpur, where it remains today. The opening lines are in the hand of Guru Arjun, and it bears the signature of Guru Hargobind at the end. There are several blank pages, left by Guru Arjun to hold the writings of Guru Teg Bahadur. Apart from many handwritten copies of Sri Guru Granth Sahib possessed by various persons and found in some gurdwaras the most important is the Birrecension at Kartarpur, near Jullundur in the custody of Sodhi Amarjit Singh, a descendant of Dhirmal.
- *Bhai Banno Vaali Bir*: After completing the AdiGranth, Guru Arjun asked one of his Sikhs, Bhai Banno, to take the manuscript to Lahore to have it bound. During this journey, Bhai Banno had a copy made for his own use. He inserted a few Shabads of his own choosing, however. This version remains with his descendents. Hand written Manuscript of Bhai Bannowali Bir is said to be available at Gurdwara Banno Sahib in Kanpur city in India.
- *Damdama Vaali Bir*: This is the volume dictated by Guru Gobind Singh at Damdama Sahib to Mani Singh. In it, Guru Gobind Singh included the Shabads of Guru Teg Bahadur. The volumes of the Siri Guru Granth Sahib which preside over our Gurdwaras now are copies of this edition.

Using the Gurmukhi Bir and the English Translation

In the West, it has become common to use the English translation of the Siri Guru Granth Sahib in Gurdwara programmes and Akhand Paaths, because many of the Western Sikhs are not fluent in Gurmukhi. This has served to bring many to the Feet of the Guru who otherwise may not have had the opportunity to experience the Shabad Guru. It should be noted, however, that it is ideal to install the full Gurmukhi Bir in the Gurdwara in order to fully experience and develop a relationship with the Guru. The English translation can be installed on a separate Palki on the side and serve to illuminate the sangat in the meaning of the Words of the Guru. The English translation may be used during an Akhand Paath in which the participants are not fluent in Gurmukhi. However, if a special Gurdwara programme is being planned, the English Akhand Paath days can be accommodated so that the full Gurmukhi Bir of Siri Guru Granth Sahib presides.

A Sikh is encouraged (but not a must) to learn to read Gurmukhi so as to deepen his or her experience of Gurbani and so that the full body of the Guru may be installed in the Gurdwara.

Note: English and other translations of the Sre Guru Granth Sahib Ji should be considered as just another 'style' (language) of talking/deitating/praising the guru. Trying to force a person to learn punjabi/gurmukhi is highly undesirable.

CHAPTER

6 Educational Prescriptions of Islam

INTRODUCTION

Islam, with more than 1,900 million out of 6 billion adherents, is the second largest world religion. Historically, Islam is viewed as a religion, which originated in seventh century with the Prophet Muhammad (570-632 A.D.) and the revelation of the Quran. Muslims do not regard Islam as a new religion. They believe that Allah is the same God who revealed himself to Abraham, Moses, Jesus and Muhammad. Hence Jews, Christians and Muslims are followers of the same living God – in a common family with ancestor, Abraham.

The name of this religion is Islam, which means submission, resignation, reconciliation or surrender to the will of God. Hence a Muslim is one who submits to God and lives in peace and harmony with all. All Muslims in the world constituted one community (umma) of believers, based upon a shared faith, which should transcend all other loyalties. Islam, after Judaism and Christianity, is the third and latest monotheistic religion. Historically it is an offshoot of Judaism and Christianity. All the three are the products of one spiritual life, the Semitic life. The term 'Semitic' comes from 'Shem' (Noah's son) in the Old Testament (Gen.10:1).

The Muslims both reject and protest the use of 'Mohammedanism' and 'Mohammedans' because it implies that the religion takes its name after Muhammad. Muslims believe that the founder of Islam is Allah (God) and the date of founding goes back to the age of Adam.

Faith in Prophets

Islam is founded with six fundamental beliefs ordained by God (Allah) and taken together represents the objects of faith (imam). Each belief is an integral part and essential of True Faith. In their absence there can be no religion. Faith in Prophets is one of the fundamental beliefs. The six fundamental beliefs are:

The Belief in the Oneness of God (Allah) or the belief in Tawhid (Islamic Monotheism)

This belief embodies the fundamental doctrine of Islam as the foundation of all other beliefs. A Muslim believes that God alone is the Lord, the Creator, the Sovereign and the Master of all affairs. He alone is Absolute, the Ever-Living, the Eternal, the Organizer, the Originator, the Fashioner and the cause of everything in the Universe. (Qur'an 112:1-4; 59:23; 2:107; 25:2; 19:65; 11:6; 42:11-12; 3:26).

The Belief in All the Revelation of God (Allah)

A Muslim believes in all the original Scripture or Messages revealed to mankind through the Messengers. All the messages were essentially one and the same divine Guidance because their essences were the same and their source was the same Omnipotent God. Sacred Scriptures are the guiding light, which the messengers received to show their respective people the Right path of God. Every Muslim has to believe in the four Holy Books of Allah:

Taurah (Torah)	Pentateuch	revealed to Moses
Zabur	Psalms	revealed to David
Injil	Gospels	revealed to Jesus
Qur'an	Qur'an	revealed to Muhammad

Muslims believe that the only authentic and complete book of God in existence today is the Qur'an. The Qur'an is the final revelation, which confirms earlier scriptures, clears up all uncertainties and perfects the truth. It is given to the Muslims as the standard or criterion by which all the other books are judged (Qur'an 15:9; 2:75-79; 5:13-14; 6:91).

The Belief that there are Angels Created by God (Allah)

Muslims believe that there are angels (Malak Pl. Malaikah) who are purely spiritual beings whose nature requires no food or drink or sleep. They are under God's command and God employs them to administer His kingdom. They surround us and are always in our company. If we listen to them they become our guardians and protect us from evil ways. On the Day of Judgment they will present a full report or our life work on earth.

When God created Adam, the devil refused to prostrate before him and he was expelled from Eden. According to a tradition from the prophet, this species consists of five orders, namely: *(i)* Jann, *(ii)* Jinn, *(iii)* Shaitans, *(iv)* Ifrits, and *(v)* Marids (16:49-50; 21:19-20; 35:1).

The Belief in the Day of Judgment and in the Resurrection of the Dead

A Muslim believes in the final reckoning, a day when the present world will come to an end and the dead will be raised up for a final and fair trail in the divine court of Justice. The righteous will be rewarded a life of bliss in Paradise, full of delights and border line are, is the solution to the problem of the children of the Polytheists who died at a tender age. They cannot be guilty of serious sin, so they cannot be sent to hell. They do not have faith in one God, so they cannot go to heaven. (14:48; 36:12; 3:185; 39:42; 20:55; 17:13; 42:40).

The Belief in Fate and Divine Decree

A Muslim believes that whatever happens whether good or bad, God (Allah) knew it beforehand. It has already been pre-recorded or foreknown by him through His foreknowledge and Wisdom before it happens. Everything in the universe has a predetermined course, which we call it in Arabic Al-Qadr. Nothing in the whole universe can happen without Divine Will. God knows the past, the present and the future of every action. The fact that God by his foreknowledge already knew what one is going to do, yet does not in any way diminish man's freedom. God's mere knowledge does not affect man's course of action. Good and bad actions are the product of man's voluntary actions solely influenced by his own choice of action (18:29; 41:46; 53:33-62; 54:49; 65:3).

The Belief in all the Prophets of God (Allah)

A Muslim believes in all the Prophets of God without any discrimination or precedence among them. God sent Prophets who brought divine guidance to every people. They were chosen by God to teach mankind and deliver His divine message. Since God is taken to be a transcendent being, He could commune with His chosen people only through the intermediaries. The prophet Muhammad declared that there are 124000 prophets who have been sent to the various people at different times. In the Qur'an itself 25 prophets have been named who were sent to the Jews (Sura 6:83-86) and later on three prophets were added from the New Testament. Abraham and Moses are most prominently mentioned and Jesus has been mentioned at least twenty five times in the Qur'an. But the prophet Muhammad has been called the last and final prophet of God to all mankind.

The prophet is a messenger of God to teach people about pure monotheism and law to guide the people (Sura 10:48; Sura 14:4). Prophets served the divine purpose of correcting the people and warning them against disobedience of His message and social law. Usually the prophets were God-intoxicated men who spoke things in their emotional outbursts and at times in poetic utterances, as in the use of Prophet David and Prophet Muhammad. The utterances were about God and warning against social injustice. They certainly were inspired men who were committed to God with a great deal of self-involvement.

Muhammad the Prophet

Muhammad means praised one. He was the posthumous son of Adullah by his wife Aminah. Abdullah belonged to the family of Hashim, which was the noblest tribe of the Quraysh section of the Arabian race, and said to be directly descended from Ishmael. The father of Abdullah and the grandfather of Muhammad was Abdul Muttalib, who held the high office of custodian of the Kabag (the house of God believed to be built by Adam). Muhammad was born in Makkah on August 20, 570 A.D. He lost his mother Aminah when he was about six years old. It therefore, fell to the lot of his grandfather Abdul Muttalib to bring up the boy and two years later, after the grandfather's death the duty was upon his paternal uncle Abu Talib.

When twelve years old, it is related, Muhammad accompanied his paternal uncle and patron Abu-Talib on caravan journey to Syria in the course of which he met a Christian monk Bahira. With his marriage at the age of 25 to the wealthy widow Khadijah, 15 years his senior, Muhammad steps upon the threshold of clear history. Khadijah was a Qurayshite and was conducting business independently and had taken young Muhammad into her employ (steward). As long as Khadijah lived, Muhammad did not have another wife. According to the traditions after Khadijah's death, Muhammad took to himself eleven lawful wives and two concubines.

Muhammad was often noticed secluding himself and engaging in meditation within a little cave (ghar) on a hill outside of Makkah called Hira. It was in the course of one of these periods that he heard a voice commanding, 'Recite thou in the name of thy Lord who created' etc. (Qur'an 96:1-5). This was his first revelation. The prophet had received his call. The night of that day was later named 'the Night of Power' and fixed towards the end of Ramadan (610 A.D.) After a brief interval when the second vision came, Muhammad under the stress of great emotion, rushed home in alarm and asked his wife to put some covers on him. Then the following words of revelation descended: 'O thou, enwrapped in thy mantle! Arise and warn'. (Qur'an 74:1ff).

Muhammad Preached

God is one. He is all-powerful. He is the creator of the universe. There is a judgment day. Splendid rewards ın Paradise await those who carry out God's commands and terrible punishment in hell for those who disregard them. Such was the gist of his early message.

Muhammad now went among his own people teaching, preaching and delivering the new message. Khadijah his wife, predisposed by her cousin Waraqah, Muhammad's cousin Ali and his kinsman Abu Bakr were the few who responded to his call. But the Quraysh leader considered it a heresy which went against the best economic interests of the custodians of Ka'ba the pantheon of deity and centre of a pan-Arabian pilgrimage. Many slaves and lower class people were converted to Islam. Khadijah died about three years before the Hijrah. Within this pre-Hijrah period there also falls the deamatic 'isra', that nocturnal journey in which the prophet is said to have been instantly transported from a;-Ka'ba to Jerusalem preliminary to his ascent (miraj) to the seventh heaven. Thus Jerusalem has become and ramined the third holiest city after Makkah and Madinah in the Muslim world.

The Hijrah (622 A.D.)

With which the Makkan period ended and the Madinese period began, proved a turning point in the life of Muhammad. Leaving the city of his birth as a despised prophet, he entered the city of his adoption as an honored chief. The statesman gradually overshadows the prophet. There hundred Muslims under the leadership of the prophet, defeated one thousand Makkans at Badr, 85 miles south west of Madinah in 624 A.D. This victory laid foudtation of Muhammad's temporal power. This victory was interpreted as a divine sanction of the new faith. Circumstances of time and place favoured Muhammad. There was the social unrest in Makka and Madinah the reaction against Hellenism in Syria and Egypt the decline of Persian and Byzantine empires and a growing realization by the nomadic Arabs of the opportunities for plunder in the settled lands round them.

The Jews of Khaybar, a strongly fortified oasis north of Madinah, surrendered in 628 and paid tribute to Muhammad. In this Madinese period the Arabianization, the nationalization of Islam was effected. The new prophet broke off with both Judaism and Christianity; Friday was substituted for Sabbath the adhan (call for prayer) was decreed in place of trumpets and gongs, Ramadan was fixed as a month of fasting the Qibla (the direction for ritual prayer) was changed from Jerusalem to Makkah, the conquest of Makkah was completed in 630 A.D. Entering its great sanctuary Muhammad smashed the many idols (360 numbers), exclaiming: 'Truth has come and falsehood has vanished'. The territory around Ka'ba was declared by Muhammad haram (forbidden, sacred) and non-Muslims were not permitted to go there. The native Jews and Christians were taken under the protection of the newly arising Islamic community in consideration of a payment later called Jizya (Poll tax, Capitation tax). Arabia seemed now inclined to be dominated by Muhammad. In 632 A.D. Muhammad entered peacefully at the head of the annual pilgrimage into his new religious capital Makkah. This was his last visit and was therefore, styled 'the farewell pilgrimage'. Three months after his return to Madinah, he unexpectedly took ill and died on June 08, 632 A.D.

Muhammad, in addition to his spiritual function, exercised the same temporal authority that any chief of a state might exercise. Before the Prophet died, he had created the conditions for a universal brotherhood on the basis of faith, a principle he vigorously substituted for the old blood ties and tribal loyalties of the Arabs. Thus the *ummamuslima* (the Muslim Community), as a fabric of society, with its principle of internal solidarity, was brought into being under his own hands. The new community was to have no priesthood, no hierarchy, and no central see. *Hazrath* (His Excellency) Muhammad is seen as *Insan al kamil* (Perfect Man), *Al-Amin* (the trustworthy). Had it not been for his gift as 'seer', 'statesman', and 'administrator', a notable chapter in the history of mankind would have remained unwritten.

- *Muhammad the Seer*: Through the revelations made to him the Arab world was given a framework of ideas within which the resolutions of its social tensions came possible. Quran was suited to the needs and conditions of the day. Muhammad's skill and tact as an administrator, is manifested by his wisdom in the choice of right men for the right jobs.

Emil Brunner says "Had Muhammad been a Pre Christian prophet of Arabia, it would not be easy to exclude him from the ranks of the messengers who prepared the way for revelation." In the light of the positive values of Muslim monotheism one can legitimately accept that Muhammad has some prophetic charism, which enabled him to communicate to his followers certain fundamental and biblical truths about God and man.

Pillars of Islam (ARKAN)

SHAHADA (KALIMA)	=	Profession of faith.
La ilahaillallah	=	No god whatsoever but Allah.
Muhammadun Rasul-ullah	=	Muhammad is the messenger of Allah.
La ilahailla'Allah	=	Ther is no god but god.

This first part is a clear, uncompromising affirmation of monotheism. This formula begins with the absolute negation (*La*) of the Pseudo-deities, polytheism, idolatry, superstition, pantheism, etc.

Muhammadunrasul-ullah. Alllah and rasul were bracketd, inseparsably, in the shahada or witness of faith. Throughout the Qur'an there is a steady reiteration of the juncture between the concern of God and of the prophet. (5:56; 8:46; 33:22, 40; 72: 23). These are the first words to strike the ear of the new born Muslim babe; they are the last to be uttered at the grave.

SALAT (NAMAZ IN PERSIAN)

Ritual prayer is the supreme act of worship in Islam. Five times a day is the faithful Muslim supposed to turn his face towards Makkah and recite the ritual prayer. It is the devotional exercise, which every Muslim is requited to render to God. Arabic is the language used for ritual prayer because Allah's mother tongue, the Muslims believe, is Arabic.

Salat comprises five daily services

Timings

1. *Fajr* = The early morning prayer, offered after the dawn and before the sun.
2. *Zuhr* = The noon prayer, after 12-00 noon.
3. *Asr* = The mid afternoon prayer.
4. *Maghrib* = The sunset prayer, to be offered immediately after sunset.
5. *Isha* = The evening prayer, usually two hours after sunset.

The offering of Namaz is obligatory upon every Muslim, male and female, who is sane, relatively mature and free from serious sickness. Purity is the first requirement for valid prayer.

Azan (The call to Prayer)

This is usually chanted by the *muezzin* (the caller) in Arabic five times a day. The *muezzin* stands facing the *Qibla* (the direction of *Ka'ba)* and sings:

- *Allahu Akbar* = God is great (four times).
- *Ashhaduan la ilahailla-llah* = I bear witness that there is no god but God (twice).
- *Ashhaduanna muhammadar rasulullah* = I bear witness that Muhammad Is the Messenger of God (twice).
- *Hayya 'ala-s-salah* = Come for prayer (twice).
- *Hayya 'ala-l-falah* = Come to prosperity.
- *Allahu Akbar* = God is great (twice).
- *La ilahailla-llah* = There is no god but God (once).

The prayer is always preceded by *Wuzu* (the ablution) of the face, hands and feet after declaring the intention that the act of ablution is for the purpose of worship and purity. Muhammad says: "The five stated prayers erase the sins which have been committed during the intervals between them, if they have been not mortal sins."

ZAKAT (Almsgiving)

It is an institution of Islam and founded upon an express command in the Qur'an, (2: 43,110,177; 4: 77,162; 5: 12,55; 9: 5,11,18,60,103; 21:73; 22:41,78). The technical meaning of the word Zakat is the annual amout in kind or coin which a Muslim with means must distribute among the rightful beneficiaries. The rate of Zakat is 2.5 per cent of the income.

Quran 9:60 gives the list of the beneficiaries of Zakat:

- The poor Muslims, to relieve their distress.
- the needy or destitute.
- The official appointed in connection with the collection and expenditure of zakat.
- For ransoming of captives of for the emancipation of Muslim slaves.
- For relieving a Muslim from the burden of debt.
- For Muslim new converts who are to be settled down.
- In the service of God, fighting in the way of God (Jihad).
- Muslim travelers who are stranded and in need of help.

Sawm (Roza, Persian) Fasting

The fast of the thirty days of the month of *Ramazan* is regarded as a divine institution, being enjoined in the Quran and is therefore compulsory (2:185). Fasting means abstinence from food, drink, smoking and sexual activity from dawn to sunset, during he entire month of Ramadan, the 9th month of the Islamic year. Fasting is obligatory for all Muslims, male or female, who are adults, sound in mind and physically fit.

Hajj (Pilgrimage)

The final pillar and one of the finest institutions of Islam is the Hajj or pilgrimage to Makkah. The performance of the Hajj is obligatory, at least once in a lifetime, upon every Muslim who is financially and physically fit. It is a wholesome demonstration of the universality of Islam and the brotherhood and equality of the Muslims. It is to confirm the commitment of Muslims to God and their readiness to forsake the material interests in His service.

INFLUENCE OF ISLAM ON INDIAN CULTURE

Hitinued. These ages in Indian history may be fixed and numerated. In the first place, Indian history may be broadly divided into three epochs ancient, medieval and modem; the first Beginning from the earliest times to the eighth century of the Christian era, the second consisting of the one thousand years olio wing the eighth century, and the third commencing with he nineteenth century and still running.

The ancient epoch may be subdivided into four ages the/edic ending in the seventh century B.C., the Buddhist in the second century B.C., the early Hindu in the middle of the third century A.D., and the later Hindu in the eighth century A.D. The medieval epoch is divisible into two ages the early medieval from the eighth to the thirteenth and the later from the thirteenth to the end of the eighteenth century. In the first age India is discovered as an agitated scene of conflicting tribes and races in which one group attempts to impose its civilization on the other. The Aryans and the non-Aryans meet in struggle and the war is waged not merely on the plane of politics and economics but also on that of cult and culture. The literature of the Vedic age is a mirror of this vast social conflict; it reflects its various stages (not necessarily successive): the commencement of the Aryan onset when the victor's warriors and priests exhilarated by their triumph sing joyous paeans in praise of the shining gods who confer the boons of victory, prosperity and long life; then the process of settlement and spread over Northern India when sobered by reflection and the responsibility of administering newly acquired lands they give utterance to hymns which embody their thinking on problems of social organization, of cosmic origins, of human destiny and of ultimate reality; and lastly, the assimilation of the victors and the vanquished, when the magic and the ritual attain a position ride by side with speculation and philosophy in the sacred arcane of die scriptures, when animistic beliefs and fetish worship lie cheek by jowl with the sublime and subtle concept of cosmic older up pantheistic godhead

EDUCATIONAL PRESCRIPTIONS OF ISLAM AS EVIDENCED THROUGH QURAN

The Arabic word Islam literally means 'Surrender' or 'Submission'. *i.e.,* 'Submission to God'. Thus one who has surrendered is a Muslim. In theory, all that is necessary for one to become a Muslim is to recite sincerely the short statement of faith known as the 'Shahadah'. *I witness that there is no god but God (Allah) and that Muhammad is the messenger of God.*

Although in a historical sense Muslims regard their religion as dating from the time of Muhammad in the early 7th century AD, in a religious sense they see it as identical with the true monotheism which prophets before Mohammad, such as: Abraham, Moses and Jesus had bought. The followers of these and other prophets are held to have corrupted their teachings, but God in his mercy sent Muhammad to call mankind yet again to the truth.

"We have not sent there (But as a Messenger) *To all mankind*, giving them Glad tidings and warning them (against Sin), but most men know not" (Qur'an, 34; 28).

Qur'an

Qur'an (Arabic, Al-Qur'an), the chief sacred text of Islam. The Arabic name indicates something 'read' or 'recited'. It contains the revelations made by Allah (God) to Muhammad during his career as a prophet in Mecca and Medina in the first decades of the 7th Century.

The Qur'an is divided into 114 chapters (Suras), each known by a different title. The chapters are divided into *vs.* (Ayas).

The Qur'an's Importance and Interpretation

Qur'an is regarded as one of the two main sources of Islamic law (the other being the Sunnah, the divinely guided behaviour and practice of the prophet).

Much of the work of interpretation is concerned with the occasions of revelation. The individual *vs.* and groups of verses are related to the life of Muhammad and are understood as having been revealed in connection with specific incidents in this life or to solve particular problems which he faced. Thus the text is understood as having an immediate context in the life of Muhammad as well as more universal and timeless significance.

Qur'an begins with Iqrah (Recite), "Recite in the name of your lord who created, created man from Blood congealed. Recite! Your Lord is the most beneficent, who taught by the pen, taught men that which they did not know…".

Qur'an was not authored by Muhammad or by any other human being Muhammad was an illiterate, unable to read or write, and remained so till his death.

What is Qur'an About?

The Qur'an, the last revealed word of God, is the primary source of every Muslim's faith and practice. It deals with all the subjects which concern human beings: Wisdom, doctrine, worship, transactions, law etc., but its basic theme is the relationship between God and His creatures. It provide guidelines for a just society, proper human conduct and an economic system.

Knowledge According to Islam

Prophet Mohammed says, 'He who goes out in search of knowledge is in God's path till he returns'. 'The search of knowledge is an obligation laid on every Muslim' (Hadith). "The one who would have the worst position in God's sight on the Day of Resurrection would be a learned man who did not profit from his learning" (Hadith).

The basis of knowledge, according to Islam, is through *Vahia* (revelations); which is revealed through messengers of God. At the age of forty, Muhammad received his first revelation from God through the Angel Gabriel. The revelations continued for 23 years, and they are collectively known as the Qur'an. A person can acquire knowledge through Ijthi had. *i.e.,* a person has the freedom to acquire new knowledge. The source of these acquired knowledge is human imagination and sensory experience. Social science, natural science and applied science are all included in this.

The classification of knowledge is both logical and psychological, because the first, knowledge acquired through revelation, is on the basis of faith and second, acquired knowledge through imagination and sensory experience, is acquired through inspirational faith and human resources.

Acquired knowledge is only temporal in nature whereas knowledge acquired through revelation stands as the ultimate truth. Prophet Mhammed says, "If anyone pursues a path in search of knowledge, God will thereby make easy for his a path to paradise".

How to Acquire Knowledge

"And Allah brought you out of your mother's wombs devoid of all knowledge, but he has endowed you with hearings and sights, and minds-hearts, so that you may be graceful" (Quran, 16:78).

In the above *vs.* three words: *(i)* 'Sama', *(ii)* 'Basar' and *(iii)* 'Fu'ad' are used for the three faculties of hearing, seeing and thinking. Hearing is through the ears, seeing is through the eyes and thinking is through heart and mind.

Sama means to procure the information and knowledge acquired by others. Basar means to acquire information and knowledge oneself through observation Fu'ad means to extract results by compiling, analyzing and interpreting the information and knowledge procured by Sama and acquired by Basar.

Those who utilize these three faculties collectively with much enthusiasm and vigour. They are dominant and they emerge in this world as leaders.

Aim of Islamic Education

- The educational system should be in such a way that the learner should attain the status of the representative of God.
- Behold, thy Lord said to the angels.
- 'I will create a vicegerent on earth' (Qur'an 2;30).
- It should aim at the development or growth of a balanced personality through training of soul, intellect, reason, emotions and senses. It helps him to attain the title of 'Khaleefathullah'.
- Education should satisfy spiritual, intellectual, physical, scientific and linguistic aptitudes and thus paving the way for his complete development.
- Basic aim of education is the submissal of oneself to the wish of God in his personal, social and humanistic spheres.
- Educational system should be moulded in such a way that it should bring dynamism in society.
- All should get equal opportunity for growth and development as according to his own ability and intellect.
- Education should provide the learner as the true servant of God to guide himself and the universe and it should not happen by entering a conflict against nature.
- As a means of plunging into the mysteries of the universe and as a means of opening up the mind to the love and awe towards God, education in theory and practice should encourage self-restraint, self purification and for the cultivation of holiness (sacredness) in our mind.

Prophet Muhamad says, Nawas bin Saman told that; he asked God's Messenger about righteousness and sin and he replied, "Righteousness is good character and sin is that which revolves is your heart and about which you do not want people to know".

Women's Education

The importance of women's education needs to be emphasized. It is as important as men's education. A community cannot progress unless it provides the best education to women, who constitute a vital segment of communal life.

The programme for women's education must be designed in accordance with the teachings of Islam. It must be clearly understood that Islamic culture is totally different from western culture. In the west, a women is not entitled to any right or honour unless she succeeds in performing the functions of a man. Islam on the other hand protects her rights and confers dignity upon her as a woman. It assigns her those responsibilities which suit her feminine nature. As for co-education, there is no scope for it in an Islamic education system at any level.

The primary responsibility of a woman is to look after her home and family, as well as to rear worthy children. The education for women should therefore equip them to discharge these responsibilities efficiently.

Islam and Science

And they say; "What is there but our life in this world; we shall die and we live, and nothing but time can destroy us" But of that they have no knowledge: they merely conjecture. (Quran, 45;24)

It is regarded that modern science as absolute and true religion, and want to impose this views to all humankind. In other words '*experimental knowledge*' is the unique guide for mankind, experimental knowledge is the knowledge that can be proved or disproved through experiment.

According to this belief of science, all religious information is considered as unreal and questionable. For this reason modern science considers the existence of Allah, the existence of the hereafter are questionable, because they can neither be proved nor observed through an experiment. "Science and Religion have their different fields, and should not interfere one another".

This science-religion balance isolates humanity from religion, because humanity can be explained by 'experimental knowledge and observation'. These remains only two limited areas for religion which are personal ethics and belief. Quran says, Say: Truly my prayer and my service of sacrifice, my life and my death, Are (all) for Allah, The cherisher of the worlds (Quran: 6: 162).

Islam is a complete way of life and it interfere in all the activities in which man engage. Islam and logic are not in the opposite poles.

The Real Meaning of Science

There is no constant universal science above religion, cultures and ideologies. Science is not a universal guide, certainly, science is guided. For *e.g.*, Newton's scientific hypothesis is a scientific paradigm. With the rise of Einstein's paradigm that is valid today, Newton's paradigm lost its validity. Paradigm is nothing but conjecture that is accepted to be true for a temporary period of time.

According to Paul Feyerabend it is absolutely the result of a subjective preference to consider science as being superior than any other teaching that human kind has put forward. Therefore the government should give up the education policy that regards science as the guide and assumes it is superior than other branches.

Science is neither a guide, nor an aim within itself, but only a tool – a tool that can be used in favour of an intention.

Method: Science and Islam

While most other substances contract when they are cooled, water expands as it freezes. Ice, being less dense than water, flows on it. This fact can be described differently by two persons. An atheistic scientist describes this scientific fact as being essentially inherent in the quality of water, whereas a God-fearing scientist describes this scientific phenomenon as the manifestation of divine wisdom to make life possible in the rivers and seas. The two approaches build different impression on the minds of students. The one approach is intended to undermine the existence of Allah and his providence, whereas the other approach strengthens belief in the existence of Allah and His providence. Instruction along the first line will produce atheistic scientists. Where as instruction along the second line will produce Good-fearing scientists.

Conclusion

Islam is not a religion and Mohammad is not the founder of Islam. It is a total and unified way of life it is a set of beliefs and a way of worship; it is a vast and integrated system of law; it is a culture and civilization; it is an economic system and a way of doing business; it is a polity and a method of governance; it is a special sort of society and a way of running a family; it prescribes for inheritance and divorce, dress and etiquette, food and personal hygiene. It is a spiritual and human totality, this worldly and other-worldly.

The Holy Quran

The word Qur'an is derived from the Arabic 'Qara' which has the same meaning as the Hebrew 'Kara, 'to read', or 'to recite'. Qur'an is the verbal noun of 'Qara' and thus denotes the act of reciting, presumably from memory. The Qur'an is the Word of God (Kalam Allah) and is His inspired work and revelation. The Qur'an is shorter than the New Testament and is divided into 114 Ṡuras (Chapters) of which 86 were revealed in Makkah and 28 in Madinoh. The 'Suras' in the Qur'an are arranged not in the order of chronology but length. Thus with the exception of the firt 'Surah'., titled 'Fatiha' the Suras are arranged according to length, the latter ones being the shortest. Each 'Sura' in the Qur'an begins with a heading and a statement about its date. After the heading comes the pharse, 'Bismillahi r-rahamni r-rihim' (In the name of god, the merciful, and the compassionate).

The Words which came to Muhammad, when in a state of trance, are held Sacred by the Muslims and are never confounded with those which he uttered when no physical change was apparent in him. The former are the sacred book (Qur'an), the latter the 'Hadith' (sayings of the prophet) or 'sunna' (traditions) of the prophet. According to the Islamic doctrine, throughout the Qur'an the speaker is God and the Prophet is addressed as the recipient of the revelation.

Copies of the Qur'an are held in the greatest esteem and reverence among Muslims. They dare not touch it without being first washed and purified. They never hold it below their girdles and always place it on the highest shelf or in some place of honor in their houses. Muslims believe that the Qur'an is uncreated and eternal, subsisting in the very essence of God. Islam the doctrine of the infallible Word of God is an article of faith. One who has committed the whole Qur'an to memory is a 'Hafiz'. The Qur'an is the most widely read book ever written, for besides its use in worship, it is the text book from which every Muslim learns to read Arabic.

During the Caliphate of Uthman (A.D. 644-656, there were different copies of the Qur'an in use. Hence Uthman commissioned Zaydibn-Thabit to collect the Qur'an. The whole Qur'an was carefully revised and compared with the copy, which had been in Hasfsa's keeping. Hafsa, the daughter of Caliph Umar, was the prophet's wife and she was In touch with the Qur'anic revelations. Uthman made several copies of this authoritative text of the Qur'an and distributed them in the Islamic Empire. The previously exiting copies of the Qur'an were destroyed. Uthman's edition to this day remains the authoritative Word of God to Muslims.

AL-FATIHA (The Opening Chapter)

- Bismillahi r-rhmani al-rahim (In the Name of God, the Compassionate, the Merciful).
- Al-Hamdu Lillahi Rabbil Aaamie'n (Praise be to Allah, Lord of the Words).
- Ar-Rahmmnir-Rahim (The Beneficent, the Merciful).
- Maaliki Yaumid – Diirs (Ower of the day of judgement).
- Iyyaakara-budu WA iyyaakanaasta-iin (Thee (alone) we worship; Thee, We ask for help).
- Ihidina s-Siratal-Mustaquim (show us the straight path).
- Siraatal – laziina an-amta day- him (The Path of those whom Thou hast favoured).
- Gayril – Magzuubi Alay him WA AZ – Zaallihin. (Not (the Path) of those who earn Thine anger nor of those who go astry).

This opening chapter of Praise (Al-Fatiha) is the equivalent of 'Our Father' for Muslims. It is known as the seven recitals as it contains seven verses. Muslims recite this prayer over the sick for healing. This is intercession for the souls of the departed.

Almost all historical narratives of the Qur'an have their Biblical parallels. Among the Old Testament characters, Adam, Noah, Abraham, Ishmael, Lot, Joseph, Moses, Saul, David, Solomon, Elijah and Job and Jonah figure prominently. Qur'an shows more parallelism to the Pentateuch than to any other part of the Bible. Of the New

Testament characters Zachariah, John the Baptist, Jesus and Mary are the only ones emphasized. Mary the Mother of Jesus is also the daughter of Aaron. The Arabic forms of the names of the Old Testament characters seem to have come through Syriach and Greek rather than directly from Hebrew.

Sources of Qur'an

1. Judaism.
2. Christianity.
3. Neo-Platonism.
4. Zoroastrianism.
5. Gnosticism.

Rabbi Abraham Geiger (1810-1874) is of opinion that the Qur'an depends almost exclusively upon Jewish sources that were passed on orally. Michael The Syrian maintained that Muhammad took all his teachings from the Jews.

Christian Orientalists place the explanation on Christian influences. St. John Damascene said that Muhammad found his religion after long conversation with Arian Monk.

Muhammad had access to the Apocryphal Gospels like the Gospel of Barnabas. Muslims assert that Muhammad obtained his account Christianity from this spurious Gospel. This Gospel of Barnabas contains a complete history of Jesus Christ, from his birth to His ascension, consisting of 222 chapters. According to this Gospel it was Judas, in the place of Jesus, crucified. When they came to arrest Jesus, God took Jesus to heaven and changed Judas into the same figure and speech with Jesus. At that time the Soldiers entered and seeing Judas so like every respect to Jesus, laid hands upon him. Then he cried out "O My God, Why hast thou forsaken me that I should die unjustly, when the real malefactor has escaped?" But those who stood firm were oppressed with grief, seeing him die whom they understood to be Jesus. And they took him down from the cross, and buried in the new sepulcher of Jesus. And the disciples went by night and stole the body of Judas, and hid it'; spreading a report that He (Jesus) had risen again, from whence sprang great confusion among the people. And the angles who were the guardians of Mary went up to heaven the third day and told Jesus what was passing. And Jesus, moved with compassion for his mother, entreated of God that His disciples might see him. Jesus descended surrounded with light, into the house of his mother where the disciples were present. They were astonished at seeing Jesus because they thought Him dead. Jesus told them, 'I have not been dead'; for God has reserved me for the end of the World. All the disciples were in prayer at midday on the Mount of Olives while Jesus came with many angels, He disappeared with angels.

CHAPTER

7 Christian Thoughts and their Influence on Education

INTRODUCTION

There are so many great and intelligent persons form ancient days to now-a-days. They are having history in connection with their greatness and intelligence. Sc many books are published about their history and there are so many cinemas also. As per their history no one lived in righteousness. They were not living in the right way. Among them only Jesus Christ saved from the sins of sinners. He changed the history of the world. The era stars from the birth of Jesus Christ as before the Jesus Christ and after the death of Jesus Christ. He was born in the centre point of the world of Jerusalem and in the small village Bethlehem. His life history is example to every human being in the world. He taught the good way from bad.

His life history makes every one happy and enjoyment to poor and great rich people. The name of Jesus signifies savior. The word Christ signifies anointed. He is one among Holy Trinity. No doubt that he is God. His qualities and characters are same as God. Especially he came to the world from heaven to save the sinners.

Jesus Birth and Childhood

Luke gives an accurate time frame for the birth of Jesus that is based on several historical events. It took place during the reign of Ceaser Augustus when Quirinius governed the province of Syria. More specifically it occurred during the year Caesar Augustus had ordered a census to be taken. Our problem is that we don't know when the records of this census have been found. Such is often the case. Time destroys many records. Until recently we did not know the names of most of Rome's governors.

The Birth of Jesus (Luke 2: 4-7)

Both Joseph and Mary, being of the lineage of David, traveled to their home town of Bethlehem. It wasn't a convenient time as Mary was close to her time delivery. It here that we learn that Joseph and Mary are still engaged, but they have not yet completed their marriage. It is likely that this did not occur until after the child was born (Mathew 1:24-25).

The demand that everyone go to their birth place put a strain on the temporary accommodations in the small town of Bethlehem. While waiting for the census to be completed, Joseph and Mary were staying in a stable. A manager served as the child's cradle. Mary wrapped him in strips of cloth and laid him there. This is a foreshadow of a later event when Mary, along with others, wrapped the body of Jesus in strips of cloth before laying him in a tomb (John 19:40). His common practice of that day was to bathe a newborn, rub his skin with salt, and then wrap them in strips of cloth.

Deity of Jesus Christ

There is only one God Jesus said in (John 10:30 KJV) I and my father are one: trying to explain God in human terms is only possible through what we know from His Word, the Holy Bible. The Bible gives us just what we need to know, and enough information to know that we can trust that God the Father, and the Son of God, Jesus Christ are one. I believe that what unifies them is that they share the same Spirit, the Holy Spirit; making them always in agreement, making them one. A crude human analogy would be man, being made in the image of God, has a spirit, a soul, and is in a physical body; but is still one person.

The deity of Jesus Christ is what separates true Christianity from the cults that hold to much of the other doctrine contained in the Bible. These cults have one other thing in common they discourage their members from reading the Bible except through the interpretation of their headquarters. Just reading the Holy Bible alone, the way God intends us to, sets people free from cults.

(Colossians 2: 8-10 – NKJV) Beware lest anyone cheat you through philosophy and empty deceit, according the tradition of men, according the basic principles of the world, and not according to Christ. {9} For in Him dwells all the fullness of the Godhead bodily; {10} and you are complete in Him who is the head of all principality and power.

(1 John 5:20 NKJV) And we know that the Son of God has come and has given us an understanding, that we many know Him who is true; and we are in Him who is true, in His Son Jesus Christ. This is the true God and eternal life.

Miracles

Definition: A miracle is an unusual and significant event (Teresa) which requires the working of a supernatural agent (dunamis) and is performed for the purpose of authenticating the message or the messenger (semeion).

Changing Water into Wine (John 2:1-11)

The first miracle of Jesus took place in the village of Cana, in Galilee. Jesus, His Mother Mary, and His disciples were quests at a wedding. The wine supply ran out, and through the urging of His Mother, Jesus had six water pots filled to the brim with water. He then had the master of ceremonies taste the water that was now wine. The master of ceremonies then called the bridegroom over and said to him, "Everyone serves the good wine first, and then the inferior wine after the quest have become drunk. But you have kept the good wine until now".

Healing of the Royal Official's Son (John 4:46-54)

A royal official who had a sick son in Capernaum, came to Cana when he heard Jesus was there, and begged Him to come down and heal his son, who was at the point of death. After a brief conversation, Jesus told the man 'Go your son will live'. The man believed Jesus and started on his way. On his way to Capernaum he was met by his servants who told him his child was alive. So he asked the hour when he began to recover, and they asked him, 'Yesterday at 1:00 in the afternoon the fever left him'. The father realized that this was the hour when Jesus had said him 'Your son will live'.

Healing of the Capernaum Demoniac (Mark 1: 21-28, Luke 4:33-37)

As Jesus was preaching in a synagogue in Capernaum, a man possessed by a demon was present and began shouting "Why are you bothering us, Jesus of Nazareth – have you come destroy us demons? I know who You are – the Holy Son of God!" Jesus commanded the demon to say no more and to come out of the man. The evil spirit screamed and convulsed the man violently and left him.

Healing of Peter's Mother-in-law (Mathew 8:14-15)

After Jesus healed the possessed man in the synagogue in Capernaum, He and His disciples went over to Simon and Andrews's home, where they found Simons mother-in-law sick in bed with a high fever. Jesus took her by the hand and helped her sit up, the fever suddenly left, and she got up and prepared dinner for them.

Catching a Large Number of Fish

Stepping in Simon's boat, Jesus asked Simon to push out a little into the water, so that He could sit in the boat and speak to the crowd on shore. It was during this miracle Jesus to Simon "Do not be afraid, form now on you will be fishing for the souls of men."

Healing a Leper (Mathew 8:1-3)

After preaching the 'Sermon on the Mount', Jesus came down the hillside followed by a large crowd. A leper approached Him, knelt before Him worshipping, and pleaded, 'If you want to, You can heal me'. Jesus touched the man, and said to him 'I want to, be healed' and instantly the leper was healed.

Healing a Centurions Servant (Mathew 8:5-13)

In Capernaum, a Centurion came to Jesus asking to have his servant, who was close to death, healed. When Jesus said He would come and cure the servant, the Centurion answered that he was not worthy to have Jesus come under his roof. Jesus was amazed at this and told 'Go, let it be done for you according to your faith' and the servant was healed in that hour.

Healing a Paralytic (Mathew 9:1-8)

There was a large crowd around the house Jesus was staying, in Capernaum. With no room left in or outside the house, four men dug through the roof and lowered a paralyzed man on a mat, right in front of Jesus. Jesus said the sick man 'Son your sins are forgiven!' and 'I say to you stand up, take your mat and go home'. The man stood up took the mat and went out.

Healing a Withered Hand (Mathew 12: 9-14)

In a Synagogue Jesus entered, a man was there with a withered hand. Being it was unlawful to work on the Sabbath; they watched to see if Jesus would cure him. Jesus knew what they were thinking and said to them 'I ask you, is it lawful to do good or to do harm on the Sabbath, to save life or to destroy it?' he then told the man to stretch out his hand, and as he did so, his hand was restored.

Raising a Widow's Son (Luke 7: 11-17)

Approaching the town of Nain, the dead and only son of a widow, was being carried out. When Jesus saw this He had compassion for the widow and told her not to weep. He then told, 'Young man, I say to you, rises!' The dead man sat up and began to speak.

Calming the Stormy Sea (Mathew 8: 23-27)

Jesus got into a boat with His disciples to cross the Sea of Galilee. A great windstorm arose. He rebuked the wind and said to the sea, 'Peace! Be still'. Then the wind ceased and there was a dead calm.

Healing the Gerasene Demoniac (Mathew 8:28-32)

After Jesus calmed the wind and the sea, He and His disciples landed in the country of Greasiness. A man full of demons, who lived among the tombs, met them. Jesus told the demons to leave the man and gave them permission to enter the swine. The unclean spirits came out and entered the swine, and the herd.

Healing a Woman with Internal Bleeding (Mathew 9:20-22)

A woman who had been suffering from hemorrhages for twelve years, and had spent all that she had on many physicians, and was no better, but rather grew worse, had heard about Jesus, and came up behind Him in a crowd and touched His cloak. Jesus said to her, "Daughter, your faith has made you well, go in peace and be healed of your disease".

Raising Jairus' Daughter (Mathew 9: 18-19)

A leader of the synagogue named Jairus came to Jesus, and begged Him to come and lay hands on his little daughter who was near death. As Jesus went, the crowds pressed in on Him and He felt power had gone forth from Him. It was at this point He healed the woman who had been hemorrhaging for twelve years. While He was still speaking to the woman, someone came from Jairus' house and told him his daughter had died. When Jesus heard about this He replied, "Do not fear. Only believe, and she will be saved". Jesus entered the house with Peter, John, James and the child's father and mother. The people in the house were all weeping and wailing for her, but Jesus said "Do not weep, for she is not dead but sleeping." He then took her by the hand and called out 'Child get up.' Her spirit returned, and she got up at once. Then He directed them to give her something to eat. Her parents were astounded, but He ordered them to tell no one what happened.

Healing a Mute Demoniac (Mathew 9: 32-33)

After the two healed blind men in miracle 15 left, demoniac who was mute was brought to Jesus. And when Jesus cast the demon out, the one who had been mute spoke, and the crowds were amazed and said they had never seen anything like this in Israel.

Healing two Blind Men (Mathew 9: 27-31)

Two blind men followed Jesus, crying loudly, 'Have mercy on us, Son of David!' Jesus asked them, 'Do you believe I am able to do this?' They answered Him 'Yes, Lord!' Then He touched their eyes and said 'According to your faith let it be done to you' and then their eyes were opened.

Healing a 38 year Invalid (John 5:5-17)

Jesus saw a man who had been ill for 38 years, lying by the pool of Bethesda. Jesus knew the man had been ill for a long time and asked him if he wanted to make well. The sick man answered Him that he had no one to put him the pool when the water is stirred up, and while he is making his way someone else steps down ahead of him. Jesus told the man 'Stand up, take your mat and walk.' The man was made well at once, and he took up his mat and began to walk.

Feeding 5000 Men and their Families (Mathew 14:16-21)

A large crowd gathered around Jesus at a deserted place on the shore of the Sea of Galilee. It was late and the people had no food. Jesus told His disciple to give them something to eat. They replied there is nothing here but five barely loaves and two fish that was carried by a boy. Jesus had the food brought to Him, and ordered them to sit on the grass. Then He took the five loaves and two fish, and looked up into Heaven, and blessed and broke the loaves and gave them to His disciples to set before the people, and He divided the two fish among them all. The food was multiplied and all 5000 men and their families ate and were filled.

Walking on Water (Mathew 14: 22-33)

After feeding the 5000, Jesus made His disciples get into a boat and go ahead to the other side of the Sea of Galilee. He then dismissed the crowds and went up the mountain by Himself to pray. By this time the boat was far from land, and was being battered by wind and waves. Early in the morning He came walking towards His disciples on the sea. When His disciples saw Him walking on the sea, they were terrified, saying 'It's a ghost'. But Jesus spoke to them 'Take heart, it is I, do not be afraid.' Peter answered Him 'Lord if its you, command me to come to you on the water'.

Healing Demoniac Girl (Mathew 15: 21-28)

Jesus set out and went away to the region of Tyre. A woman whose little daughter had an unclean spirit heard about Jesus and she came and bowed down at His feet. Jesus told her, "I was sent to only the lost sheep of Israel, it's not fair to take the children's food and throw it to the dogs". The woman answered "Yes Lord, but even the dogs eat the crumbs that fall from their masters table." Then Jesus answered 'Woman, great is your faith! Let it be done as you wish.' She went home, found her child laying on the bed and demon gone.

Healing a Deaf man with Speech Impediment (Mark 7: 31-37)

Jesus left Tyre, and in the region of Decapolis, a deaf man who had a speech impediment was brought to Him. He took the man aside away from the crowd, put His fingers into the man's ears and He spat and touched his tongue. The looking to heaven, He sighed and said to him 'Ephphatha', that is 'Be opened'. Immediately his ears were opened.

Feeding the 4000 Men and their Families (Mathew 15: 29-39)

Jesus passed along the Sea of Galilee, and went up into the mountain, where He sat down. Great crowds came to Him, bringing their sick, and He cured them. The crowd was with Jesus for three days and had nothing to eat. Feeling compassion for the crowd, he asked His disciples if they had any loaves. They came up with seven leaves and a few small fish. Then ordering the crowd to sit down, He took the seven loaves and the fish, and after giving tem to the crowds. And all of them ate and were filled, and the scraps were picked up, filling seven baskets. Those who had eaten were 4000 men besides women and children.

Healing a Blind Man (Mark 8: 22-26)

In Bedside some people brought a blind man to Him and begged Him to touch him. Jesus took the blind man out of the village, and when He had put saliva on his eyes and laid His hands on him, He asked the man if he could see. The man answered he could see people but they looked like trees walking. Then Jesus laid His hands on his eyes again, and the man's sight was restored, he saw everything clearly.

Healing a man Born Blind (John 9:1-4)

Jesus saw a man who was blind from birth. He then spat on the ground and made mud with the saliva and spread the mud on the man's eyes, saying to him 'Go wash in the pool of Siloam." When the man done this he came back able to see.

Healing a Demoniac Boy (Mathew 17:14-21)

After the transfiguration in which Moses and Elijah appeared with Jesus on a mountain, Jesus, Peter, James and John came down form the mountain and were met by a man who pleaded with Jesus to remove the demon from his son. The disciples at the of the mountain had tried to cast out the demon, but could not. Jesus rebuked the demon and it came out of him, and the boy was cured instantly. When His disciples asked Him why they could not cast out the demon, He said to them 'This kind can come out only through prayer.'

Catching a Fish with a Coin in its Mouth (Mathew 17:24-27)

When they reached Capernaum the tax collectors came to Peter and asked 'Does your teacher not pay the Temple tax?' Peter said 'Yes He does.' And when he came home, Jesus spoke of the tax first and told Peter to "Go to the sea and cast a hook, take the first fish that comes up, and when you open his mouth, you will find a coin, take that and give it to them for you and Me".

Healing a Blind and Mute Demoniac (Mathew 12:22)

A demoniac was brought to Jesus who was blind and mute. Jesus cured him so that the man could speak and see the crowds were amazed and said 'can this be the Son of David?'

Healing a Woman with an 18 year Infirmity (Luke 13:10-13)

Jesus was teaching in a Synagogue on the Sabbath. A woman appeared with a spirit that crippled her for 18 years. She was bent over and unable to stand upright. When Jesus saw her, He called her over and said, 'Woman, you are set free of your ailment.' When He laid hands on her, immediately she stood up straight and began praising God.

Healing a Man with Dropsy (Luke 14:1-6)

Jesus was going to the house of a leader of the Pharisee's to eat a meal on the Sabbath just then, in front of Him there was a man who had dropsy. Jesus asked the lawyers and Pharisees, "is it lawful to cure people on the Sabbath, or not?" Everybody was silent. So Jesus healed him and sent him away. Then He said to them "if one of you has child or an ox that has fallen into a well, will you immediately pull it out on a Sabbath day?" And they could not reply to this.

Healing 10 Lepers (Luke 17:11-19)

On the way to Jerusalem, Jesus entered a village and was approached by 10 lepers. Keeping their distance, they called out to Jesus for mercy. When He saw them, He said to them 'Go and show yourselves to the Priests.' And as they went they were made clean. Then one of them, when he saw he was healed turned back, praising God with a loud voice. He prostrated himself and thanked Jesus.

Raising of Lazarus (John 11: 1-44)

Mary and Martha, the sisters of Lazarus of Bethany, sent Jesus a message that His friend Lazarus was ill. Jesus stayed two days longer in the place He was, before setting out Bethany. When Jesus arrived, he found that Lazarus had already been in the tomb for days. Martha told Jesus that if He had been here, her brother would not have died, but Jesus said to her 'your brother will rise again.' Jesus asked where Lazarus was laid out. Jesus began to weep as they walked to the tomb. The tomb was a cave with a stone lying against it. He asked to have the stone removed. Martha said to Him Lord already there is a stench because he has been dead four days." Jesus answered "Did I not tell you that if you believed, you would see the Glory of God?" when the stone was removed, Jesus looked upward and prayed to the Father. He then cried out in a loud voice 'Lazarus comes out.' The dead man came out with his hands feet and face wrapped in a cloth. Jesus said to them 'Unbind him, and let him go.'

Healing Bartimaeus of Blindness (Mark 10: 46-52)

As Jesus and a large crowd was leaving Jericho, Barimaeus, a blind beggar, was sitting by the roadside. When he heard that it was Jesus of Nazareth passing by, he shouted to Jesus to have mercy on him. Although he was told to keep quiet by many, he shouted louder. Jesus stood still and called Bartimaeus to Him. Throwing off his cloak the man sprang up and came to Jesus, asking Jesus to let him see again. Jesus said to him 'Go your faith has made you well.' Immediately Bartimaeus regained his sight and followed Him on the way.

Restoring a Severed Car (Luke 22: 45-54)

Jesus and his disciples were on the Mount of Olives after the Passover dinner. After He prayed a short distance form His disciples, He came to them and found them sleeping. While He was awakening them, a crowd came led by Judas. Judas approached Jesus to kiss Him. Jesus said to him "Judas is it with a kiss that you are betraying the Son of Man?" When those around Jesus saw what was coming they asked "Lord should we strike with the sword?" then one them struck the servant of the High Priest and cut off his car. But Jesus said 'No more of this!' and He touched his ear and healed him. They then seized Jesus and led Him away, bringing Him to the house of the High Priest.

Catching a Great Number of Fish (John 21:4-11)

After the resurrection, Jesus stood on the beach of the Sea of Galilee while several of His disciples were fishing, but the disciples did not know it was Jesus. He called out to them and asked if they caught any fish. They answered 'No'. He then told them to cast the net on the right side of the boat, and they will find some. So they cast it, and now they were not able to haul it in because there were so many fish. Realizing the man on the shore was Jesus, the disciples brought the boat to shore with the net full of fish. There was 153 large fish in the net, and though there was so many the net was not torn.

Resurrection and Appearances of Jesus

Jesus was crucified. He died. He was buried and He rose again. The resurrection is an essential part of Christianity. There is no Christianity without the resurrection (1 Corinthians 15). This page explains some details of the resurrection of Jesus Christ.

The resurrection of Jesus Christ was the beginning of Christianity. If Christ had not been resurrected and seen by many people (more than 500). Christianity would not exist today. Jesus made twelve appearances after his resurrection:

- His first appearance was to Mary Magdalene, on that early Sunday morning. (Mark 16:9; John 20:10-18)
- Jesus appeared to the women returning from the tom. (Mathew 28:9-10)
- Jesus appeared to two disciples on the road to Emmaus. (Luke 24: 13-32; Mark 16:12-13)

- He appeared Peter in Jerusalem. (Luke 24:34; 1 Corinthians 15:5).
- He appeared to his disciples and other followers, and also a second time to the two men from Emmaus, in a locked room in Jerusalem. The apostle Thomas wasn't there at that time. (Luke 24:36-43; John 20:19-23).
- A week later, Jesus again appeared to his disciples behind locked doors. (John 21:1-24)
- Jesus appeared to seven of his disciples on the shore of the Sea of Galilee. (John 21:1-24)
- Jesus was seen by 500 believers at one time. (1 Corinthians 15:6)
- (1 Corinthians 15:7) he appeared to James.
- He appeared to eleven disciples on a mountain in Galilee. (Matt. 28:18-20).
- He walked with his disciples along the road to Bethany, on the Mount of Olives, and then ascended into Heaven. (Luke 24:50-53)
- He was seen by Paul on the road to Damascus. (Acts 9:3-6; 1 Corinthians 15:8)

John 20:24-29

Some people had doubts that Jesus had risen from death, that he had been resurrected. After all, the Roman drove nails through Jesus' hands and feet and later pierced his side with a spear to make sure he was dead. And now there were people claiming to have seen Jesus alive again. Even the Apostle name Thomas had doubts, as explained in John 20:24-29 (NIV translation).

Now Thomas (called Didymus), one of the twelve, was not with the disciples when Jesus came. So the other disciples told him. 'We have seen the Lord!' but he said to them, "Unless I see the nail marks in his hands and put my finger where the nails were, and put my hand into his side, I will not believe it."

A week later his disciples were in the house again and Thomas was with them. Though the doors were locked, Jesus came and stood among them and said. 'Peace be with you!' then he said to Thomas, "Put your finger here; see my hands. Reach out your hand and put it into my side. Stop doubting and believe."

Thomas said to him, 'My Lord and my God!' then Jesus told him, "Because you have seen me, you have believed; blessed are those who have not seen and yet have believed."

The Significance of the Resurrection
1 Cointhians: 15

In the New Testament of the Bible, there is a book called 1 Corinthians, which was written by a disciple named Paul. The 15th chapter of this book explains the significance of the resurrection of Jesus. It says that Jesus died for our sins. (See 1 Corinthians 15:3). It also says that our faith would be meaningless if there had been no resurrection (see 1 Corinthians 15:20). Paul is one of the people who saw Jesus after the resurrection.

CHRISTIAN THOUGHTS AS EVIDENCED THROUGH 'BIBLE' AND THEIR INFLUENCE ON EDUCATION

The Bible is the name given to Christian scriptures. The word Bible is derived from Greek through Latin, which means the books or the roots. It consists of old 'Testament' and the New Testament. Old testament was mostly in Hebrew language written during six or seven hundred years and completed before 150 BC. It contains thirty nine books incorporating traditions, stories and records of sematic tribes of Egypt and Palestine. David and Solomon were powerful kings of this area. Old Testament Contains history, myth, instruction, legislation, prophecy etc. It is written in prose as well as in poetry. The concept of 'covenant' is very important in these books. It is a kind of special relationship between man and God. In convenant, God expressed his choice of Israelite people. Wandering of people between Egypt and Palestine from the part of old Testament which is divided into three sections *viz*; the Law, the prophets and writings. The law is found in first five books attributed to Moses. The Hebrew word for law is Torah. Laws relating to nomad shepherd life and also to settled agricultural life are contained in them.

The New Testament was written in the second half of the first century. It consists of 27 books written in Greek. Some of the books are brief that they are written in a page only. The first four books are called Gospels. The word gospel is derived from the old English word god spell meaning *good news*. Gospels contain the life and teaching of Jesus Christ.

The Bible has a central and significant place in the life and worship of a Christian church. The faith of Christianity is centered in Jesus Christ who is a historical person and who was born of a

Jewish mother in Palestine whose earthly ended with his death on a cross on Good Friday but only to rise again with his resurrection on Easter Sunday. Jesus Christ is called the Lord who is everywhere.

The world is the realm of our earthly life and the world also signifies the arena of existence opposed to God. Man is fallen. His self-assertion is the root of Sin. Sin includes an individual and a cosmic dimension. God is related to the world in creations as well as redemption.

Man, according to Bible is made in the image and Likeness of God. He is a fallen creature and is redeemed by Jesus Christ. He is made a member of new humanity by Jesus Christ.

Educational Implications

Education is regarded as a significant activity in Christianity. Churches came forward to educate the masses by establishing schools in the beginning and universities later. Education to a Bible is a means to true moral life. An important aim of education is to enable the child to learn how to serve the individual as well as society. Christianity not only emphasizes the idea of social service but also tries to translate this idea into action by opening schools, hospitals and by training individuals to man them.

Aims of Education

Christian Education aims at brotherhood. Koinonia is a new Testament word used for followship. The human solidarity of forgiven sinners forms the source of a new type of community life and an important aim of education would be to enable the child to become a member of this community. One of the tasks of education is to make the individual understand the real purpose of sex and marriage.

The child has to know and practice Eucharist which means thanks giving. It was also called Lord's supper. It is a Christian act of worship now different forms of worship have developed. Liturgy is the name given to these forms. Originally it meant public service. Thus we can say that Christianity aims at multi-dimensional development of the personality of the child through education.

Curriculum

So far as curriculum is concerned Bible directs that individuals should have mastery over theology. Religion because an important part of Christian curriculum in the beginning but later on when church schools were established three R's *viz*; Reading, Writing and Arithmetic were emphasized. Thus language and mathematics were included in the curriculum as important subjects. Apart from Christian theology, Bible, three R's, ethics and some individual activities were included in the curriculum: *E.g.*, helping the neighbours, serving the sufferers, nursing the patients in the hospital, treating the sick persons, preaching in the church, giving free education and teaching Bible in church and schools.

Method

Coming to method of teaching we can underline oral method since Bible contains oral sessions. Sometimes the ethical concepts are taught orally in the positive from and sometimes in the negative ones. Do not steal, do not be greedy are the examples of negative preaching and love they neighbour, obey they parents and elders are the examples of positive ones. Revelation may be cited as another method which has been indicated in the Bible. Psalm and proverbs are also used as devise in the Bible apart from letters which were aimed at giving divine messages. Later on self-learning, seminars, symposia, workshops, tutorials, monitorial system, activity oriented methods were also included in the methods of teaching in Christian schools. Christianity tries to develop modesty, humbleness, sincerity, honesty, dutifulness, obedience and simplicity in the students.

The Holy Bible

The Origin of the Term 'Bible'

The term 'Bible' is derived from the Greek work 'biblia' which literally means 'books'. In the 3th century the neuter plural 'biblia' came to be regarded as a feminine singular and thus 'the books' without qualification indicated the special position, which it enjoys among all the books of the world. St. Jerome's name for the Bible was 'the divine library'. This designation is significant, because the Bible is not a single book, but a collection or library of 73 books.

There is no name in the NT for the completer body of the scripture, the only scriptures then known being those of the OT. The common designations for the O T books by Jesus Christ and his apostles were:

'The scriptures' – Graphai, 'the holy scriptures' – graphaihagiai, 'The sacred writings'.

THE DIVISION OF THE BIBLE INTO OLD TESTAMENT AND NEW TESTAMENT

The term 'old testament' and 'New Testament' came into general use since the time of Tertullian, by the end of the 2nd cent. A.D. however, the two parts of the Bible are not 'testaments' in the ordinary sense of the term 'Testament' in its ordinary sence, means the last will of a person where he gives a legal expression of his wishes for the term for 'testament' or 'last will' is diatheke. In this secular meaning diatheke is used only in two places in the NT that is in Gal: 3:15 and Heb: 9:16:17. The Greek word diatheke, in all other instances in the NT and almost always in the LXX means 'covenant' rater than "testament". The corresponding Hebrew word for 'covenant' is berith. It was Tertullian who rendered the Greek tormdiatheke into Latin often by 'Testament' which came into general use.

When we consider the content of the OT and the NT it is more significant to designate them as 'the Old coveant'. A Covenant is an agfeement or contract between two parties, by which they enter into a relationship of enduring character. The biblical writers, in both the OT and the NT, speak of a 'covenant' between God and man.

In the OT we find God making covenants with Noah, with Abrqham, with Moses on Mt. Sinai. In all these covenants the initiative always came from God's side. The covenant is God's doing and God's gift. Convenants between God and man, however, differed from purely human convenants in that they were not agreements between equals. God was always the giver and man the receiver. God's promises originated in his sovereign grace alone, and man could do nothing but accept God's favours and directions.

Covenant is a relationship and the effect of this relationship is love and friendship. To establish a covenant means to enter into a relationship. God wishes to lead all men to a life of communion with himself. It is a relation go in beyond that fundamental creaturely relation which all his works necessarily bear to their creator. As in the covenant with Abraham, so in the covenant with his descendants, the central blessing was communion with God, for he was their God and they were his people. It is this idea which underlies the covenant theme of the Bible. In the OT it dominates all religious thought and in the NT it acquires an unparalleled fullness, because it has now as its content the total mystery of Jesus Christ. Jesus Christ is the mediator of the new covenant.

In the OT we find God making or better establishing convenants with individuals and with the nation if Israel. The covenant witch God established with Noah and the first covenant with Abraham are unilateral and unconditional. God's second convenant with Abraham and the sinaitic covenant are bilateral and conditional. The Davidic covenant, however, is unilateral and therefore unconditional.

The prophets Jeremiah and Ezekiel have proclaimed the 'new' and eternal covenant. This 'new' covenant God will make with the 'faithful remnant'. God's law would be written on their hearts which would be an inner and dynamic principle of action. What we find in Jeremiah and Ezekiel is the 'interiorization of religion' or the 'religion of the spirit'. It is to be remembered here that the 'new' covenant will not abolish the 'old', but will supersede in the sense that through the new covenant the old is fulfilled and its purpose achieved.

BIBLE AS A BOOK OF FAITH

Bible is a book. That is it is written 'from faith', 'for faith'. In fact, the Bible is an interpreted history. A history interpreted through faith. The inspirited authors of both the OT and the NT were not historians in the modern sense of the term but were primarily theologians. They were not interested in the every for their own sake. Rather they were more interested in the meaning and significance behind an event or action than in giving the details of the event.

THE DIVISION OF THE OT BOOKS

(a) *The Traditional Division*: According to Greek and Latin tradition the OT book are divided into there:

1. *the historical books*: the Pentateuch, Jisgya, Jydges, Ruth, 1,2, Samuel, 1,2, kings; 1,2, chronicles, Ezra, hehemiah, tobit, Judith, esther, 1,2, maccabees.
2. *the wisdom books*: job, psaims, proverbs, ecclesiasted, Ecclesiastes, Song of Solomon, book of wisdom.
3. *the prophetical books*: the four major prophets and the twelve minor prophets.

(b) *The Jewish division of the Hebrew Bible*: The Jews divide the herbrew Bible into three:

1 *the law*: the Pentateuch;

2 the prophets;

- The former propohets are the historical books of josha; judges; 1,2 samuel; 1,2 kings which relate Israel's history from the conquest of canaan to the Babylonian captivity. These books are called" former prophets" because these writings record the ministry of the great non writing prophets such as Samuel, Elijah and Elisha and also reflect an interpretation of Israel's history similar to that of the great writing prophets. These historical books have a prophetic message and are designed to guide future generations.
- The latter prophets are the great preachers of Israel: Isaiah, Jeremiah and Ezekiel who are known as Major Prophets, and the 12 Minor Prophets. These prophets are known as 'writing prophets'.

3 *the writings*: psalms, proverbs, job, song of Solomon, Ruth, lamentation, Ecclesiasted, Esther, Daniel, Ezra, Nehemiah, 1 and 2 chronicles.

This Jewish division of the Hebrew Bible into the law, the prophets and the writings is recognized in the NT in the expression 'in the law of Moses, and the prophets and the psalms' since the third division, the writings, begins with the book of psalms, the mention of psalms in LK: 24:44 refers to writings. Sometimes the whole OT is summed up under the expression the law and the prophets. In Judaism the five mosaic books are considered the core books and later books of the Bible are viewed as commentary on them. The Jews call their Bible as TANAK (*Tanak = torach, nebiim, and ketubim*).

THE DEUTEROCANONICAL BOOKS (NOT FOUND IN THE HEBREW AND PROTESTANT BIBLES)

The Hebrew Bible does not contain the following books of the old testament: Tobit, Judity, the wisdom of Solomon, Sirach, baruch, 1-2 maccabees. Besides, it also does not contain part of Esther; Danv 3:1-68 (the prayer of Azariah and the song of three young men from the furance) Dan 13 (the story of Susanna) and Dan. 1 (the story of Bel and Dragon.

The above mentioned books are called douterocanonical in the catholic bible and we accept them as inspired books. They are called deuterocanonical because their place in the canon was at some time denied or doubted in the church (the 'canon' of the bible means the authoritative list of he books contained in the bible and recognized by the church as inspired.) the deuterocanonical books are found only in the Greek old testament, called the septuagint.

The protestant churched accept only the books of the Hebrew bible for the OT and therefore they do not accept the deuterocanonical books as inspired. They call these books as 'apocrypha'. The word 'apocrypha' literally means 'hidden' or 'concealed' what we. Catholics, call apocrypha, they call 'pseudepographa'. The word 'pseudepographa' literally means 'false writings', that is writings attributed to someone who did not write them. The books that are found in the Hebrew bible are called by the Catholics and 'protocanonical. Protestant OT has only 39 book where as the catholic OT have 46 books.

THE ORIGINAL LANGUAGES OF THE BIBLE

The original languages of the bible are Hebrew, Aramaic and Greek. Hebrew and Aramaic belong to the Semitic family of languages and Greek belongs to the into European family.

The OT was written mostly in Hebrew language. Hebrew was, in fact, a Canaanite language which the Israelites took over as they settled down in Palestine, and it is at present the official language of the state of Israel. The mention of Hebrew as a language occurs for the first time in the prologue to the book of Ecclesiasticus or Sirach. Hebrew was a living language rough between 950-100 B.C.

Some part of the OT was written in Aramaic two words in Gen 31:47 on verse in Jer 10:11 and the sections Ezra 4:8-6:18,7:12-26; and Dan 2:4-7:8 are written in Aramaic language, which is a dialect related to Hebrew. After the Babylonian exile the Aramaic gradually displaced Hebrew as the spoken language of the Jews.

Jesus and his disciples spoke the Galilean variety of Jewish Aramaic with a Galilean accent some of the Aramaic expressions are abbatalithaqumi (MK: 4:41).

Wisdom fsolomon 10-51; 2 macc; Dan 13 and 1 and all the books of the NT where written in Greek wisdom of Solomon 1-9, Judith, Baruch, Sirach, I Macc. Were originally written in Hebrew but are preserved only in Greek. The Greek of the bible is not classical but popular, known as koine," the common which prevailed from c.335 B.C. to the 6th century A.D.

The Hebrew bible: the ancient Hebrew text was without the vowel marks. But after the 6th century A.D. as a result of the works of the masoretic scholars the consonantal text was given vowel marks and this text is called mesoretic text (MT). Masoretes were those who test is the basis of the printed Hebrew OT the complete Hebrew bible was published in 1488.

THE CHAPTER AND VERSE DIVISIONS IN THE BIBILE

The division of the biblical books into chapters and verses is of late origin. The division of the biblical books into chapters is generally ascribed to Stephen Langton by others to cardinal Hugo Stephen Langton was a lecturer at the university Paris and later he became the archbishop of Canterbury. The verse division in the OT is attributed to the Dominican Sanctes Paginus of Lucca and the verse division in the NT is attributed to Robert Stephen.

THE MANUSCRIPTS OF THE BIBLE

It was in the middle of the 15th century AD that the printing was invented. Before its invention all the copies of the bible had to be made by hand. These hands written copies of the bible are known as manuscripts. The original manuscripts of the biblical books were lost. What we possess today are the copies of the copied manuscripts of the original.

In very ancient times the materials used for writing were stone. Wood and clay tablets. The materials used for copying the biblical books were papyrus and parchment or vellum. Papyrus was very commonly used at the beginning of the Christian era and continued up to 4th century A.D. papyrus is a tall aquatic plant growing in river shallows and in marshes. The pith of the papyrus was used in the manufacture of paper.

(a) *Scrolls and Codices*: The finished sheets of paper were either joined together to form a continuous 'roll' or folded to form a 'codex' (book). When the ancient manuscripts had the form of rolls they were called 'scrolls'. The ancient manuscripts had also the form of 'codices' but the general custom was to write on the scrolls and then roll them up.

(b) *Parchment or Vellum*: From the 6th century onwards 'parchment' or 'vellum' was used as the material for writing. Parchment or vellum was specially prepared skins f animals

for the purpose of writing. Parchment was an expensive material. The 'parchments' that Paul asked timothy to bring to him; were more like the OT or parts of it. Parchment texts have the form of codices.

The manuscript tradition of the bible is far superior to that of all other books of antiquity, both in the matter of age and number. If in 1707 only 91 manuscripts of the bible have come to light, in 1989 more than 5488 manuscripts of the bible, especially of the NT have been discovered. As years go by more and more manuscripts are coming to light of the 3100 manuscripts of the NT only 42 manuscripts contain the entire NT.

(c) *The Manuscripts of the Hebrew Bible*: All the major Hebrew manuscripts date from the middle aged (that is between 476 and late 15th century). We mention some important manuscripts.

1. *the cairo codex*: it contains the former and the latter prophets. I dates back to the year 895 A.D. this is the oldest of the dated Hebrew manuscripts and was found in Cairo and hence the name " The Cairo codex;
2. *the aleppo codex*: it originally contained the whole Hebrew bible with punctuation. It is generally dated c. 900-925 A.D;
3. *the leningrad codex*: it contains the whole Hebrew bible and is a copy made from the manuscript written by Aharon Ben Asher. The copy was made in Cairo in the year 1008 or 1009. It is important to note that the 'Leningrad Codex' is the basis of the printed edition of the present day Hebrew Bible. The Leningrad codex is still the oldest dated manuscript of the complete Hebrew Bible.

THE DEAD SEA SCROLLS

The dead sea scrolls are also known as 'Qumran texts' or 'Qumran manuscripts'. Qumran is the name of the site on the Northwest of deadsea. It is generally believed that a Jewish sect, called Essenes, settle in Qumran and lived a community life. Essenes were an ultra conservative sect of Jews who has broken away from official Judaism and regarded themselves as the faithful remnant of the true Israel and the core of God's eschatological community. They adopted a communal life style including common meals, daily study of the bible etc. all property was held in common they believed in the imminent coming of God. Some Essenes practised celibacy.

The essences lived in Qumran from c.140 B.C. till 68 A.D. when their settlement was destroyed by Roman armies. The Essenes with the intention of recovering after the departure of the invaders, hid away their manuscripts in inaccessible caves; but unfortunately their hopes were never realized they were all mercilessly killed by the Romans and their deposit f he manuscripts remained hidden till 1947.

It was in the year 1947 that the Dead Sea scrolls were accidentally discovered by some Bedouins in a cave near the Dead Sea. Archaeological work on the site started in 1951 and by 1956 ten more caves were discovered and they have been given the name cave 1, cave 2, cave 3, etc., or 1Q, 2Q, 3Q etc., from all these caves some 600 manuscripts have been identified they include biblical and non biblical writings. About 100 scrolls are books of the OT in Hebrew, among these all the OT books are represented these biblical manuscripts date from the last few centuries B.C. and the earlier part of the first century A.D.

The non-biblical manuscripts relating to the Qumran community are the following.

1. The rule of the community or the manual if discipline (IQS).
2. The Damascus document of the zodokite document (60D).
3. The war scroll (10M).
4. The Hymn scroll (10H).
5. Pesharim or commentaries on Habakkuk (Qp. Heb.), Nahum, Micah etc.
6. Targum on Job (11 Qtg. Job).

The Qumran texts are the greatest manuscripts discovery in modern times they are important for the light they shed on three areas: Palestinian Judaism before and at the beginning of the Christian era, the transmission of the OT text in the same period. And the Palestinian background of the NT.

CHAPTER

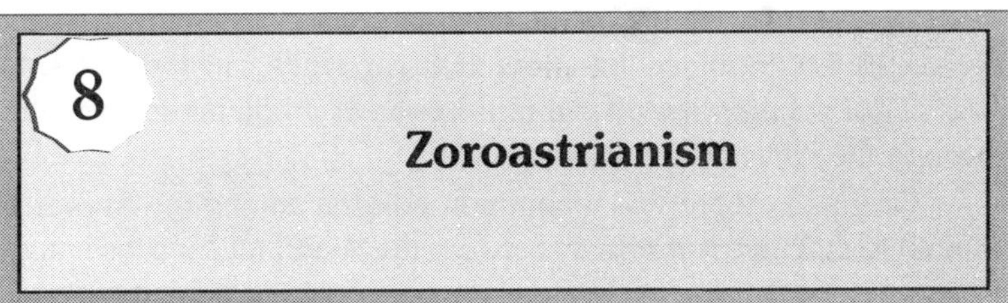

8 Zoroastrianism

INTRODUCTION

Hinduism, Christianity, Buddhism are world religions but Zoroastrianism is just a national religion now though it was a world religion in days of yore. It is the religion of the Parsees. The correct name for the religion established by Zoroaster is Mazdayasnism which means the worship of Mazda or the Lord.

Mazdayasnism was first revealed by Homa to King Jamshid. Afterwards it was revealed to King Fiedoon. Then it was revealed to Thirta. Lastly it was revealed to Zoroaster.

After the death of Zoroaster his son in-law Jamaspa became his successor. Jamaspa wrote down the teachings of Zoroaster which are known as Zend Avesta, the scriptures of the Zoroastrians. Frashaoshtra, father-in-law of Zoroaster, was the first apostle of this faith. He expounded the tenets of this religion. Zoroastrianism became the state religion of Persia.

After the time of Zoroaster, Zoroastrianism underwent many changes at the hands of the priests who were called Magi. The priests re-introduced ritualism and the worship of the old nature-deities in a new garb by making them archangels of Ahura Mazda.

Persia is now a Mohammedan country. A few Zoroastrians are found there. They were persecuted and driven out of Persia. They took refuge in India. They are called the Parsees. They have become a self-contained community in India.

Zoroaster was not a philosopher or a metaphysician. He was only a Prophet who had the divine revelation.

Zoroastrianism is not a system of philosophy. It is a revealed religion of faith and devotion. During the days of Zoroaster there was an urgent need for ethics and virtuous life. The need for philosophy did not arise. At all times the need to lead a virtuous, divine life is far more imperative for the vast majority than the need to understand the various philosophical problems. If one leads the divine life according to the instructions of sages and scriptures, he will find a solution for all the philosophical problems from within through the voice of the Indweller.

Originally there was a common religion among the Aryans in Central Asia. There is similarity between the Vedic and Zend languages. Even the versification of the Zend Avesta is closely related to that of the Vedas. There is identity of divine names in the Zend Avesta and the Vedas.

The principal truths taught by Zoroaster were based on and derived from the Vedas. Zoroastrianism is based on the Vedic religion. The doctrines and ceremonials of the Zoroastrians have a mostly remarkable similarity to those of the Vedas.

Origin and Development

The religion's priests, successors to the pre-Zoroastrian Magi, acquired great power by their command of the techniques of purification. The priests also had great influence on the government in the first period of Zoroastrianism, that under the Achaemenids, when it was for a time the state religion. Alexander's conquest of Persia and the collapse of the Achaemenids destroyed the privileged position of Zoroastrianism. Little is known of the religion for the next 500 years, except that an offshoot, Mithraism (stemming from the worship of Mithra), was taking hold farther west. Zoroastrianism reemerged (c. AD 226) under Ardashir I, who established the Sassanid dynasty and fostered a general revival of Achaemenian culture. For four centuries Zoroastrianism was the state religion of the Sassanids, and it successfully met the challenge of nascent Christianity and, later, of heretical Manichaeism. In the mid-7th cent. Persia fell to Islam, and Zoroastrianism largely disappeared. The Parsis of India, centered on Mumbai, probably form the largest group of modern

Zoroastrians, who are estimated to number between 124,000 and 190,000. Estimates of the number of persons (concentrated in Yazd, Tehran, and Kerman) who practice the religion in Iran today vary widely. Zoroastrianism affected Judaism (particularly during the time of the Captivity) and, through Gnosticism, Christianity.

In its origins Zoroastrianism appears to have been the religious expression of the peaceful, sedentary communities of N Iran as opposed to the animistic polytheism of their enemies, the nomadic horsemen. Zoroaster consistently contrasts these two peoples as the People of Righteousness (asha) and the People of the Lie (druj). The religion was concerned with increasing the harvest and with protecting and treating kindly the domestic animals whose labours accomplished the production of food.

Gradually certain practices that Zoroaster appears to have deplored, such as the use of haoma (a narcotic intoxicant) in prayer and the sacrifice of bulls in connection with the cult of the god Mithra (a lesser god in Zoroastrianism), became features of the religion. It is not surprising, however, that former customs should be thus revived, because Zoroaster appears to have incorporated in his religion the old Persian pantheon, although very much refined. Instead of tolerating the worship of all the deities, however, he divided them into those who were beneficent and truthful and those malevolence and falseness made them abhorrent.

Heading the good spirits was Ahura Mazdah (also Ormazd or Ormuzd) [sovereign knowledge], in primitive Zoroastrianism the only god. Six attendant deities, the Amesha Spentas, surround him. These abstract representations, formerly the personal aspects of Ahura Mazdah, are Vohu Manah [good thought], Asha Vahista [highest righteousness], Khshathra Vairya [divine kingdom], Spenta Armaiti [pious devotion], Haurvatat [salvation], and Ameretat [immortality]. In time the Amesha Spentas became archangelic in character and less abstract. Opposing the good *ahuras* were the evil spirits, the *daevas* or *divs,* led by Ahriman. The war between these two supernatural hosts is the subject matter of the fully developed cosmogony and eschatology of Zoroastrianism.

The entire history of the universe, past, present, and future, the religion teaches, is divided into four periods, each of 3,000 years. In the first period there was no matter; the second preceded the coming of Zoroaster; and in the third his faith is propagated. The struggle between good and evil rages during the first nine millennia and humans help Ahura Mazdah or Ahriman according to whether their conduct is good or evil. Each person after death crosses the Chinvato Peretav [bridge of the separator], which spans hell. If he is reprobate, the bridge narrows and he tumbles to perdition, but if he is worthy of salvation he finds a wide road to the realm of light. In the fourth period of the universe a savior, Saoshyant, will appear, the dead will rise for their final reward or punishment, and good will regin In its origins Zoroastrianism appears to have been the religious expression of the peaceful, sedentary communities of N Iran as opposed to the animistic polytheism of their enemies, the nomadic horsemen. Zoroaster consistently contrasts these two peoples as the People of Righteousness (asha) and the People of the Lie (*druj*). The religion was concerned with increasing the harvest and with protecting and treating kindly the domestic animals whose labours accomplished the production of food.

Zoroastrianism should be regarded as quasi-dualistic, rather than (as sometimes described) wholly dualistic, since it predicts the ultimate triumph of Ahura Mazdah. This god may be represented in the form of the pure natural substances that he has created notably fire but also water and earth. The special veneration shown to fire and its use in religious ceremonies has led to the erroneous belief that the Zoroastrians were fire worshipers. The care taken to avoid contaminating these natural substances led to great elaboration of the purification, ritual.

Zoroaster – The Prophet

General

Just as the Jews place their hope in Messiah, the Hindus on the coming Kalki Avatara, so also the Parsees have been looking forward to the birth of Saoshyant who will establish on earth righteousness and happiness. There is no Tapas or austerity in Zoroastrianism in order that the body may not be weakened and rendered unfit for work. Reincarnation is not found in the scriptures as accepted by orthodox Parsees, but it is taught in the fragments preserved by the Greeks and in the Desatir. Parsees perform prayers for the dead at stated fixed periods. They perform ancestor-worship and do anniversaries for the dead in an elaborate manner.

Zoroastrianism teaches that Ahura Mazda created man and gave him his body and mind. Ahura Mazda is the protector and nourisher of all. Man is responsible for his thoughts, speeches, and actions. Individual will and individual intellect are connected with the cosmic will and cosmic-intellect.

Ahura Mazda created this world in six periods. Mashya and Mashyana are the first man and woman created by God. During the deluge an underground palace 'Vara of Yima' was built for the protection of all creatures.

Zoroastrianism is a religion of absolute faith and unswerving devotion to Ahura Mazda. A devotee bows, prays, and sacrifices. He makes offerings unto the Lord. He prays and Ahura Mazda grants all his wishes. He prays to remove his sins by repentance.

Zoroastrianism teaches that the goal of life is to attain perfect eternal happiness through companionship with Ahura Mazda. The means for attaining the everlasting bliss is Asha or holiness. Holiness or purity is the soul of Zoroastrianism.

Pure thoughts, pure words, and pure deeds this is the famous axiom of Zoroastrian religion. This is the constantly reiterated rule of the Zoroastrian life. Pure thoughts, pure words, pure actions can be practised only through faith in the Ahura Mazda, the Lord of righteousness. The word Asha includes all the principles of morality. The word Asha comes in almost every chapter of the Zend Avesta. Zoroastrianism teaches that holiness is happiness, and that is the most precious gift of Ahura Mazda and that is the best offering to be presented to the Lord by the virtuous.

A Zoroastrian must act in harmony with the will of God. He should study the scriptures and perform his duty to God and his fellowmen. He should strictly observe the divine laws. Then only he will attain holiness and happiness.

The Prophet

Zoroastrianism teaches that Ahura Mazda created man and gave him his body and mind. Ahura Mazda is the protector and nourisher of all. Man is responsible for his thoughts, speeches, and actions. Individual will and individual intellect are connected with the cosmic will and cosmic-intellect.

Ahura Mazda created this world in six periods. Mashya and Mashyana are the first man and woman created by God. During the deluge an underground palace 'Vara of Yima' was built for the protection of all creatures.

Zoroastrianism is a religion of absolute faith and unswerving devotion to Ahura Mazda. A devotee bows, prays, and sacrifices. He makes offerings unto the Lord. He prays and Ahura Mazda grants all his wishes. He prays to remove his sins by repentance.

Zoroastrianism teaches that the goal of life is to attain perfect eternal happiness through companionship with Ahura Mazda. The means for attaining the everlasting bliss is Asha or holiness. Holiness or purity is the soul of Zoroastrianism.

Pure thoughts, pure words, and pure deeds this is the famous axiom of Zoroastrian religion. This is the constantly reiterated rule of the Zoroastrian life. Pure thoughts, pure words, pure actions can be practised only through faith in the Ahura Mazda, the Lord of righteousness. The word Asha includes all the principles of morality. The word Asha comes in almost every chapter of the Zend Avesta. Zoroastrianism teaches that holiness is happiness, and that is the most precious gift of Ahura Mazda and that is the best offering to be presented to the Lord by the virtuous.

A Zoroastrian must act in harmony with the will of God. He should study the scriptures and perform his duty to God and his fellowmen. He should strictly observe the divine laws. Then only he will attain holiness and happiness.

Zoroastrian Scriptures

Zoroastrianism's scriptures are the *Avesta* or the *Zend Avesta* [Pahlavi *Avesta* = law, *Zend* = commentary]. The *Avesta* consists of fragmentary and much-corrupted texts; it is written in Old Iranian, a language similar to Vedic Sanskrit. The major sections of the *Avesta* are four – the *Yasna,* a liturgical work that includes the *Gathas* ('songs'), probably the oldest part of the *Avesta* and perhaps in part written by Zoroaster himself; the *Vispered,* a supplement to the *Yasna;* the *Yashts,* hymns of praise, including the *Khurda* ('little') *Avesta;* and the *Videvdat,* a detailed code of ritual purification, often erroneously called the *Vendidad.* Other sources of information on Zoroastrianism are Achaemenid inscriptions, the writings of

Herodotus, Strabo, and Plutarch, and the commentaries on the *Avesta* written (6th cent. AD) in Pahlavi, a Persian dialect used as a priestly language, under the Sassanids.

The Yasna and the Visparad are the Vedas of Zoroastrianism. The first part of Yasna consists of Gathas or hymns which came from the mouth of the prophet. The Gathas are five in number. The Gathas are written in metres which correspond to the metres of the Sama Veda. The second part of Yasna contains prayers addressed to the Supreme Lord and other deities who form the spiritual hierarchy.

Visparad is a collection of invocations or litanies which are recited before other prayers and scriptures. The twenty-one Nasks deal with all kinds of Sciences, *viz*; medicine, astronomy, agriculture, botany, etc. They correspond to the Vedangas of Hinduism. Then there is the Khordah Avesta or little Avesta which contains *Yashts* (invocations) and prayers for the use of lay persons. The modern Parsees recite these prayers daily.

Zoroastrian scriptures are called Zend Avesta. They contain three parts. The first is Vendidad. This contains religious laws and ancient mythical tales. The second is Visparad. The third is Yasna. The Avesta contains direct conversations between Zoroaster and Ahura Mazda, the Supreme Lord.

Fire, the Symbol of God

People believe that the religion of Zoroaster was fire-worship. This is a mistake. "Do not say that the Iranians were fire-worshippers. They were worshippers of one God." These are the utterances of the great Firdusi. Fire is a sacred and supreme symbol of God. It is a sacred symbol in the Avesta. Fire is considered as the son of Ahura Mazda. The prophet of Iran did not teach fire-worship. He taught the worship of the one Supreme Lord of the universe, Ahura Mazda. Fire is the symbol of divine in all sacrifices. It is a sacred object. It is the symbol of divine life. It is the sacred symbol most reverenced by the Zoroastrians of today.

In every religion, fire has been the symbol of the Supreme Lord. Brahman is fire in Hinduism. Ahura Mazda is fire. The Jews worship their God as a pillar of fire. The Christians declare that their God is a consuming fire. Fire symbolised the brilliance of the Lord. It is purifying. Fire stands for effulgence, illumination. The worship of Agni or Fire comes in the Vedas also. In the Bible it is said, 'God is light.' Upanishads declare 'Brahman is Jyotirmaya (full of light).' In every religion fire finds a place in rituals. Fire brings the message that God is Light of lights. Zoroaster himself held Fire in great sanctity as a noble gift from God. He summoned Fire from the sky and pointed it to heaven. The Heavens burst into fire. Some of the flames darted downwards and fired the altar at his side. Sacred fire in the altar of a temple is a symbol that reminds the Parsee of the glory of Ahura Mazda. It is called Atar in the Avesta.

Fire is declared to be the most helpful of all the spiritual intelligences or archangels. He is the friendliest. He comes down from Ahura Mazda. He is acquainted with all heavenly secrets.

The Jews received for the first time the ideas of heaven and hell, of angels and archangels of Messiah, of the resurrection and the last Day of Judgment from Zoroastrianism. These have laid the foundation to the doctrines of Christianity and Islam also.

Ahura Mazda

Ahura Mazda is the Supreme Universal Lord. He is All-pervading. He is the source and the fountain of life. He corresponds to the Hiranyagarbha of the Hindus. He is the Brilliant, Majestic, Greatest, Best, most Beautiful, the strongest, most intellectual, the Highest through Holiness, the Holiest among the heavenly who created the world. He is changeless, mighty, just, merciful, and most beneficial.

The prophet of Iran preached that all that is good and beneficial to mankind is the creation of Ahura Mazda and everything that is malignant is the creation of Ahriman or Satan.

The following are the commands which Ahura Mazda, the supreme Lord has sent to the followers of Zoroastrianism through His prophet Zoroaster. To know God as one, to know the Prophet Zoroaster as His true prophet, to have perfect faith in the religion and the Zend Avesta, to have unswerving faith in the goodness of God; not to disobey any of the commands of Zoroastrianism, to shun all evil actions, to do virtuous actions, to pray five times a day, to face some bright object like sun while worshipping God, to have perfect faith in the justice on the fourth morning after death, to exert for attaining heaven and to fear hell, to think always that God has done what He willed and shall do what He wills.

Morality and Ethics

Ethics of Zoroaster

The following are the ethical teachings of Zoroaster: To do good actions; to be pure in thought, word, and deed; to have a clean heart; to wish others' good; to speak the truth; to do charity; to be kind; to be humble; to attain knowledge; to control anger; to be pious; to respect parents, the teachers, and the old and the young; to utter sweet and pleasant words; to be patient; to be friendly towards all; to be contented; to feel shame for doing forbidden actions.

CHAPTER

9 Educational Importance of Holy Books of Hinduism

UPANISHADS AND BHAGAVAT-GITA

INTRODUCTION

Education is a growing science and its foundations are to be explored for a study of the subject as an inter-disciplinary approach. Philosophy is the corner stone of the foundation of Education. But thus does not mean that education should be enslaved to philosophy or some set of values created by human society. Philosophy should be interpreted as a vision in a wider prospective. This being so, education should be wedded to some philosophy in general. We need some frames of reference in which education has to fit. There have been various schools of philosophy presenting their views with much optimism. Education is the process of enabling people not merely do live but to live adequately. There are various facts of education: academic, aesthetic, moral, physical, social and spiritual. Theories of education have been formulated and different values emphasized.

Every educational practice is illuminated with the backdrop of philosophy. The speculative, normative and critical function of philosophy affects not only the direction of moral guidance that the teacher gives but also affects the direction of moral guidance that the teacher gives but also affects the direction and the emphasis of the curriculum, the colour of the teachers attitudes from day-to-day, even from hour to hour.

Education in the Vedic Period

The present education has its roots deeply embedded in the past. India's has been singularly glorious. Its refulgence has not only in the present but also aroused faith in the future. In the ancient period, all the political, economic and social current emanated from spiritualism. Social life was solidly founded upon good conduct, love, non-violence etc. Co-operation and co-existence formed its spirit. The fundamental unit of society was the individual.

Education in India had its beginnings in the need to satisfy man's innate curiosity, while he lived in the lap of nature. It is usually argued that the elements, methodology and organization of education in India originated during the vedic period. India's educational and cultural traditions are the most ancient in the world's history. In ancient India, the tradition of society and the nation were preserved in schools. India's ancient period has been so glorious and rich that foreign scholars have praised it lavishly.

Characteristic of education are – knowledge, aims of education, the method of education, the 'upanayana' ritual, celibacy or brahmacharya, service of the teacher, accepting aims, practicality education for the individual, duration of education, curriculum, method of teaching, relations between student and teacher, women's education, vocational education, educational achievements etc.

Upanishads

The word Upanishad means sitting near devotedly. It brings to the mind the picture of co earnest disciple or learner learning from his spiritual 'guru' or teacher. Apart from Indian scholars and seers, European also have sung the glory of the Upanishads. The Upanishads deal with knowledge (vidya) destroys ignorance (avidya) and takes the seeker to salvation (moksha) and to Brahma (God) and help him to understand him in the true sense and thus liberates him from the bondage of the world (Freedom from the cycle of births and deaths). The Upanishads are recognized as 'Shruthi' or Revelation. The total number of unpanishads are 108. Ten are the most important among them.

Educational Implications

Educational implications of Upanishads may be worked out keeping in view aims, content, methodology, school administration and other educational process.

Aims of Education

Education during upanishadic period was related to social norms and it tried to conserve the cultural tradition of the society of those days. The society was divided on the basis of 'Varanas' and 'Ashramas'. But education did not only conserve that social ethos, it is also bring about social change. Aim of education are summarized as follows:

(a) Character building.

(b) Development of personality.

(c) Knowledge of social roles and status.

(d) Vocational efficiency.

(e) National integration.

The Content

The content was related to the needs of individual and society. Philosophy, Theology, History, Geography, Astronomy, Astrology, Arithmatic, Algebra, Geometry, Language, Literature, Ayurveda, Dhanurveda and the like: were taught and learnt by Upanishadic philosophers and students. Psychology was being studied with greater interest.

Methodology

Methods of Upanishadic philosophy analyzed by Prof. R.D. Ranade in to ten categories: Etymological method, mythical method, Dialectic method, Synthetic method... etc. All the above method of teaching was discovered by Upanishadic philosophers according to the need of the hour. They were suited to the content of education and educational goals.

Teaching was done at that time at all the three levels *viz*; *(i)* memory *(ii)* understanding and *(iii)* reflective. The emphasis was laid on discussions, questioning, induction and deduction. Commentaries, illustrations, descriptions, narrations and practical demonstrations may be easily inferred from the text of Upanishads.

System of Education

The teacher pupil relationship was ideal. A teacher taught about 15 to 20 pupils at a time he was prepared to teach even one pupil. The pupil was well disciplined, courteous, modest and humble. He pleased the teacher by his service as well as through study.

Sanskrit was the medium of instruction and oral discussion formed the basis of teaching-learning which were suplimented by text-books in post-literacy period. The schools were of three types. *Firstly*, ashramas or 'Gurukulas' which may be said to be primary schools, 'charanas' may be compared roughly with our secondary schools and 'parishads' were meant for higher studies and researches. Upanishads contain doctrines of self-realization and the implication is that both teachers and students were devoted to learning, study, meditation through which they tried to realize the self.

The Teachers of Upanishadic Period

The teachers who lived, thought and taught in the upanishadic period made real contribution to the development of upanishadic thought. Some of the teachers who are mentioned in Upanishads do not seem to be historical personalities. They are mythological personages. For example, Indra, Virochana, Prajapati, Varuna, Yama seem to be unhistorical persons.

None of some great teachers (historical persons) are: Svetasvatara, Trishanku, Mantri, Kaushitaki, Uddalaku, Ajatsatru, Vamadeva, Sandilya, Sanatakumara, Aruni, Vajnavalkya...etc.

The Upanishadic teachers were the symbols of 'simple living and high thinking'. They were embodiment of character and knowledge. They may be source of inspiration to the teachers of all the places and at all the times.

The Student – Teacher Relationship

The Guru and his wife had to perform respectively the role of the father and that of the mother for the disciple accepted in the Gurukul. The pupil accepted the teacher and his father and mother as well, and he never dared to oppose him in any way. The manusmirit explains this relationship thus in a clear manner — 'A dwija is born twice. *First* after his mothers conception and secondly at the time of his initiation ceremony when he is made fit to acquire the knowledge of the Brahma.

The Guru also performed his duty honestly. He taught his student the truth exactly as he knew it. He never concealed anything from his disciple. The disciple also did not conceal his weakness from his Guru.

Implications of the Upanishadic Era for Modern Education

The importance of the Upanishadic Era for modern education are – the ideal of development of the whole man, the ideal of good moral character, the concepts of the ideal teacher and the ideal student, the high ideals of the Upanishadic Gurus to be achieved, college and universities, hostels to be re-patterned on the great upanishadic ideals of Gurukula and the Upanishadic ideals for modern students.

The Ideal of Development of the Whole Man

We have seen in the foregoing pages that the educational system during the Upanishadic period stood for on all-sided development of the pupil in such a way that he realized himself as a full man and ultimately attained immortality. Educationalist like: Mahatma Gandhi, Rabindranath Tagore, Swami Vivekananda and many others in our country have also emphasized the ideal of the development of the whole man. But the words of our wise men have not made any impact on our modern educational system. With the result that today we happen to see many stinted specimens of humanity in the forms of graduates of our colleges and universities.

The Ideal of Good Moral Character

An ideal man doesn't not live for himself alone. The aim of education during the upanishadic age was also to enable the pupil to develop himself in such a manner that he might contribute to the development of society. He find the practice of highest moral ideal during the upanishadic period. Today many of our youths happen to be misguided as to work as social miscreants disturbing the peace of our society. So we must incorporate in our modern educational system the ideal of high moral character.

The Concepts of the Ideal Teacher and the Ideal Student

We have seen in the foregoing pages that the Unpanishadic Guru assumed the roles of ideal teachers and they derived spiritual pleasure in helping their pupils to understood the truth of human existence. In our modern educational system we have to incorporate the concept of ideal teacher and the ideal pupil.

The High Ideals of the Upanishadic Gurus to be Achieved

Our modern teacher education colleges preparing teachers for schools profess to develop in the trainees the ideals which were actually praised by the Upanishadic preceptors. Many of the educational departments of the various universities in our country have fallen short of everything that are desirable for an ideal teacher.

College and Universities to be Repatterned on the Great Upanishadic Ideals of Gurukula

During the Upanishadic period the house of the preceptor (the Guru or Acharya) used to function as a residential university for pupils who were there for seeking the *Aparavidya*. The modern colleges and universities having hostels are now no more centres of learning. In order to make them ideal residential centres for our students we should look towards the great grand traditions of the Gurukuls of the Upanishadic age and remodel them on the same pattern under the strict supervision of some really good teachers.

The Upanishadic Ideals for Modern Students

The pupils during the upanishadic age were admitted to a Gurukul of the preceptor's Ashram after his deservingness was fully tested by the preceptor. Today many students join college and universities in order to become film-starts. Today students come to college and universities to learn new fashions. Our students may be saved from these undesirable things if we assimilate the ideals and principles followed by the upanishadic preceptors.

Education in the Vedic Period is –

1. Education was conducted in the gurukul or teacher's house.
2. Students lived as members of a family.
3. The emphasis was upon the study of the Vedas.
4. Sanskrit was the median of education.
5. Brahmanas were the teachers.
6. Education was not available to every class of society.
7. The students life was rigorous.
8. Education was free.
9. Sanskrit was taught.

Upanishads sources of all Indian philosophies. It means knowledge and for salvation knowledge about self is necessary. In modern education, the concept of the ideal teacher and the ideal student to be incorporated. The student should learn the upanishadic ideals to build the highest form of moral character for the social good.

Bhagavad-Gita and Education

Bhagavad-Gita is a part of Mahabharatha. It consists of 700 couplets in 18 chapters. The relation of Gita and the Upanishads has been only too well-known to the Indian philosophers. According to the Vaishaviya Tantrasara "The Upanishads are like: cow, Krishna like: a milkman, Arjunalke the calf that is sent to the udders of the cow before milking and the Bhagavat Gita like the milk-rector that is churned from the udders of the cow". Thus it has been traditionally well-known that Gita is the essence of the philosophy of the Upanishads. Gita is helpful to the ordinary man in understanding his duties. Thus Gita has a very important place in Indian Philosophy.

Principal Teaching of Gita is

- Doing duty as dharma.
- Death is certain.
- Soul is immortal.
- Incarnations.
- Social welfare.
- Karmayoga.
- Two ways of liberation.
- Renunciation on attitude of mind etc.

Educational Implications of Gita

The main implication of Gita is – True meaning of education, objectives of education and pupil teacher relationship.

The True Meaning of Education

The true meaning of education through the virtuous knowledge as emphasized by Krishna. True education is that which helps one to see the existence of God in the soul of an individual. Arjun was delusioned of the start of the battle. Krishna helps him to see two whole epitomized in one individual. Thus Krishna tries to help Arjun to see the point that he cannot kill any one's soul which resides in the Brahma himself.

The Ideal of Education

The ideal of education into six parts, such as:

1. To develop virtuous knowledge – our students suffer from ignorance of various knowledge. In Gita Krishna removes Arjuna's ignorance and motivates him towards performing his duty. It from this position we many take up the idea that the ideal of education should be remove ignorance and to provide the virtuous knowledge.

2. To develop and effect sublimation of personality – Everyone's personality is equipped with evil and virtuous traits. Kauravas and Pandavas exist in each of us.
3. To co-ordinate between the individual and social aim.
4. To develop the inner consciousness.
5. To develop intellectual and logical ability.
6. To establish the importance of duty are the ideal of education.

The Curriculum

Gita refers to two types of knowledge – the *Para vidya* and *Aparavidya*. The knowledge about spiritualism alone can give eternal peace to man. Hence in an educational system "the spiritual aspects of man's life should be given its due place along with subjects related with worldly affairs".

The Concept of Moral Education According to Gita

In the forgoing pages we have said that the performance of one's duty has been principally emphasized in Gita. It was the fulfillment of this ideal that Arjun takes the decision to fight in the battlefield. Through practicing this ideal a person will reach the peak of his development and he will overcome all worldly attachment. This is exactly what is needed in our youths of these days. We impress upon them to practice the above ideal we shall be giving them the noblest moral education.

Gita helps a person to see the existence of God in all creatures. Education to develop virtuous knowledge personality, innerconsciousness, intellectual and logical ability and importance of duty in one's life. Along with knowledge of mundane affairs, spiritual knowledge to be imparted.

Education should aim at acquisition of supreme knowledge and complete development. In modern education, the concept of the ideal teacher and the ideal student to be incorporated. The student should learn the upanishadic ideals to build the highest form of moral character for the social good. Gita helps a person to see the existence of God in all creatures.

BHAGWAD-GITA AND EDUCATION

Shreemad Bhagawad-Gita is an epitome of the Vedic culture and literature. It is the essence of all Indian scriptures. In this unique holy book we find a clear analysis of the various Yogas. The relationship between the Jeeva (the being) and Ishwar (God) has been clearly explained in the Yoga, *viz*; Karma Yoga, Bhakti Yoga and Gyan Yoga. All these three types have been clearly defined in Gita. But how has it been possible to envelop the various Yogas in such a short book? It may be said that Gita covers all the scriptures (Shastras). It is a wonderful collection of boundless ideas and feelings (Bhava). It is because of these boundless ideas that the various commentators have succeeded in propounding various 'isms' and ideas. Shri Shankaracharya has advocated Gyan Yoga through his commentary on Gita. Shri Ramanujacharya has propounded Bhaktiyoga on Gita. Lok Manya Tilak has considered Gita chiefly as Karmayoga.

Exploration of the Basic Elements of Life

1. *The Chief Motivation Free of Life*: We do not live in a vaccum. We reside in a very wide environment which is full of complexities and intricacies. There is always an inevitable interaction between us and the environment. This interaction is a sign of life. Every living being is subjected to this interaction. Of course, variations are found in the interactions of various living creatures. A dog seeing a monkey reacts in a certain way, but the human baby seeing a monkey becomes excited and shows different reactions. In the nature of on there is an element of intelligence. This element brings in change in the situation. Due to his intelligence, man is not bound to follow a certain path. He is able to make a choice from various alternatives before him. This ability of making a choice creates for him a complex problem. Now arises the issue of policy. The exploration of elements of life attempts to resolve the arisen issue.

Arjun places his difficulty before Krishna who expresses his view point for helping him to solve his difficulty. The battle between Kauravas and Pandavas was to begin. Armies of both the parties were present in the battle ground of Kurukshetra. Krishna brought the chariot with Arjun in between the two armies. As a signal to start the battle, drums were beaten and Shankhas (conches) were blown. Now a doubt arises in Arjun's mind whether to fight or not to fight. Arjun was a Kshatriya. It was his duty to fight. But the doubt arose because of the uniqueness of the situation. In a battle one party is an enemy of another and wants to destroy it. In Kurukshetra close relations were standing before each other. The family bond duty was not to shed blood of each other, but at the same time 'duty' warranted that the prestige must be also maintained. In the very beginning of Gita, Kurukshetra has been termed as Dharmaskhetra (*i.e.,* the place of performing sacred duties). Now there is a clash between the blood-relationship and the Dharma. *i.e.,* the duty, Arjun is not able to decide his course of action. The morality viewpoint arises and the policy is now that of morality. When there is a policy matter, there are alternatives.

Arjun tells Krishna, what is the use of Kingdom which is to be obtained by killing close relations consisting of elders and revered persons? It is better to earn a living through begging. Arjun further asks Krishna: "What is the certainty of our victory in the battle? Should we then shed blood in this uncertain situation? Now Krishna says," "Arjun, why are you expressing this ignorance? This conduct is neither praiseworthy nor can it lead you to heaven, nor will it give you glory".

Krishna says, "Oh Arjun you say that so many relatives will be killed. But the fact is that you, I and all others were present previous to this birth and we shall remain even after this life is finished.

The one who thinks that he can kill a soul, and the one who considers it as dead, both do not know. The soul neither kills nor is it killed (2-19).

Even if soul is under bondage of birth and death even then death is no cause of grief. All these have to die, just there is a difference after or before (2-26).

To desist from battle is not noble. Battle is your life mission. If a warrior dies as a duty, the heaven's doors become open for him.

For a Kshatriya there is nothing higher than dying for a righteous (Dharmayudha) battle (2-3-2).

Your argued cause for desisting for battle is unheavenly. If you do not fight you lose both glory and your duty (Swadharma). All will decry you. And for a good man infamy is worse than death. And who will know that you left the battle ground for love of your relatives. All will say that you have run away from the battle due to fear.

You say that you do not know whether you will win or lose in the battle, but at least you know this that if you are killed you will go to heaven, and if you win you will get the Kingdom (2-31-37).

Giving the above reasoning Krishna says to Arjun. Treat gain and loss, victory and defeat as the same thing, get ready for battle. By doing this you will be committing no sin (2-38).

The main substance of the entire reasoning of Krishna in this is that if duty (Dharma) draws one side and another motivating force to another, then in every situation one should act according to duty (Dharma). The demand of duty is above everything else. This idea is an original concept of moral education in Gita.

Krishna says that to treat gain and loss, and 'victory and defeat' as equal is extremely difficult. Pleasure and pain are experienced in the present, harvesting the benefit of gain and victory is matter for future. In accepting guidance of the intellect, the main obstruction is from the attachment of the outcome. In Gita several times it has been observed that one should be indifferent (Udasin) to attachment and outcome. A duty should be performed with the feeling of doing a duty.

The philosopher Kant of Germany has also accepted the above view point of Gita. He has also said that in the performance of one's duty, one should be indifferent to attachment and outcome.

2. *The Door of Hell*: When the attachment (Bhava) is a very powerful, and it is not momentary, then it is called wordly pleasures (Vishaya). Five wordly pleasures are famous. They are lust (Kam), anger (Krodh), Greed (Lobha), delusion (Moha), and Pride (Ahamkar). Lust, anger and greed are regarded as doors to hell. In the face of these, the intellect becomes very weak. In all stories lust (Kam) has been considered as blind. When in just, a person does not look either forward on backward. Anger is generated when justful desire is not fulfilled, In greed, the intellect, being powerless, becomes a handmaid to attachment and becomes helpful in realizing the objective. In greed one wants to enjoy the fruit of another man's labour, in the same way as it is the horse who runs, but it is rider who reaches the destination. In human being greed is a powerful casue of friction. The domain of greed is much wider than of lust and anger.
3. *The Path towards Fall*: In Gita lust (Kam) has been given the first place in the doors of hell. The word lust may be used both in narrow and in wider sense. Within the wider sense all types of desires are included in it. A desire or Kama is a basic motivation

in human nature. When a desire is unfulfilled we become unhappy and, if possible, we attempt to remove all the obstacles in the way of realizing the same. If our attempt is very risk, we get anger also. Desire is an element our human nature. But the things that come within the objectives of our desire are not definite in the beginning. They may be very few or many and of varying nature. The thing for which one has an attachment may not be within the desires of another person. When we feel attachment for a certain thing that enters into our consciousness and gradually we become more and more conscious about it. When we fail in achieving our desire we get anger. In anger the intellect becomes covered and we are not able to see the concerned thing in the right perspective. What is the reason for this inability?

A thing that we happen to see is not in a vaccum. That thing is encircled by other things which are continually influencing it. This kind of action and reaction is an element of its existence. Nothing is momentary. That which appears to be momentary has its past also. When we thing about a thing we are also related with things that are related with it. When Arjun expressed his difficulty before Krishna, his intellect could understand the situation in its various aspects. He was reminded of the blood-relationships and of his attachment for Bhishma and great regard for his Guru Dronacharya. At this time his intellect was working. He know that when engaged in the battle he forget all these things. In anger, a person forgets the past and does not think above future. When a person reaches this stage, his intellect vanishes and he comes up at the brink of all (2-62-3).

4. *The Significance of Self-duty (Swadharma)*: Krishna tells Arjun that a duty (Swadharma) has to be performed for the sake of duty itself. The desire for outcome and attachment pulls down the work from the moral view point. It is said in Gita that it is excellent if one performed his duty, even if the work done is lower than that of any other person. Even to die is auspicious while performing one's duty, to act according to another person's duty is dreadful (3:35).

Educational Implications of Gita

1. *The True Meaning of Education*: We may derive the true meaning of education through the virtuous knowledge (Satwika Gyan)

as emphasized by Krishna (18:20). Virtuous knowledge is that through which we perceive unity in diversity and sense the Brahma (*i.e.,* God or Parmeshwar) in all the creatures on this earth. Thus we may accept according to the philosophy of Gita that true education is that which helps one to see the existence of God (*i.e.,* Brahma) in the soul of an individual. Arjun was delusioned at the start of the battle. Krishna (his Guru) helps him to see the whole epitomized in one individual, Krishna, *i.e.,* God Himself. Thus Krishna tries to help Arjun to see the point that he (Arjun) cannot kill any one's soul which resides in the Brahma (God) Himself.

2. *The Ideals of Education*: We may analyze the ideals of education into six parts, such as:
   - *(i)* to develop virtuous knowledge;
   - *(ii)* to develop and effect sublimation of personality;
   - *(iii)* to co-ordinate between the individual and social aim;
   - *(iv)* to develop the inner consciousness;
   - *(v)* to develop intellectual and logical ability;
   - *(vi)* to establish the importance of duty in life;

Now we try to understand how Gita refers to the above ideals of education.

- *(i) to develop virtuous knowledge*: our students, like all of us, suffer from ignorance of virtuous knowledge. In Gita Krishna removes Arjun's ignorance and motivates his towards performing his duty. From this position we may take up the idea that the ideal of education should be to remove ignorance and to provide the virtuous knowledge;
- *(ii) to develop and effect sublimation of personality*: everyone's personality is equipped with evil (Asuri) and virtuous (Daivi-godly) traits. In other words, Kauravas (Asuri) and Pandavas (the virtuous) exist in each of us. Krishna awakens in Arjun the virtuous powers inherent in him and motivates him towards the right path. This is exactly what a Guru should do for his disciple. Thus the ideal of education should be to develop and sublimate the personality of the student;
- *(iii) to co-ordinate between the individual and social aim*: in the battle-field Arjun is lost between his individual freedom

and the social responsibility. His individual freedom was to fight or not to fight. The social responsibility warranted his participation in the battle for punishing the evil-doors for establishing peace in the land. Krishna impresses upon him to sacrifice his individual freedom and take up the Gandeev for annihilating the wicked persons and their allies. Thus we may say that according to Gita 'one of the chief ideals of education should be to effect a co-ordination between the individual and social aspects of things';

(iv) *to develop the inner consciousness*: arjun desires to keep himself away from the ghastly battlefield. Krishna does not want to force him against his will. Instead, he (Krishna) takes recourse to logical reasoning and tries to convince Arjun about his sacred self-duty (Swadharma). Ultimately, on his own, Arjun decides to fight against his opponents. Thus Krishna, his Guru and Friend, succeeds in awakening the inner consciousness (Anthahakaran). This is exactly the ideal that we should follow in the fields of education;

(v) *to develop intellectual and logical ability*: arjun expresses his doubt regarding the utility of battle. His doubt is at the root of preachings of Gita. Krishna employs his intellectual and logical ability for removing Arjun's doubt. Thus the main purpose of the philosophy of Gita is to develop the intellectual and logical ability of Arjun (the common man) in order that he may be able to take his own decision in the face of alternatives. This should be our ideal of education also;

(vi) *to establish the importance of duty*: one can be happy only by establishing a balance between one's rights and duties. Krishna tells Arjun that nothing is greater than performance of one's duty (Swadharmapalan). It is very necessary to emphasize this viewpoint before the students of these days. If our students develop this attitude towards life, then this very earth will become a heaven.

3. *The Curriculum*: Gita refers to two types of knowledge (Gyan) – *(i)* the Apara Vidya, *i.e.,* the knowledge about mundane affairs and *(ii)* the Para Vidya, *i.e.,* the spiritual knowledge or the knowledge about the supreme self. In the knowledge about

mundane affairs we may include all types of subjects in various disciplines of arts, science and engineering etc., which are generally taught in our education centres. Within the Para Vidya – the spiritual realm – is generally ignored. This was resulted in the predominance of acquisition of worldly wealth of various types at the utter neglect of spiritual realm. The knowledge about the spiritualism alone can give eternal peace to man. Hence in our educational system. "the spiritual aspects of man's life should also be given its due place along with subjects related with worldly affairs".

4. *The Concept of Moral Education According to Gita*: In the foregoing pages we have said that the performance of one's duty (Swadharma-Palan) has been principally emphasizes in Gita. It was towards the fulfillment of this ideal that Arjun takes the decision to fight in the battle-field. Krishna has impressed upon him that one's duty should be performed without taking into consideration its outcome and attachment (Rag) for the same. It is extremely difficulty to think of any higher moral ideal for a man than this. Through practicing this ideal a person will reach the peak of his development and he will overcome all worldly attachment. This is exactly what is needed in our youths to these days. So if we impress upon them to practice the above ideal with shall be giving them the noblest moral education.

Conclusion

Because of his intelligence, man can make a choice, when faced against various alternatives. The choice is to be made according to one's study. No desire of outcome and attachment. Gita helps a person to see the existence of God in all creatures. Education to develop virtuous knowledge, personality, inner consciousness, intellectual and logical ability and importance of duty in one's life. Along with knowledge of mundane affairs, spiritual knowledge to be imparted.

THE UPANISHADS

Vedas speak of divine found in the nature outside of man. Upanishads meditated on the inner nature of man, from the many he goes to the ONE from polytheism to henotheism and monotheism. Up deals with the great questions of man and their answer. It is summarized in two words: BRAHMAN and ATMAN. They are two names for one truth; the two are one and the same. In Tamil it is called 'andam and pindam': *andathiliruppathupindathilulladu.* Our inner truth of the Universe is BRAHAMAN. Sacred OM is the name for both Brahman and Atman. It is divided into three sounds, but the three roll into one, AUM. One of the meanings of Aum is YES. Brahman, Atman and OM are the positive truth, in yes of all it is related to SAT, CIT, and ANANDA *i.e.,* being, consciousness and Joy.

Upanishad deals with many life questions and answers. It is the system of Gurukula, the disciples learning through the guru. Often in the Upanishad tradition the guru rarely gives direct answers to the questions raised by the disciple. It is to be noted that the disciple has to find the right answer.

(a) *Kena Upanishas*: Who sends the mind to wander afar? Who first drives life to start on its journey? Who impels us to utter these words?

What cannot be spoken with words, but that whereby words are spoken know that alone to be Brahman, the spirit and not what people here adore.

(b) *Ketha Upanishad:* The boy, Nachiketas asks the spirit of death the questions when he first meets. When a man dies this doubt arises some say 'he is' and some say he is not teach me the truth.

(c) *Chandogya Upanishad Says*: There is a spirit which is mind and life, light and truth and vast spaces. He contains all works and desires and all perfumes and all tastes. He enfolds the whole universe, and in silence loves to all. This is the spirit that is in my heart, smaller than a grain of rice, or a grain of barley, or again of mustard seed or again of canary see, or the kernel of a grain of canary seed. This is the spirit that is in my heart greater than the earth greater than the sky, greater than heaven itself, greater than all these worlds. This is the spirit that is in my heart, this Brahman.

If we ask where Brahman, the spirit of the universe, is the answer is from kena Upanishad: he is seen in nature in the wonder of a flash of lightening. Who comes to the soul in the wonder of a flash of vision? Madukya Upanishad, the shortest Upanishad, explains the paradox that Brahman is all and Brahman is nothing or nothing.

OM the eternal word is all: what was what is and what shall be and what beyond is eternity all is OM Brahman is all and Atman is

Brahman. Atman, the self has four conditions. The first condition is the waking life of outward-moving consciousness, enjoying the seven outer gross elements. The second condition is the dreaming life of inner moving consciousness enjoying these even subtle inner elements in its own light and solitude. The third condition is the sleeping life of silent consciousness when a person has no desires and beholds no dreams. The fourth condition is Atman in is own pure state the awakened life of supreme consciousness. It is neither outer nor inner consciousness neither semi consciousness nor sleeping consciousness.

By its official designation the Gita is called an Upanishad since it derives its main inspiration from that remarkable group of scriptures the Upanishad. Though the Gita gives us a vision of truth impressive and profound though it opens up new path for the mind of man it accepts assumptions which are a part of the tradition of past generations and embedded in the language it employs the fratricidal struggle is made the occasion for the development of a spiritual message based on the ancient wisdom prajnapurani of the Upanishads the different elements which at the period of the composition of the gita were competing with each other within the Hindu system are brought together and integrated into a comprehensive synthesis the teacher refines and reconciles the different currents of thought the Vedic cult of sacrifice the Upanishad teaching of the transcendent Brahman the Bhagavata theism and tender piety the Samkhyadualsm and the yoga meditation he draws all these living elements of Hindu life and thought into an Organie unity.

The Isa Upanishad and the Bhagavad-Gita

The ideas found in Isa Upanishad equally seen in the Bhagavad-Gita let us look at Isa Upanishad behold the universe in the glory of God and all that lives and moves on earth leaving the transient find joy in the eternal set not your heart on another's possession. Working thus a man may wish for a life of a hundred years. Only actions done in god bind not the soul of man. There are demon haunted worlds regions of utter darkness whoever in life rejects the spirit goes to that darkness after death. The spirit without moving is swifter than the mind the senses cannot reach him. He is ever beyond them standing still him over than those who run to the ocean of his being the spirit of life leads the streams of action. He moves and he moves not he is far and he is near, he is within all and he is outside all. Who sees all beings in his own self and his own self in all being loses all fear when a sage sees this great unity and his self has become all beings what delusion and what sorrow can eve be near him?

Vedas

The Gita draws the spirit of Vedas and carries on the light of Vedas and enlightens the seekers who are searching for liberation and the people in conflict situations. It raises questions about Truth and offers the ways for finding it.

Gayatri mantra found in Vedas:

Om Bhur Bhuvasvah
Tat Saviture Vareniam
Bhargo Devasya Dhimahi
Dhiyo Yo Nah Pracondayat, Om Shanti, Shanti.

"Let our meditation be on the glorious light of Savitri. May this light illumine our minds".

Rig Veda x.129 and in the one arose love. Love the first seed of soul. The truth of this the sages found in their hearts: seeking in their hearts with wisdom, the sages found that the bond of union between being and non being. Who knows in truth? Who can tell us whence and how arose this universe? The gods are later than its beginning: who knows therefore whence comes this creation? Only that god who sees in highest heaven: he only knows whence this universe comes, and whether it was made or uncreated. He only knows, or perhaps he knows not.

There is a philosophical inquiry. The progress of the mid requires doubt and faith, questions and answers. Upanishads is full of these questions so too is the Bhagavad Gita.

In the Vedas we have the dawn of spiritual insight. In the Upanishads we have the full splendor of an inner vision.

The Bhagvath-Geetha

The Bhagavad is more a religious classic than a philosophical treatise... it gives utterance to the aspirations of the programmes of all sects who seek to tread the inner way to the city of God. Millions of Hindus for centuries have found comfort in these great books which sets forth in precise and penetrating words the essential principles of a spiritual religion. Hauer, a Sanskrit German Scholar stated of Gita. We are not called to solve the meaning of life but to find out the Deed demanded of us and to work and so, by action, to master the riddle of life.

It represents not any sect of Hinduism but Hinduism as a whole, not merely Hinduism but religion as such its universality, without limit of time or space, embracing within its synthesis the whole gamut of the human spirit from the crude fetishism of the savages to the creative affirmations of the saint'.

Aldous Huxley: "the Gita is one of the clearest and most comprehensive summaries of the perennial philosophy ever to have been made. Hence it's enduring value, not only for Indians, but for all mankind. The Bhagavad-Gita is perhaps the most systematic spiritual statement of the perennial philosophy".

Historical Perspective of the Gita, Author and Krishna

With to regard to the historicity of the Gita, three views to be kept in mind. Some hold that the data of the Gita is Pre-Buddhist. Others hold that it is of Post-Buddhist. Some others are not concerned about the historical perspective of it.

Historicity of the Gita

There is no doubt that the war described in the Mahabharata is not symbolic and that it may even be based on historical fact; but the problem is different when we find the dialogue between Krishna and Arjuna set in a background of war. The Mahabharata was a way of securing its importance. The Bhagavad-Gita is like a little shrine in a vast temple, a temple that is both a theatre and a fair of this world; and whilst the war in the Mahabharata may be meant as a real war it is obvious that the war in the Bhagavad-Gita has a symbolic meaning. In Mahabharata Arjuna and Krishna are different beings. In Gita there is a battle for the kingdom of heaven. Will we surrender to the forces of evil within us? Should we not fight it out courageously/yet we often give up the fight and find good reasons to withdraw from it. In the Gita Arjuna becomes the soul of man and Krishna the charioteer of the soul.

Gandhiji believes that the historicity of the Gita is not much of concern. He says: 'personally, I believe that Duryodhana and his supporters stand for the satanic impulses in us, and Arujna and others stand for God ward impulses. The battlefield is our body Sri Krishna is the Lord dwelling in everyone's heart who is ever murmuring his promptings in a pure chitta like a clock ticking in a room.

The date of the Bhagavad-Gita is disputable. Since there is no reference to Buddhism in the Gita and there are a few archaic words and expressions, some scholars considered it pre Buddhist *i.e.,* about 500 B.C. the Sanskrit of Gita is simple and clear, like the oldest part of the Mahabharata. This could be for an early date. There are others who consider it as later development of Buddhism. Many spiritual insights of Buddhism are incorporated. It is to stem the influence of Buddhism ad to purify the caste system; an effort is made in Gita. Hence it could be around 200 B.C. to 20A.D.

The Bhagavad-Gita is later than the great movement represented by the early Upanishads and earlier than the period of the development the philosophic stems and their formulation in sutras. From its archaic constructions and internal references. We may infer that it is definitely a work of the pre Christian era. Its date may be assigned to the fifth century B.C., though the text may have received many alterations in subsequent times.

Garbe considers that Gita was originally a smkhya-yoga treatise with which the krsnavaasudeva cult got mixed up and in the third century B.C. it became adjusted to the Vedictration by the identification of Krishna with Vishnu. The original work arose about 200 B.C. and in the second century A.D. a follower of Vedanta gave the present form according to Radhakrishnan this theory is rejected.

Hopkins regards Gita a Krishnaite version of an older Visnuvite poem, and in the beginning it was an unsectarian work. Holtzmann views it as a Visnuvite remodeling of a pantheistic poem. Keith believes that it was originally an Upanishad of the Svetasvatara type but it was later adapted to the cult of Krishna. Otto believes that the doctrinal treatises are interpolated. Jacobi holds that the original nucleus was elaborated by the scholiasts into its present form. These different opinions arose from man apparently conflicting beliefs that were brought into a simply unity to meet the needs of the time in the author a brilliant synthesis emerged.

Authorship

We do not know the name of the author of the Gita. Almost all the books belonging to the early literature of India are anonymous. The authorship of the Gita is attributing to Vyasa, the legendary compiler of the Mahabharata.

It is argued that the teacher, krsna, could not have recited the seven hundred verses to Arjuna on the battlefield. He must have said a few pointed things which were later elaborated by the narrator into an extensive work.

Historicity of Krishna

For the Gita the historicity of Krishna is immaterial. The emphasis of the Gita is the eternal incarnation of the divine which comes to human assistance.

There is however, ample evidence in favour of the historicity of Krishna according to Pro. Radhakrishnan. He says that Chandogya Up. Referes to Krishna, devakiputra, the son of Devaki. It speaks of him as the pupil of Ghora Angirasa who is a priest of the sun, according to kausitakibrahamana. Ghora Angirasa explained to Krishna that in the final hour one should take refuge in these three thoughts." Thou are the indestructible, thou art between the teaching to Ghora Angirasa in the Upanishad and of Krishna in the Gita.

Krishna is an important person in the story of Mahabharata. He is the friend of Arjuna. Panini refers to Vasudeva and Arjuna as objects of worship. Krishna belongs to the family of Yadu whose home was perhaps in the neighbourhood of Mathura, a town with which Krishna is associated in history, legend and tradition. In the Mahabharata Krishna is portrayed as an historical individual and as an incarnation. In 4th century B.C. the cult of Vasudeva was well established. Thus cult is referred in Niddesa the Buddhist work. The book is called Bhagavadgita because Krishna is known in the Bhagavata religion as Sri Bhagavan. In the Gita, Krishna says that he is not expressing Vivasvan to manu and by manu to Ishvaku.

A historical individual is identified with the supreme God. This identification is common in Hindu thought. In the Gita, the author says: delivered from passion, fear and anger absorbed in me, taking refuge in me, many purified by the austerity of wisdom have attained to my state of being as an individual Krishna is one of millions of forms through which the universal spirit manifests itself. The author of the Gita mentions Krishna of history as one of many forms along with his disciple, Arjuna. The avatara is the demonstration of man's spiritual resources and latent divinity. It is not so much the contraction of Divine majesty into the limits of the human frame as the exaltation of human nature to the level of Godhead by its union with the divine. Again and again he is born to bring people to higher plane. According to a passage in the Mahabharata. The supreme who is ever ready to protect the worlds has four forms. One of them ells on earth practicing penance; the second keeps watch over the actions of earring humanity; the third is engaged in activity in the world of men, and the fourth is plunged in the slumber of a thousand years. The Hindu tradition makes out that the avataras are not confined to the human level. The presence of pain and imperfection is traced not to man's rebellious will but to a disharmony between the creative purpose of God and the actual world the theory of avatara is an eloquent expression of the spiritual world.

Though the Gita accepts the belief in avatara as the Devine limiting him self for some purpose on earth, possessing in his limited form the fullness of knowledge, it also lays stress on the eternal avatara, the God in man the Divine consciousness always present in the human being. The two views reflect the transcendent and the immanent aspects of the Divine and are not to be regarded as incompatible with each other. Krishna's avatara is an illustration of the revelation of the spirit in us, the divine hidden in gloom. According to the Bhagavata," at midnight in the thickest darkness, the Dweller in every heart revealed himself in the divine Devaki for the lord is the self-hidden in the hearts of all beings. Krishna the teacher, gently and slowly guides Arjuna". He is fighting with the forces of darkness, falsehood, limitation, and mortality which bar the way to the higher world. When his whole being is bewildered, when he does not know the valid law of action, he takes refuge in his higher self, typified as does not know the valid law of action, he takes refuge in his higher self, typified as Krishna. The rider in the chariot of the body is Arjuna but the charioteer is Krishna and he has to guide the journey. Every individual is a pupil, an aspirant for perfection, a seeker of God and if he seeks earnestly, with faith, God the goal becomes God the guide. Indian tradition is not much concerned about the figure of historicity but of the message that is imparted.

The Mahabharata and the Gita

The Bhagavad-Gita was included in the Mahabharata this vast epic of one hundred thousand slokas or couplets is the longest poem in the world 140 times long in comparison to Bhagavad-Gita. The word Mahabharata meaning the great Bharata. The son of Bakuntala the founder of a dynasty of India kings Salidasa wrote great drama called 'Sakuntal' the Bhagavad-Gita is found in Bhismaparva of Mahabharata it contains 18 chapters. Mahabharata is an epoc which contains seminal elements from the local politics these are dramatized and made into a myth. Mahabharata has eighteen books and the great battle where Duryodhana and all his armies were destroyed lasted eighteen days. The most important Upanishads printed in Sanskrit are about 18. The two longest Upanishads are Brihadaranyaka and the Chandogya 10 pages each others around three to thirty pages each is a Upanishad one of the most important has only 18 verses.

The main story of the Mahabharata centres around forces of good and evil on the whole, as the pandavas and the Kuravas. The father of Dhrita-rashtra and Pandu was king of Hastinapura about fifty miles north east of modern Delhi. At his death Pandu, since his eldest brother, Dhrita-rashtra, being blind succeeded to the throne. He married kunti and madri. The former bore him the sons of Yudhishthira, Bhima, and Arjuna. Madri born two sons called Nakula and Sahadeva. The sons of Dhrita-rashtra had on hundred sons through kunti. The eldest son was Duryodhana the incarnation of evil. Pandu died and along with him Madri died. The eldest brother, dhristra-rashtra, became the king and brought up his younger brother's children. Dhristra-rashtra appointed the eldest Yudhishthira as eir apparent and divided the kingdom and asked him to rule his portion of kingdom. This was the cause of great rivalry and the beginning of the Great War. Duryothana being worried about the streangth of his cousin brothers tried cunningly to usurp the other half as well with the help of his uncle, Sakuni. The eldest brother of Arjuna had the weakness of gambling with dice. Sakuni lured him to play the game. In betting Yudhisthira lost ever thing even his wife, Draupadi. Dutshodana tried to derobe hands to God instead of holding to her robe. Dhristra-rashtra intervened and restored back the honour and the kingdom to Yudhisthira. Once again at the game of dice he lost his kingdom. This time the punishment was that he had to go to forest for twelve years and live there and another year in incognito. During this one year if they were discovered the punishment would be repeated. After completing the term of contract, when the sons of

Pondu asked Duryodhana to resotre the kingdom. He refused to oblige Krishna was sent cities five rooms. Duryodhana told Krishna that only by force even an inch of land would be parted with thus a just war became the necessity. The Pandavas the khatraiays were called to perform their duty to fight for their right. Arjuna who came earlier seated himself at the foot Krishna who seemed to rest. Duryodhana with pride sat at the head of Krishna which would be the greatest source of victory. Relieved by the simple request Duryodhana was happy to get the army of Krishna and the promise that Krishna would of army, seven divisions on the side of Arjuna and eleven divisions on the opposite. The terms of number. But with Krishna as the charioteer the matter is different seven hundred versed were strung together as a song celestial of Krishna taking the short period before the commencement of the battle the advice given to Arjun, could not be too long. Probably it could have been seven versed which ere developed into seven hundred verses later on. The battle took place for eighteen days. To represent this there are 18 chapters of the Gita. The place of was called kurukshtra, near Delhi. Symbolically this takes place inevery one's heart, hence the battle of Dharmashetra. The author of the Gita as of the Mahabharata, so too of gita which is found in it.

The Gita is called an Upanishad. It is viewed that it is an Upanishad of Upanishads. Some believe that this Upanishad to be revered and remembered was inserted into Mahabharata. For it contains the essence of self knowledge. It contains the threefold yoga, *viz;* Karma Yoga (work), Upassana (devotion) and Jnana (knowledge) as means of liberation.

According to George Ferstein, the Bhagavad-Gita is the cenral text the ancient tradition of Vishnusim. It is the most popular work of Hinduism. The Gita is not fully developed philosophical system, yet its world view and darshana is intrinsically coherent and meaningful. It primarily deals with the vital issues of life like: life and death, doubts and faith, immorality and morality, ignorance and wisdom, action and sannyasa. It is of poem of spiritual experience.

The problem and the conflict of Arjuna and sets the stage for resolving the conflict of him, a representative of humanity. All the Upanishads are the cows, Krishna is the miler, Arjuna is the calf, people of purified intellect are the drinkers, and the supreme nectar

Gita is the milk, nectar. Knowing the gita getting the rich mixture of different philosophical traditions of India. The Gita could be divided into three sections. The first six chapters with the path of work. It is the path of desireless action deal with the 'thou' the next six chapters deal with the 'that' the path of devotion. The last six deal with the highest knowledge and the nature of the middle term 'art'. Thus it is interpreted as the exposition of Mahavakaya 'thou art that' thus the Gita is perceived by an Advaitin.

Vinoba says: I live and move in the atmosphere of the Gita. The Gita is my life's breath. To vary the image, I swim in the sea of the Gita when I speak of it but when I am above I dive to the depths of this ocean of nectar and there at peace. According to him the Gita throws light on the whole of the Mahabharata. Mahabharata is the comprehensive treatise on the science of society. It is like Ramayana an enthralling ethical poem.

The Gita teaches that God is only one without blemish. There is no one an embodiment of absolute evil. Some evil is pointed out at Bhisma and Yudhisthira. Some good aspects are seen on karna and duryodhana. Life is a mixture of good and evil. The Gita is the is to enhance the purity of heart and to destroy the illusion.

What is the relevance of the Gita to our life today? Let us have the mind of Arjuna and listen as a disciple of Krishna the Indian spiritual experience.

Concept of Reality Found in Gita

Reality is normally discussed from the intellectual categories of God, world and man. The relationship between these three fold aspects is the field of thinking person. At times they are clearly stated. The problem of one and many has been the issue of resolution for many jnanis and philosophers. Here in the gita we try to understand the reality from these categories.

Concept of Brahman and God

Veda also of God. He is the God who is in fire, in water, who pervades the entire universe. He who in plants, trees, to him we make our obeisance again and again.

The Upanishads affirm the reality of supreme Brahman, one without second, without the attributed, identical with the deepest self of man. Strictly speaking there is no definite description of Brahman, called Nirguna Brahman. The austerity of silence is the only way in which we can bring out the inadequacy of our halting descriptions and imperfect standards. The Tao which can be named is not the true Tao. Buddha maintained silence when he was questioned him as to the nature of truth. The root word, vis. Means to pervade. Vishnu the pervade is found in the Rig Aranyaka says 'to narayana we bring worship' to Vasudeva our meditations and in this way Vishnu assist us.

Krishna the teacher of the Gita is identified with Vishnu the ancient Lord of the Sun, and Narayana, an ancient God of cosmic character. Vishnu is the resting place of gods and men.

The Gita does not give any arguments in support of its metaphysical position. It does not provide proofs for the existence of God. It Calles for the spiritual experience and surrender to absolute spirit personified in Krishna.

We can only speak of it as the non dual, adviata that which is known when all dualities are resolved n the supreme identity. The Upanishads speak of it in negative accounts. The reality is not this not this. Bhagavad-Gita supports this view of the Upanishads in many passages. The supreme is said to be unmanifest, unthinkable and unchanging contradictory predicated are attributed to the supreme. These predicated bring out the twofold nature of the supreme as being and as becoming. He is both transcendent and immanent both inside and outside the world.

Not only is the impersonality of the absolute but the divine activity and participation in nature also seen in the Upanishads. So too in Gita there is the concept of god who exceeds the mere infinite and the mere finite. In the words of the Taittitiva up the supreme is that which these beings are born, that by which they live and that into which, when departing they enter. The theistic Svetasvatara up. He, who is one and without any color by the manifold wielding of his power, ordains many colors with a concealed purpose and in to whom, in the beginning and the end, the universe dissolves he is the god may he endow us with an understanding which leads to good actions. Thou art the woman, thou art the man thou art the youth and also the maiden; thou as an old man totterest with a stick being born his form is not capable of being seen with the eye no one sees him. They who know him thus with the heart, with the mind as abiding in the heart, become immortal.

Upanishads speak of the supreme no only immutable and the unthinkable but also the lord of universe. Though he is the unmoved in substance, yet is the active power in the world. Impersonality and personality are not fictions of mind but two ways of looking at the eternal, the Brahman and Ishwara. The Gita makes out the reality as undivided consciousness called Brahman and as the supreme self called God. The supreme is at once the transcendental the cosmic and the individual reality. In its dynamic cosmic aspect, it not only supports but governs the whole cosmic action. It is also present in the individual IShwara is not responsible for evil except in an indirect way. Since God is not a dictator, he only influences others and controls us. In the realm of freedom, there is the possibility.

Of conflict and devil. The concept of seeking has no value if there is no evil in the world. Hence there is seeking in the midst of error, ugliness and evil for truth, beauty and goodness. For the gita the world is a scene of an active struggle between good and evil in which god is interested.

The personal Ishvara is responsible for the certain preservation and dissolution of the universe. The supreme has two natures, the higher and lowe. The souls represent the higher and the material world the lower part of the supreme. God is responsible for both ideal and concrete relity. Thus the conceptual becomes the cosmic. God with his creative ideas is Brahma. God who pours out his love and work with a patience which is matched only by his love us Vishnu, who is perpetually at works with a patience which is matched only by his love is Vishnu who perpetually at work saving the world . The god is interested in the process of redeeming the world so he aspect of Vishnu is emphasized. Krishna represents the Vishnu aspect of the supreme.

The Gita speaks of personal god who creates the world by his nature he resides in the heart of everybody. He is the enjoyer and lord of the sacrifices. He inspireds us from within in the sense of devotion and grants our prayers. He enters into personal relationship in prayer and service.

Who ensouls the cosmic forms and movements? He is the parameshvara who presides over the individual souls and nature and controls the cosmos. He is also the purusottama the supreme person fills our being and illumines our understanding. All things are made up of being and non-being including purusottama. God has the element of negativity called Maya though he controls it. He controls the souls so as to work out their destinies determine by their own natures. Thus though he is involved in this changing world being immanent.

He is untouched by it and remains the impersonal absolute, the unmoved mover. The God of the Gita cannot be identified with the cosmic process for extends beyond it. Hence it is not simply antheism.

Bondage

The battle of virtues and vices is found in the battle between Kauravas and Pandavas. The kurukshetra is to be seen as dharmakshetra. The sources of suffering are many, the war within us are of different types. The effect of karma leading to the untimely death of the father of Pondavas. Blindness of the king is his fondness to his children, and his inability to control their greediness. Quite a few such blind men live within us. This is not a battle which took place so many thousand years ago; it is one which is waging all the time, even today the greedy and arrogant Duriyodhana, did believe that his army was well protected by Bhisma, Drona, Karna and other great warriors. The revengegul and deceiving attitude of saguni is the hidden struggle in each one of us. The inability of the great masters to stand up against injustice done to Pondavas behind the prison of loyalty. The saddest part of it is the ourtage of the modesty of the wife of Pandavas, a woman caught in the struggle of men. The obsession of gambling that blinds the eldest brother of pandavas and repeated gambling leading to disaster. There is a failure of honesty is fulfilling the conditions agreed upon.

There are silver linings in the dark clouds of delusion, illusion and ignorance. Faithfulness of utmost loyalty of Karunan and of the utter trust on Krishna of the ourtraged devotee, Draupadi, wife pa Pandavas. The simple presence of Krishna for the guidance of Pandavas, not to participate and lead the war and relying on the wealth of arms for the battle.

The art of resolving the conflict in the inner self is portrayed in the Gita. Different means of freeing oneself from these bondage and the synthesis of the different means of liberation is the unique art of living proposed in the Gita.

Arjuna is represented as a seeker, who believes in the atma. He makes the distinction between the body and atman. He has observed the sidciplines of yama-niyama. As a brahmacharya, seeks the truth. To him Krishna imparts the truth to the question raised by Arjuna the means of the atman, soul.

Krishna is the atman in us who is our charioteer. We can win only if we hand over the reins of he chariot to him. God makes us dance, like: the mater in a puppet show. The Gits does not dcide for us but if whenever faced with a moral problem, you give up attachment to the ego and then decide what you should do, you will come to no harm. This is the substance of the argument which Sri Krishna has expanded into 18 chapters.

Central themes of gita are three Jana, Bhakti and karma *i.e.,* light, love and life. Different yoga 1 chapters divided into 6 chapters for each yoga. All the there yogas are interwoven throught out the chapters of the Gita yet certain elements of particular yoga are predominant in these sections of the Gita.

Means of Freedom and Integration

Gitasadhana

Every system if Indian philosophy has a practical way to reach the ideal. To reach the awareness that man is part of the divine and reawaken his true nature. This needs technique called Sadhana. The gita gives not only the metaphysic of reality but also the discipline, called Yogasastra. Yoga's root word is yuj which mean to bind together. It means binding of psychic powers, boy and mind. It means binding of psychic powers, boy and mind. It is yoking the divise energies into one concentration and awareness called Samadhi. It is breaking through the narrow mind set to transcendent perspective.

The Gita gives a comprehensive yoga-sastra. It is flexible and many sided it includes the various phases of the development of the soul. Different yoga's are proposed for differently dominated gunas of one's personality. The three fold yogas are jnana-yoga or the way of knowledge, bhakti-yoga or the way of devotion karma yoga or the way of action.

Arjuna is a representative of the human soul which seeks to be perfect and peaceful. In the beginning of Gita he is full of confusion. How is unsettled life's anxieties lead him to great distress. Every individual goes through this process one time or the other. We are often assailed b doubt, denial and hatred of life and despair. We want to escape from this messy situation and we seek the hand of grace, though only a few of us are willing to pay the price for it. The divine within us work through the sense of insufficiency of barrenness and dust.

The way of Action [Karma-Marga]

The Gita opens up with a problem Arjuna refuses to fight and raises difficulties for it. He pleads for the withdrawal of action in the battlefront, difficult life situation to convert Arjuna is the purpose of the Gita . He raises the question whether action or renunciation of action is better. The Gita concludes that action is better with the purity of motivation Arjuna decides to fight and perform his duty with enlightenment. Ring through the episode the teacher emphasizes the need for action. He does not accept the solution that the world is an illusion and the action is fruitless. He insists on active life anchored on God. The samkhya or jnana calls for renunciation of action. As a created being we are bound by karma. To escape from karma the cause of bondage, one has to be saved by knowledge. Every deed originated from egoism and the desire to enjoy the fruits of action. Hence to be free one has to renounce all action. Hence to be free one has to renounce all action and become a sannyasi. Isa up tells that both knowledge and action have to go together, the knowledge of God and the action. The Gita adopts the same viw and invites us to the rescue the world by working in it.

Once born in this world, we are bound to perform action. Nature is at work and we cannot stop it. No one can remain idle. Idleness is not freedom. True freedom lies in the motive of action. One always acts with certain motive, both conscious and unconscious. Renunciation does not mean to give up the act proper but the selfish desire of it, the mind set one performs the action as if he is the author, kartr, of the action, forgetting the supreme. We often act with ignorance. The Gita advocated the detachment from the desire, not the cessation from work. This is called 'nishkama karma'. Every action karma done in svadharma has to become akarmaactionlessness through the process of vikarma, deatachment of desire, the purity of mind and desirelessness of the fruit of the action is the missing link to make the karma yoga equal with janan yoga. One, who embarks upon the life of sannyasa, lives a life of detachment. He is acionless in action. But karma yogi with the mind of detachment of desires acts in actionlessness. What is important in both the yoga's is the purity of mind, desirelessness and detachment for the furits of action. Both accept they are not the authors of action but only instruments of the lord.

Prepare for war with peace in thy soul. Be in peace in pleasure and pain, in gain and in loss, in victory or in the loss of a battle. In this peace there is no sin.

Just one has to act expecting not the results. Let not the results motivate the doer. Bodily activity is always necessary. Yet that activity be filled with the spirit of actionlessness. Mere physical inactivities will not deliver us. We need to work what is given to us. The 47th verse of second chapter of the Gits is very clear on this:' set thy heart upon thy work but never on its reward. Work not for a reward; but never cease to do thy work'.

One has to work ceaselessly. We should not submit to fatalism. It is important that to acknowledge that there is the hand of destiny, the unknown element. Yet we need to act often our past determines our present. Largely it all depends on our present effort. We need to be in between excessive optimism and excessive pessimism one has to perform his duty.

The man who in his work finds silence and who sees that silence is work, this man in truth sees the light and in all his works finds peace.

Arjuna has faced many battles and fought against enemies. He is concerned about the effects of war and its horrors. He sees that this fight would destroy his gurus, friends, and relatives. He is not against his enemies but his kith and kin. The very purpose of the war is defeated at the end. He seems to think correct but he is deeply ignorant and under the cover of illsusion. Arjuna the warrior, speaks like: sannyasin and is under the cover of false compassion. The purpose of the Gita is ahimsa or non-violence, a perfect state of mind, speech and body. Krishna advises Arjuns to fight without passion or ill-will without anger or attachment and if we develop such a frame of mind violence becomes impossible. We must fight against what is wrong but if we allow ourselves to hate, that ensures our spiritual defeat. We should not fight with ego. The advice is that even in performing one's duties one can achieve perfection. The aim of the Gita is lokasamgraha, world solidarity. It means to purify one's heart and mind before changing others so as to build unity among people. Though we are compassionate to some individuals when violence is done to a child or woman or animal, we often continue to de violence to the millions of people without being aware of it. We need to become aware of violence committed to brotherhood and humanity. We need to act in the world with true compassion and love to remove the evil. We have to be dedicated for he cause of unity in the world, to get rid of wars. If we act with the spirit of detachment from the results and dedication to God the spirit of sannyasin within the heart, we live without regret and with peace.

The root evil is the ignorance avidhya. Hence one needs true wisdom. The karma marga leads to this wisdom which is pure. Sankhara says: 'Liberation is accomplished by wisdom, but wisdom does not spring without the purification of the heart. Therefore for prescribed in the srutis and smrtis dedicating them to the supreme lord. This work becomes the yajna or the sacrifice. Sacrifice means making sacred for God. It is a spontaneous self giving and surrender. By this surrender one's mind is purified the source of action. Then the action becomes pure. The karma becomes pure and a sacrifice pleasing to God.

The Gita tells us that we need to transcend the order of deed and its results. We don't interfere arbitrarily with the natural order. Yet we act in this world with the transcendent attitude. Be in god and act. We become master of karma with detachment and faith in god. Here both the saga and the does without attachment and god act together in the question of right and wrong. The human person is only instrument. God's will become one's peace. Then the action with attachment which is defective becomes liberative. For the victory or defeat of that action does not affect the person. He has crossed over dualities and becomes spontaneous and free. The person acts like god who is not bound both extremes but continuously active in love and wisdom. The freed souls work for the guidance others and relish the action as adventuresome. Yet they live in this world as strangers and endure all hardships. Their citizenship is in heaven.

This karma yoga is path of wisdom. The activity of a liberated person is one of peace and bliss like other yoga's. Work is not a means but the song of joy. The karma yogi is a sannyasi in the world not of the ashram.

Some Important Verses of the Gita

M.K. Gandhi says 'I went through the whole of it immediately and was fascinated by it. From that time till now the last nineteen stanzas of chapter II have ever remained engraved in my heart. For me they contain the essence of dharma they are the key to the understanding of the Gita. They are:

Chapter 2, 54-72

54. *Arjuna*: how is the man of tranquil wisdom who abides in divine contemplation? What are his words? What is his silence? What is his work?
55. *Krishna*: when a man surrenders all desired that come to the heart and the grace of God finds the joy of God, then his soul has indeed found peace.
56 whose mind is untroubled by sorrows, and for pleasures he has no longings, beyond passion and fear and anger, he is sage of unwavering mind.
57. Who every where is free from all ties, which neither rejoices nor sorrows if fortune is food or is ill, his is a serene wisdom.
58. When in recollection he withdraws all his senses from the attraction of the pleasures of sense, even as a tortoise withdraws all its limbs, then his is a serene wisdom.
59. Pleasures of sense but not desires disappear from the austere soul. Even desires disappear when the soul has seen the supreme.
60. The restless violence of the senses impetuously carries away the mind of even a wise man striving towards perfection.
61. Bringing them all into the harmony of recollection, let him sit in devotion and union his soul finding rest in me. For when his senses are in harmony, then his is serence wisdom.
62. When a man dwells on the pleasures of sense, attraction for them arises in him. From attraction arises desire the lust of possession and this leads to passion to anger.
63. From passion comes confusion of mind, then loss of remembrance the forgetting of duty. From this loss come the ruin of reason and the ruin of reason leads man to destruction.
64. But the soul that moves in the world of the senses and yet keeps the senses in harmony, free from attraction and aversion, finds rest in quietness.

65. In this quietness falls down the burden of all her sorrows, for when the heart has found quietness wisdom has also found peace.
66. There is no wisdom for a man without harmony, and without harmony there is no contemplation. Without contemplation there cannot be peace, and without peace can there be joy?
67. For when the mind becomes bound to a passion of the wandering sense, this passion carries away man's wisdom even as the wind drives a vessel on the waves.
68. The man who therefore in recollection withdraws his senses from the pleasures of sense is a serene wisdom.
69. In the dark night of all beings awakes to light the tranquil man. But what is day to other beings is night for the sage who sees.
70. Even as all waters flow into the ocean, but the ocean never overflow, even so the sage feels desired, but he is ever on in his infinite peace.
71. For the man who forsakes all desires and abandon all pride of possession and of self reaches the goal of peace supreme.
72. This is the eternal in man; O Arjuna reaching him all delusion is gone. Even is the last hour of his life upon earth man can reach the nirvana of Brahman man can find peace in the peace of his God.

Fifteen Important verses of Gita

2:69 in the dark night of all beings awakes to light the tranquil man. But what is day to other beings is night for the sage who sees.

4:18 the man who in his work finds silence and who sees that silence is work, this man in truth sees the light and in all his works finds peace.

6:5 arise therefore and with the help of they spirit lift up they soul to fall for they soul can be they friend and they soul can be thine enemy.

6:16 yoga is a harmony. Not for him who eats too much, or for him who eats too little not for him who sleeps too little or for him who sleeps too much.

7:8 I am the taste of living waters and the light of the sun and the moon. I am OM the sacred word of the Vedas, sound in silence heroism in men.

9:17 I am for father of this universe and even the source to be known the path of purification the holy OM the three Vedas.

9:22 but to those who adore me with the pure oneness of soul to those who are eve in harmony, I increase what they have and I give them what they have not.

9:23 even those who worship the gods because of their love they worship me although not in the right way.

9:26 he who offers to me with devotion only a flower, or a fruit or even a little water, this I accept from that yearning soul because with a pure heart it was offered with love.

9:27 whatever you do, or eat, or give, or offer in adoration, let it be an offering to me and whatever you suffer, suffer it for me.

9:29 I am the same to all beings and my love is ever the same but those who worship me with devotion they are in me and I am in them.

9:30 for even if the greatest sinner worships me with all his soul, he must be considered righteous, because of his righteous will.

9:32 for all those who come to me for shelter, however weak or humble or sinful they may be women or Vaisyas or sudras they all reach the path supreme.

9:34 give me they mind and give me they heart, give me they offerings and they adoration and thus with they soul in harmony, and making me they goal supreme thou shalt in truth come to me.

16:21 there are the gates to this hell, the death of the soul the gate of lust the gate of wrath and the gate of greed. Let atman shun the three.

CHAPTER

10 Secularism and Education

Meaning

The meaning of secularism different to country to country. European secularism emerge as a protest against Christianity in 19th century. The meaning of secularism different in India and Europe. Webster says, 'Secularism, a system of doctrines and practices that rejects any form of religious faith and worship'. Gandhiji says, 'We believe in Sarva Dharma Samabhavana having equal regard for all faith and greeds'.

Dr. B.R. Ambedkar explains, "Secular state doesn't mean that it shall not take in to consideration the religious sentiments of the people. All that secular state means is that this parliament shall not be competent to impose any particular religion upon the rest of the people. This is the only limitation that the constitution recognizes (*Parliamentary Debates, 1951,* Vol. III, Part II).

This term secularism incorporated in the constitution by 42nd constitutional amendment in 1976. But the constitutional frame workers have a clear cut idea regarding since constitution framing. We are not following western concept of secularism fully, we indianise it. Secularism is a attitude and belief. It is not antireligious or irreligious. It doesn't rejecting any religion.

The Characteristics of a Secular Sate/Secularism as State's Policy

- The state as such has no religion of its own.
- It doesn't accord preferential treatment to the followers or any faith.
- It doesn't discriminate against any person on account of his faith.
- All citizens are eligible to enter government service irrespective of their faith.
- Consider religion as personal issues.
- State not support any religion and not controlled by any religion.

Educational Implications of Secularism

In a multi religious country like India, the spirit of secularism is to be developed in order to maintain the unity and integrity of the nation. Education should play a positive role in preparing people for a secular society and a purposeful life. We hope secularism will develop in to stronger force leading to the social unity of India. When institutionalized religions gradually lose their co-ersive hold on the younger generation. A process in which the dominance of religion over other institutions is reduced, is called secularization.

According to Brubacher secularism has 'no religious point of view while it has a theory of moral education'. Brubacher has also observed, "if the secularist has any religion at all it is likely that scientific doctrine constitutes the presuppositions of that religion and that scientists are its high priests".

Secularism is a philosophy of moral education. Secular behaviour springs in the school from the influence of the school, through the conduct and behaviours of the teachers themselves and little in the school community as a whole. All the activities and programmes of the schools must strive for the inculcation of values of love, truth and tolerance.

Religions and Moral Education in Secular India/Indian Constitution and Secularism

- *Article 19(1)*: "Subject to public order, morality and health and to other provisions of this part, all personas are equally entitled to freedom to conscience and the right freely to profess, practise and propagate religion".

- *Article 21*: "No person may be compelled to pay any taxes, the proceeds of which are specifically appropriated in payment of expenses for the promotion or maintenance of any particular religion or religious denomination".
- *Article 22(1)*: "No religious instruction shall be provided in any educational institution wholly maintained out of state funds".

Provided that nothing in this clause shall apply to an education institution which is administered but has been established under an endowment or trust which requires that religious instructions shall be imparted in such institutions.

- *Article 22(2)*: "No person attending any educational institution recognized by the state of receiving aid out of state funds shall be required to take part in any religious institution or to attend any religious worship that may be conducted in such institution or in any premises attached there to unless such person, or if such person is a minor his guardian has given his consent thereto".
- *Article 30(1)*: "All minorities whether based on religion or language, shall have the right to establish and administer educational institutions of their choice".
- *Article 30 (2)*: "The state shall not in granting aid to educational institutions, discriminate against any educational institution of the ground that it is under the management of minority, whether based on religion or language".

The Education Commission (1964-66) on Religious Education and Education About Religion

"We suggest that a syllabus giving all chosen information about each of the major religions should be included as a part of the course in citizenship or as a part of general education to be introduced in schools and colleges upto the first degree. It should be highlight the fundamental similarities in the great religions of the world and the emphasis they place the cultivation of certain broadly comparable moral and spiritual values".

- *Secularism in India:* India is a secular country as per the declaration in the Preamble to the indian constitution. It prohibits discrimination against members of a particular religion, race, caste, sex or place of birth. The Indian notion for the term secularism is different from the French notion for the term.

The word secular was inserted into the preamble by the 42nd Amendment. (1976) It implies equality of all religions and religious tolerance and respect. India, therefore does not have an official state religion. Every person has the right to preach, practice and propagate any religion they choose. The government must not favour or discriminate against any religion. It must treat all religions with equal respect. All citizens, irrespective of their religious beliefs are equal in front of law. No religious instruction is imparted in government or government-aided schools. Nevertheless, general information about all established world religions is imparted as part of the course in Sociology, without giving any importance to any one religion or the others. The content presents the basic/fundamental information with regards to the fundamental beliefs, social values and main practices and festivals of each established world religions. The Supreme Court in *S.R Bommai v. Union of India* held that secularism was an integral part of the basic structure of the constitution.

- *History of Secularism*: Religions of India are known to have co-existed and evolved together for many centuries predating Republic of India. Indian civilization is among the oldest and living civilizations of the modern world. India is a country where religion is very central to the life of many people. India's age-old philosophy as expounded in Hindu scriptures called Upanishads is *sarva dharma samabhava*, which means respect for all belief systems. This basic trait of *Sanatan dharma* is what keeps India together despite the fact that India has not been a mono-religious country for over two millennium. A Hindu Nationalist school of thought also proclaims that with Sanatan Dharma being the spirit of India, the very concept of western secularism is redundant and badly imposed. Some researchers believe that the history of Indian secularism begin with the protest movements in the 5th century BC. The three main protest movements were by the Charvakas (a secularistic and materialistic philosophical movement), Buddhism, and Jainism. All three of them rejected the authority of the Vedas and any importance of belief in a deity.

- *Secularism in British India*: In the 18th century, when the British East India Company began to gain total control over India that ideas of secularism began to impact on the Indian mind. Until then, religion was considered to be inseparable from political and social life. The British codified laws pertaining to practices within religions on the sub-continents. This began when the Governor of Calcutta Warren Hastings set out his Judicial Plan in 1772 and 1774, this was a judicial system that codified civil, criminal and commercial laws, while family law and some property laws were still governed by Muslim and Hindu religious law, not to mention religious laws of Christians, Sikhs, Parsis and other faiths. Some see this as a part of their divide-and-rule policy· In doing so they laid the foundation for a non-uniform civil code which remains largely unchanged to date. This is a major grouse for Hindu politicians who insist that there should be a uniform civil code for all citizens. For example, believers of all faiths other than Islam are legally bound to be monogamous while those who practice or convert to Islam are permitted up to four marriages, which is therefore not uniform behaviour. In India, right from the British period, main contradiction was not between religious and secular but it was between secular and communal. In the western world main struggle was between church and state and church and civil society but in India neither Hinduism nor Islam had any church-like structure and hence there never was any such struggle between secular and religious power structure. The main struggle was between secularism and communalism. The communal forces from among Hindus and Muslims mainly fought for share in power though they used their respective religions for their struggle for power.
- *Secularism in Modern India:* Buddhist monks at the Sera Monastery during a festival. The monastery was granted asylum by the India and relocated to Mysore after the Chinese invasion of Tibet. After independence and partition, a large body of Muslims were left in India and hence leaders like Gandhi and Nehru preferred to keep India secular in the sense that the Republic of India shall have no national religion and the people of India shall be free both in any individual and corporate sense

to follow any religion of their choice. Thus India remained politically secular and its people continued to passionately practise their religions.

Jawaharlal Nehru, the first Prime Minister of India, was a supporter of secularism and secular politics. Theoretically speaking the Congress Party was also committed to secularism. However, the Congress Party consisted of several members and leaders whose secular political principles are doubtable. But it was due to Mahatma Gandhi, Nehru, Maulana Abul Kalam Azad and B.R. Ambedkar that India committed itself to secularism and its Constitution was drafted on secular lines. Secularism in India, as pointed out before, emphasised upon the principles of equal respect for all religions and cultures and non-interference of religion in the government affairs. Also, according to the Indian Constitution no discrimination shall be made on the basis of caste, creed, gender and class. Similarly all citizens of India irrespective of one's religion, caste or gender have right to vote. According to articles 14 to 21 all will enjoy same rights without any discrimination on any ground. According to Article 25 all those who reside in India are free to confess, practice and propagate religion of one's choice subject of course to social health and law and order. Thus even conversion to any religion of ones choice is a fundamental right. In fact, in India an overwhelming majority of people are religious but are tolerant and respect other religions and are thus 'secular' in the Indian context. Even Sufis and Bhakti Saints are considered quite secular in that sense. The word secularism has had multiple interpretations, namely: an agnostic interpretation and a pluralistic interpretation. While Nehru, Mohammed Ali Jinnah, and Subhas Chandra Bose subscribed to the agnostic interpretation of Secularism, Gandhiji and others believed in pluralistic interpretation of Secularism.

The Preamble to the Constitution of India grants 'liberty of thought, expression, belief, faith and worship' immediately after proclaiming that India is a 'Sovereign Socialist Secular Democratic Republic.' This reading of the constitution suggests that the Constitution of India has a pluralistic interpretation of Secularism. Also, religious belief governs the application of laws in India (Indian law), which indicates a pluralistic interpretation of the term Secularism in the Indian legal system. The science of the concept of legal pluralism and the study of legal pluralism as it has naturally existed in India is on-going. There are some atheists and secularists who reject religion in its entirety but such people are extremely few. Though there are no census figures available but one can safely say that there are less than 0.1 per cent in India. Also, there are extremely orthodox people who exhibit rigidity and intolerance towards other faiths though of course not on communal grounds but on the grounds of religious orthodoxy but they too are in minuscule minority. Tolerance in India among people of all religions is widely prevalent. It is perhaps due to influence of ancient Vedic doctrine that truth is one but is manifested in different forms. Thus the real spirit of secularism in India is all-inclusiveness, religious pluralism and peaceful co-existence. However, it is politics, which proved to be divisive and not religion. It is not religious leaders by and large (with few exceptions) who divide but politicians who seek to mobilise votes on grounds of divisive identities like religion, caste and ethnicity. In a multi-religious society, if politics is not based on issues but on identities, it can prove highly divisive. Politicians are tempted to appeal to such identities rather than to solve-problems. The former case proves much easier. The medieval society in India was thus more religiously tolerant as it was non-competitive. The modern Indian society, on the other hand, has proved to be more divisive as it is based on competition.

Bibliography

1. Aggrawal, J. C. (1996). 10th Rev. Ed. *Theory and Principles of Education*, New Delhi, Vikas Publications.
2. Aggrawal, J. C. (2001). *Basic Idea's in Education*. Delhi, Shipra Publications.
3. Aggrwal, J.C. (2005). *Education for Values, Environment and Human Rights,* Delhi, Shipra Publications.
4. Amala, Annie, *et al.* (2006). *History of Education*. New Delhi: Discovery Publishing House.
5. Anand, C.L. (1993). *Teacher and Educations in the Emerging Indian Society*, New Delhi: NCERT.
6. Apple, M. (1979). *Ideology and Curriculum*. Boston: Routledge and Regan Paul.
7. Banerji, S. C. (1992). *Tantra in Bengal (Second Revised and Enlarged ed.), Delhi: Manohar.*
8. Basham, A L *The Origins and Development of Classical Hinduism* (1989).
9. Basham, A.L (1999). A Cultural History of India, Oxford University Press.
10. Basu, D.D. *Introduction to the Constitution of India.*
11. Bhaktivedanta, A. C. (1997). *Bhagavad-Gita As It Is, Bhaktivedanta Book Trust,* retrieved from http://bhagavadgitaasitis.com
12. Bhandarkar, Ramakrishna Gopal (1913). *Vaisnavism, Saivism, and Minor Religious Systems. New Delhi: Asian Educational Services.* Third AES reprint edition, 1995.

13. Bhaskarananda, Swami (1994). The Essentials of Hinduism: A Comprehensive Overview of the World's Oldest Religion, Seattle, WA: Viveka Press.
14. Bhatacharya and Sriniwas (1977). Society and Education Calcutta: Academic Publishers.
15. Bhattacharyya (Ed.), Haridas (1956). *The Cultural Heritage of India. Calcutta: The Ramakrishna Mission Institute of Culture.* Four Volumes.
16. Bhattacharyya, N.N (1999). *History of the Tantric Religion (Second Revised ed.),* Delhi: Manohar Publications.
17. Bowen, J. (1971). *A History of Western Education,* Vol. 2. London: Methuen and Co.
18. Boyce, *Zoroastrians* (1986).
19. Brameld, T. (1971). *Patterns of Educational Philosophy*. New York: Hold Rinehart and Winston.
20. Brubacher, John S. (1962). Modern Philosophies of Education New York, McGraw Hill Book Company Inc.
21. Brubacher, John S. Philosophy of Higher Education San Francisco, Jossey – Bass 1978.
22. Brunacher, John S. (1962). Eclectic Philosophy of Education, New Jersey, Prentice Hall, Engellwood Cliffs.
23. Chakravarti, Mahadev (1994). The Concept of Rudra-Siva Through The Ages (Second Revised ed.), Delhi: Motilal Banarsidass.
24. Chandra S.S. and Sharma R. K. 2004: Philosophical of Education.
25. Charles F. Aiken. and Joseph P. Thomas. *The Catholic Encyclopedia*, Vol. IX. 1910. New York: Robert Appleton Company.
26. Chaube, S.P. *History and Problems of Indian Education*. Agra: Vinod Pustak Mandir.
27. Chennakesavan, S *A Critical Study of Hinduism* (1980).
28. Chidbhavananda, Swami (1997). *The Bhagavad Gita, Sri Ramakrishna Tapovanam.*
29. Coombs, Philips H. (1985). The World Crisis in Education New York: Oxford University Press.
30. Curtis, S. J. and Boultwood, M. (1953). *A Short History of Educational Ideas*. London: University Tutorial Press.

31. Dhalla, *History of Zoroastrianism* (1938).
32. Dhalla, *Zoroastrian Theology* (1972).
33. Dhavan, M.L. (2005). Philosophy of Education Delhi, Editor, Isha Books.
34. Donell, *Sanskrit Literature* (New York, 1900).
35. Durkheim, Emile (1956). Education and Sociology, New York: Free Press.
36. Eliot, Sir Charles (2003). *Hinduism and Buddhism: An Historical Sketch,* Vol. I (Reprint ed.), Munshiram Manoharlal.
37. Flaherty, WD *Dreams, Illusions and Other Realities* (1984).
38. Flood, Gavin (1996). *An Introduction to Hinduism. Cambridge: Cambridge University Press.*
39. Flood, Gavin (Editor) (2003). *The Blackwell Companion to Hinduism. Malden, MA*: Blackwell Publishing Ltd.
40. Frazer, *A Literary History of India* (New York, (1898).
41. Gandhi, *the Bhagavad-Gita*, Orient Paperbacks, 2001.
42. Ghanta, Ramesh and Dash, B.N. (2006). *Foundations of Education*. Hyderabad: Neelkamal Pub (P) Ltd.
43. Government of India (1993). Education for All: The Indian Scene New Delhi: MHRD Widentry Horizons.
44. Guénon, René (1921). *Introduction to the Study of the Hindu Doctrines (1921 ed.),* Sophia Perennis.
45. *Guénon, René, Man and His Becoming According to the Vedanta (1925 ed.),* Sophia Perennis.
46. Guénon, René, Studies in Hinduism (1966 ed.), Sophia Perennis.
47. Hopkins, T J *The Hindu Religion Tradition* (1971).
48. http://en.wikipedia.org/wiki/Nyaya
49. http://en.wikipedia.org/wiki/Samkhya_philosophy
50. http://en.wikipedia.org/wiki/Secularism_in_India
51. http://www.answers.com
52. http://www.answers.com
53. http://www.ibiblio.org/sripedia/ebooks/mw/index.html
54. J.C. Aggarwal – *Teacher and Education in a Developing Society*.
55. Juan Mascaro, *the Bhagavad-Gita*, Penguin Classics, Penguin Books India, New Delhi.

56. Kabir, H. (1955). *Science, Democracy and Islam*. London: Allen and Unwin.
57. Kabir, H. (1955). *Science, Democracy and Islam*. London: Allen and Unwin.
58. Kar, N. K.: (1996). Value Education – A Philosophical Study Ambala, The Associated Publication.
59. Kashyap C.S. (2005). *Our Constitution – An Introduction to India's Constitution and Constitutional Law*. New Delhi: National Book Trust, India.
60. Kashyap, Subhash (1993). Perspectives on the Constitution Delhi, Shipra Publ.
61. Keay, John (2000). *India: A History. New York: Grove Press.* ISBN 0-8021-3797-0.
62. Kilpatrick, WH (1934). Source Book in the Philosophy of Education New York, McMillan and Company.
63. Kinsley, D *Hinduism* (1982). K KK LOstermaier, A Survey of Hinduism (1988).
64. Kornblum, William (1998). *Sociology the Central Themes*. New York: Harcourt Brace College Publishers.
65. M. Farhang, *The Zoroastrian Tradition* (1988). The Manual of Discipline in the Dead Sea Scrolls is Believed to Reflect Zoroastrian Influence.
66. Mayer, F. (1963). Foundations of Education Ohio, Charles E Merrile Books Inc.
67. Mohanti J. (1987). Democracy and Education in India, New Delhi: Deep and Deep Publishers.
68. Mohanty, J. (1982). *Indian Education in the Emerging Society*, New Delhi: Sterling Publishers.
69. Monier Williams, *Indian Wisdom* (4th ed. London, 1803); Johantgen, (Leipzig, 1863).
70. Monier-Williams, Monier (2001). *Written at Delhi,* English Sanskrit Dictionary, *Motilal Banarsidass.*
71. Naik, J. P. and Syed, N. (1974). *A Student's History of Education in India*, New Delhi: Macmillan Co.
72. Nakosteen, M. (1968). *History of Islamic Organize of Western Education*. Roulder: University of Colorado Press.

73. Nakosteen, M. (1968). *History of Islamic Organize of Western Education*. Roulder: University of Colorado Press.
74. Nayar, P. R., Dave, P.N., and Arora, K. (1982). *Teacher and Education in Emerging Indian Society*, New Delhi.
75. Nikhilananda, Swami (1990). *The Upanishads: Katha, Isa, Kena, and Mundaka,* Vol. I (5th ed.), New York: Ramakrishna-Vivekananda Centre.
76. Nikhilananda, Swami (trans.) (1992). *Gospel of Sri Ramakrishna (8th ed.), New York: Ramakrishna-Vivekananda Centre.*
77. Oberlies, T (1999). *Die Religion des Rgveda, Institut für Indologie der Universität Wien, Vienna.*
78. Osborne, E (2005). *Accessing R.E. Founders and Leaders, Buddhism, Hinduism and Sikhism Teacher's Book Mainstream, Folens Limited.*
79. Panday, V. C. (2005). *Value Education and Education for Human Rights* Delhi, Isha Books.
80. Pandey, R. S.: An Introduction to Major Philosophers of Education Agra, Vinod Pusatak Mandir.
81. Pandey, Ramshakal. *Teacher in Developing Indian Society*. Agra: Vinod Pustak Mandir.
82. Paratte, R. (1977). *Ideology and Education*. New York: McDay.
83. Passi, B. K. (2004). Value Education Agra, National Psychological Corporation.
84. *Philosophical Foundations of Education* (2014). ShriVinod Pustak Mandir Agra, UP, Sole Author, ISBN: 9789381602805.
85. Pylee, M.V. (2003). *Indian Constitution*. Thiruvananthapuram: Kerala Bhasha Institute.
86. Pylee, M.V. (2005). *An Introduction to the Constitution of India*. New Delhi: Vikas Publishing House (P.) Ltd.
87. R.N. Sharma – *History of Indian Philosophy*.
88. Radhakrishnan, S and CA Moore (1967). *A Sourcebook in Indian Philosophy,* Princeton University Press.
89. Radhakrishnan, S (1996). *Indian Philosophy,* Vol. 1, Oxford University Press.
90. Radhakrishnan, S (Trans.) (1995). *Bhagvada-Gita,* Harper Collins.
91. Radhakrishnan, S. and Moore. *Source Book of Indian Philosophy*. Allen and Uncoin.

92. Raheja, S.P. Human Values and Education.
93. Rajput J. C. (2006). Human values and Education Pragun Publisher.
94. Ram Shakal Pandey – *A Survey of Educational Thought.*
95. Rena, R. (1971). *Introduction to Indian Philosophy.* New Delhi: Tala Mac Graw Hill.
96. Ross, James (1962). Groundwork of Educational Theory, London: George Harre and Sons. 29. Ram Murti Acharya (1990). Towards an Enlightened and Humane Society – A Committee Report, New Delhi MHRD.
97. Ruhela, S. P. (1969). Social Determinants of Educability in India New Delhi, Jain Publishers. 31. Ruhela, S. P. and Vyas K. C. (1970). Sociological Foundations of Education in Contemporary India, Delhi: Dhanpat Raj and Sons.
98. Rusk R. and Robert. (1951). *A History of Indian Education.* London: University of London Press.
99. Rusk R. Robert. *A History of Indian Education.* London: University of London Press, 1951.
100. S. Radhakrishnan , *The Bhagavad-Gita*, Blackieand Son Publishers Pvt. Ltd., Blackie House, Bombay.
101. S.P. Chaube – *Foundations of Education.*
102. Saiyidain, K. G. (1970). Facts of Indian Education New Delhi, NCERT.
103. Sargeant, Winthrop and Christopher Chapple (1984). The Bhagavad Gita, State University of New York Press.
104. Sen Gupta, Anima (1986). The Evolution of the Sâmkhya School of Thought, South Asia Books.
105. Sharma, R.N. (2000). *Text Book of Educational Philosophy.* New Delhi: Kanishka Publishers.
106. Silverberg, James (1969). "Social Mobility in the Caste System in India: An Interdisciplinary Symposium", *The American Journal of Sociology 75 (3): 442-443.*
107. Smelser, N. and S. Lipset, eds. (2005). *Social Structure and Mobility in Economic Development, Aldine Transaction.*
108. Smith, Huston (1991). *The World's Religions: Our Great Wisdom Traditions, Harper San Francisco, San Francisco.*

109. Suresh Bhatnagar - *Indian Education Today and Tomorrow.*
110. Swami Dayananda, *the Teaching of the Bhaguvad Gita*, Vision Books Private Ltd., New Delhi.
111. Taneja, R.P. (2000). *Dictionary of Education*. Anmol Publishing Ltd.
112. Tattwananda, Swami (1984). *Vaisnava Sects, Saiva Sects, Mother Worship (First Revised ed.),* Firma KLM Private Ltd. Kolkatta.
113. Thamarasseri, Ismail and Sabu, S (2010). *Thoughts on Education.* Kanishka Publishers, New Delhi.
114. Thamarasseri, Ismail (2007). *Education in the Emerging Indian Society*, Kanishka Publishers, New Delhi.
115. Thamarasseri, Ismail (2014). *Philosophical Foundations of Education.*, Agra: Vinod Pustak Mandir.
116. Thomas, P Hindu Religion, *Customs and Manners* (1981). R C Zaehner, Hinduism (1962).
117. Vivekananda (1982). *Complete Works of Swami Vivekananda* (Vol. V). Advits Publishers.
118. Vivekananda (1982). *Complete Works of Swami Vivekananda* (Vol. V). Advits Publishers.
119. Vivekananda, Swami (1987). *Complete Works of Swami Vivekananda,* Advaita Ashrama, Calcutta.
120. Vivekananda. *Complete Works of Swami Vivekananda.* Advits Publishers, Vol. V, 1982.
121. Warnock, M. (1977). *Schools of Thought.* London: Faber and Faber.
122. Zaehner, *the Dawn and Twilight of Zoroastrianism* (1961).

Index

❑❑❑